IN LIEU OF IDEOLOGY

I should like to end as I began, by exhorting Singaporeans to take more interest in the history of their country — its founding, development and progress. They will then realize the magnitude of the problems that have had to be faced, and the great achievements that have been accomplished.

— Goh Keng Swee
("150 Years of Singapore", 1 August 1969)

The **Institute of Southeast Asian Studies (ISEAS)** was established as an autonomous organization in 1968. It is a regional research centre dedicated to the study of socio-political, security and economic trends and developments in Southeast Asia and its wider geostrategic and economic environment. The Institute's research programmes are the Regional Economic Studies (RES, including ASEAN and APEC), Regional Strategic and Political Studies (RSPS), and Regional Social and Cultural Studies (RSCS).

ISEAS Publishing, an established academic press, has issued more than 2,000 books and journals. It is the largest scholarly publisher of research about Southeast Asia from within the region. ISEAS Publishing works with many other academic and trade publishers and distributors to disseminate important research and analyses from and about Southeast Asia to the rest of the world.

IN LIEU OF IDEOLOGY
AN INTELLECTUAL BIOGRAPHY OF
GOH KENG SWEE

OOI KEE BENG

ISEAS

Institute of Southeast Asian Studies

First published in Singapore in 2010 by ISEAS Publishing
Institute of Southeast Asian Studies
30 Heng Mui Keng Terrace
Pasir Panjang
Singapore 119614

E-mail: publish@iseas.edu.sg
Website: <http://bookshop.iseas.edu.sg>

The responsibility for facts and opinions in this publication rests exclusively with the author and his interpretations do not necessarily reflect the views or the policy of the publisher or its supporters.

ISEAS Library Cataloguing-in-Publication Data

Ooi, Kee Beng.
   In lieu of ideology : an intellectual biography of Goh Keng Swee.
   1. Goh, Keng Swee, 1918–2010.
   2. Politicians—Singapore—Biography.
   3. Cabinet officers—Singapore—Biography.
   4. Singapore—Politics and government.
   I. Title.
   DS610.63 G61O62   2010

ISBN 978-981-4311-30-4 (soft cover)
ISBN 978-981-4311-31-1 (hard cover)
ISBN 978-981-4311-32-8 (E-book PDF)

Cover design by Chris Lim Kah Wai
Cover pictures courtesy of *The Straits Times* © *Singapore Press Holdings Limited*. Reprinted with permission.

Front cover: Dr Goh Keng Swee at the Hong Lim ward during the Hong Lim by-election, 29 April 1961.
Back cover: Dr Goh Keng Swee inspecting the troops at the Armed Forces Day parade, 1 July 1971.

Typeset by Superskill Graphics Pte Ltd
Printed in Singapore by

CONTENTS

FOREWORD

Dr Goh was the foremost among the architects of the transformation of Singapore
— Press Statement from Prime Minister's Office,
14 May 2010.

One month before Dr Ooi Kee Beng delivered his manuscript to the publisher, Dr Goh Keng Swee breathed his last.

Dr Goh's death triggered an interesting phenomenon in Singapore. On the one hand, a profusion of tributes to the great man, from high and low, arose from many who had worked with him or, as contemporaries, were familiar with his achievements. Yet, at the other end of the age-spectrum, say, among the under-40s, there was bemused surprise at that outpouring of acclaim.

A sign of collective amnesia among the younger half of the citizenry? Not really. They just may not have learned of Dr Goh, for reasons that are suggested below; or their ears did not prick up when his name or accomplishments earlier came up.

One reason is that Dr Goh was out of the public eye for some 15 years or more before his death. He did his job, retired, and had a clean break with politics. During his years of active service, Dr Goh's mission, as the book demonstrates in unmistakable terms, was to throw himself wholeheartedly into the tasks at hand. Not for him the development of a personality cult. He did not obsess over what the history books might want to say about him. He knew that his actions and their results spoke for themselves. And he understood the ancient Roman maxim: Sic transit gloria mundi.

The second reason that the younger generation may not have come up to speed on Dr Goh is the palpable state of the teaching of history in schools. Maybe, steps are now being taken to improve the situation. Time will tell. Perhaps the timeliness of publication of this book, so soon after Dr Goh left this earthly world, will stimulate interest among Singaporeans not only in its subject matter, but our nation's history.

What did Dr Goh do to justify the description by Prime Minister Lee Hsien Loong in the tribute quoted above? Dr Goh's work is normally divided into three compartments — finance and economic growth, defence, and education — corresponding to the three ministries he headed over a span of 25 years. Yet, his record in those three vital areas is not the sum and substance of what he did for Singapore. His reach penetrated virtually every area of public life. He was the ultimate policy wonk. But not just that. Because of his intellectual prowess, innovative turn of mind, and common sense combined with a degree of chutzpah, he enjoyed a moral authority that enabled him, as the saying goes, to punch above his weight. Far above his weight.

What he did, as Dr Ooi patiently and penetratingly exposes, shaped Singapore's destiny. And what he did not, or more accurately what he prevented, was equally significant. Seductive ideas and proposals always emerge from ministries and elsewhere. Particularly in those early days of straitened resources, someone with the clarity of thinking, cogency of exposition, and moral integrity of a Dr Goh was needed to sift the wheat from the chaff. The need for judgement of that calibre is still valid. Always.

Leadership in government is essentially the practice of the art of making choices. Choices not just of policies, programmes and projects, important as they may be. There are also choices of governance: the type of governance system adopted taking into account the circumstances of time and place; the values the leadership wishes to espouse; and the pertinence of concepts such as justice, egalitarianism, civil rights, the rights of the individual, the environment, as well as other more mundane policies. Those were the fundamental issues which Dr Goh, who thought deeply about moral philosophy, wrestled with in his public life.

Those issues were pertinent in his early years in public life, in the 1960s, as the foundation of the new nation was being set; and they continue to be valid, as existential issues. So, it is interesting to speculate on how Dr Goh may have addressed some of the more intriguing questions of the day: the distribution of the national pie, population, immigration, the falling fertility rate, and so forth. While he kept out of the public eye for some two decades before his death, there is enough known about him and his thought process, which the author has explored so assiduously in his scholarly work, to project that Dr Goh would have conceived radical ideas. He is sorely missed.

Dr Goh's interests were wide ranging, and his mind rapier sharp. That combination enabled him to take a kaleidoscopic perspective of the issues before him. He was truly a renaissance man, a humanist, and would wholeheartedly have subscribed to the sentiments of Tagore in these lines from the Gitanjali:

"Where the mind is without fear and the head is held high;
Where knowledge is free;

. . .

. . .

Where the clear stream of reason has not lost its way into the
dreary, desert sand of dead habit;
Into that heaven of freedom, my Father, let my country awake."

No one is perfect. With all his many virtues and attributes,
Dr Goh was subject to human foibles and failings. Out of timber
so crooked as that from which man is made, nothing entirely
straight can be built, said Immanuel Kant. So Dr Goh had his
irascible moments, the faltering of judgement, and the occasional
rash, lamented act. They can be forgiven, and most of his victims
probably did forgive. Because of his generosity of spirit and
sterling character, those who worked closely with him, and earned
his confidence, were prepared to go the last mile for him. They
recognized him for what he was: a selfless leader who always put
the public interest before his own. Truly, "He was the noblest of
them all".

A word about the author and his opus. When the manuscript
arrived and the sub-title, "*An Intellectual Biography of Dr Goh Keng
Swee*", popped up, so did my eyebrows. I wondered who that
intrepid author was, whom I had then not met, that ventured
to probe that lofty mind. As I scanned the text, I realized that
Dr Ooi was not exaggerating. I later learned from him that,
astonishingly, he had never met Dr Goh, a fact that enhanced
my esteem for him. He clarified that he had attempted to gain
second-hand insights through interviews with several personalities
that were contemporaries of Dr Goh, but gave up the idea in
favour of a scholarly search of primary sources.

That task he has accomplished in spades. Even to someone
like me who had worked with Dr Goh on-and-off for some thirty
years, the result of Dr Ooi's labour is a revealing tome. Befitting
his scholarly background, Dr Ooi has painstakingly researched
dozens of references, indeed well over a hundred. And he has

strung his material and his thoughts together cogently and convincingly. The product is worthy of patient perusal, but even Dr Ooi may concede it is not for the faint-hearted.

All who knew Dr Goh well owe the author a debt of gratitude for so diligently and successfully undertaking the project. We should thank as well ISEAS and its perspicacious director, Mr K. Kesavapany, for promoting this project and selecting a very able scholar to write it.

It is ISEAS' declared intention to produce biographies of other leading Singaporeans, particularly the founding fathers. It is an aspiration that will be applauded by Singaporeans of a reflective disposition.

J.Y. Pillay
Chairman
Singapore Exchange Limited

PREFACE

Dr Goh Keng Swee passed away on 14 May 2010, just as I was finishing Chapter Seven. It was very sad news, of course. I had hoped to present him with a copy of this book, more for the symbolism than anything else, you understand. He had after all been bedridden for many years, following a series of strokes.

I decided then that the next best thing for me to do was to shift to top gear and finish the book within a month of his death. I have a weakness for symbolisms.

And so, I hand in my manuscript to ISEAS Publishing now, on the morning of 14 June 2010. With that, a project that took three years to do is brought to completion.

It has been a great and undeserved honour for me to study and to write about this unique man. Being of foreign origins, I had to discover this Singaporean for the first time. I knew nothing about the great deeds he performed in his life, and so was able to be properly awed by them.

I went to his wake at his home in Dunbar Walk. His son, Goh Kian Chee, was there to receive me, as was his widow, Dr Phua Swee Liang. Seeing Dr Goh in his casket that day, I wished that my children were there with me so that I could point to him and talk to them about who he was. I had after all been filling my mind with his thoughts for months on end.

Dr Goh's body was laid in state at Singapore's Parliament House for three days, beginning on 19 May. So that morning, my wife and I took the opportunity to bring along a group of home-educating families, including our own children, to pay our final respects. We sat on the granite steps outside Victoria Theatre for a couple of hours while I talked to the group about this man, whose passing was prompting young and old Singaporeans to revisit their national history.

Most of the children present, aged between 4 and 15, had not heard about Dr Goh, and if they had, knew of him only as a name they were supposed to recognize for some unclear reason. The people who were most interested in what I had to say were not the kids; it was their mothers.

And so, it is to them, and to all Singaporeans, that I dedicate this book; my humble contribution to the complex saga of The Little Island that Roared.

ACKNOWLEDGEMENTS

A half century has passed since the two decades that followed the Second World War saw colonies throughout the world transform themselves into sovereign states. A new generation is now grown who benefits — and suffers — from the actions of post-colonial nation builders, but who has no detailed knowledge about the complexities of their national history. What has also appeared is a sense of urgency among members of the older generation who lived through those times, to capture whatever can be captured of the past. They fear that the young will not understand their own situation and jeopardize the nation-building process through that ignorance.

And so, there has been an explosion of books about Southeast Asia's past leaders, many of them coming out of ISEAS Publishing. The latter is largely due to ISEAS Director Ambassador K. Kesavapany, whom I wish to thank before anyone else for giving this project to me, and for all the help he rendered along the way.

I thank him also for graciously allowing me to structure this book in a unique fashion. This volume is unlike other recent ones written about past leaders which are based on interviews with friends, relatives and colleagues, but is instead a narrative built around the subject's original writings.

I wish also to express my gratitude to Dr Goh Keng Swee's family members for assistance given to me over the last three years.

This project is also the first to make full use of the digitized version of *The Straits Times*, made available to me a year before the official launching of the NewspaperSG initiative that now provides scholars with easy access to Singaporean and Malaysian media printed before 1989. I heartily thank Singapore Press Holdings for that privilege.

That access to key material would not have been possible without the trust and generosity of Singapore's National Library. I would especially like to thank Ms Lim Soo Hoon, Chairman of the National Library Board (NLB) and Permanent Secretary of Singapore's Public Service Division; NLB Director Ms Ngian Lek Choh; Ms Judy Ng, Head of the Lee Kong Chian Reference Library; Ms Noryati A. Samad, Senior Manager of the Singapore and Southeast Asia Collections at the Lee Kong Chian Reference Library; Ms Ang Seow Leng, Senior Reference Librarian at the Lee Kong Chian Reference Library; and Ms Kartini Binti Saparudin, Associate Librarian at NLB.

Ms Kartini offered valuable help in my quest for articles written by Dr Goh Keng Swee before 1960, saving me a lot of time and headache through her kind and warm assistance.

The National University of Singapore's Singapore/Malaysia Collection put useful and rare material at my finger tips, and I am grateful to the librarians there for their competence and warmth.

My hunt for details about Goh Keng Swee the schoolboy was made easy through the kind assistance of the Archivist at the Anglo-Chinese School, Mr Earnest Lau, formerly Principal of Anglo-Chinese Secondary School, and his assistant, Ms Jenny Ng.

My debt of gratitude to colleagues at ISEAS goes without saying. ISEAS Library is one of the best stocked in the world, and this book would have taken a much longer time to write if I had not had such easy access to the books and journals found there, as well as special collections such as the Gerald De Cruz Papers and the Tun Dr Ismail Abdul Rahman Collection. I thank Library Head Ms Ch'ng Kim See, Ms D. Gandhimathy, the head of Systems Development, Reference and Circulation Services, Ms Susan Low, head of Special Projects, and all other ISEAS librarians for their kind and ready assistance.

A great debt of gratitude is owed to Mrs Triena Ong and all the staff at ISEAS Publishing for their warm and dedicated professionalism. Without them, this volume would not be as error-free and elegant as it is. As with all my earlier books handled by ISEAS Publishing, the final product always comes out looking more stylish than I could have imagined when handing in the manuscript.

I am also indebted to Dr Audrey Kahin and the Division of Rare and Manuscript Collections at Cornell University Library for permission to access the George McTurnan Kahin Papers, and to my friend and colleague Dr Hui Yew-Foong for help rendered on that front and for many valuable comments made on our daily trips to work.

Thanks must also be given to the National Archives, Kew Gardens, where invaluable documents concerning Malaya's and Singapore's history are easily kept available by a competent staff.

A special word of thanks must also go to colleagues at ISEAS who provided me with advice and relevant material, especially Dr Terence Chong, Dr Francis Hutchinson, Dr Lee Hock Guan, Dr Loh Kah Seng, Mr Daljit Singh and Mr Tan Keng Jin.

When I started on this project, I also interviewed several people who knew Dr Goh Keng Swee well. Although the approach I finally chose did not make direct use of those interviews, I wish them to know that my conversations with them provided me with solid knowledge about the man whose thoughts I was about to analyse. Many thanks to Mr Ngiam Tong Dow, Mr Lim Ho

Hup, Prof Lui Pao Chuen, Mr Phua Bah Li, Dr Soon Teck Wong and Dr Moses Yu.

Inspiration comes from unexpected directions and in all shapes, sizes and subjects. This makes it difficult to give credit where credit is definitely due, and I am bound to leave many unmentioned to whom I am in truth indebted. So, even if their names are not included in this short note, I wish them to know that I am grateful for their help, kindness and friendship. They contributed in more ways than they will ever know.

Last and certainly not least, I wish to thank my wife, Laotse Sacker, for her patience and assistance throughout the years. She scrutinized the chapters before they were finished, and gave precious pointers that are all now incorporated into the final product.

INTRODUCTION

This project suffered a few false starts. I began by looking for books about Dr Goh. These are surprisingly few, the most prominent of them being his daughter-in-law Tan Siok Sun's recent *Goh Keng Swee: A Portrait.* It took some time for me to realize that a book on Dr Goh could not possibly build on secondary sources and on what interviewees remember about him, regardless of the state of their memory and how well they knew him. Although people were most willing to help, useful documented sources about him were a scarcity.

Besides, Singapore's historiography suffers a narrative bind caused not only by the minute size of the island, its small population and its short history, but also by widespread concerns about national security and legal consequences. Such conditions persuade political biographers and historians to rely on interviews with an ever diminishing group of aging insiders and on limited access to official documents.

After some ingestion of information about Dr Goh, I saw that what was lacking once Siok Sun's book had come out in 2007 was a volume that dealt at length with the man's thoughts. After all, he was a thinker above all else, with the qualifier of course that thought and action were intertwined in his personality. What better way is there to understand Dr Goh then than through his own words?

And so, the concept for this book became clear. What was also gratifying was to learn that he wrote a lot throughout his life, and already as a young teenager. Furthermore, he was an old-world politician who had a wonderful command over his language of choice and who personally wrote practically everything he allowed to be publicized. He was also highly respected by his colleagues for his scope of knowledge, and his need to do research on anything he was to give a talk on.

From that point onwards, the book developed with a dynamic of its own. All I had to do was find the material, sieve through them, pick out texts that I found representative of his major trends of thought, and analyse them within a historical context.

A natural demarcation in Dr Goh's life was when he became an elected politician. This occurred exactly when Singapore's political situation changed dramatically. I therefore divide this book into Section One and Section Two — the first dealing with writings done before he was openly a politician, and the second with the rest of his life when his thoughts were fully concerned with the building of the nation. To be sure, the last chapter is somewhat different and deals largely with his understanding of the modern world and China's economic reforms.

Section One is written in a chronological fashion, and covers, as far as I am able to ascertain, everything that Dr Goh wrote before winning the Kreta Ayer seat for the first time in 1959. The same procedure could not be used for Section Two. His thinking and his achievements were too interlocked throughout the coming years for them to be represented chronologically. I therefore chose a thematic approach for the period after Singapore's gaining of self-government. What I finally ended up with was a chapter each on economics, finance, defence, education, the human element and China. Admittedly, these extended beyond the concerns of the three portfolios that he was officially in charge of at different times in his life; and acts poignantly as testament to the holistic and practical frame of mind that he possessed.

The result is what is best called an intellectual biography. The narrative weaves selected works by Dr Goh with historical and biographical details in an attempt to do justice to the richness of his thinking and in acknowledgement of the fact that his achievements can only be fully appreciated alongside the imperatives he experienced.

For the period before 1959, the biographical element is stronger than the intellectual, and provides the reader with an account of his early thinking. In Section Two, the latter element is definitely more prominent.

No doubt, as in all of us, his thinking evolved over time. However, what is surprising is how consistent his basic ideas seemed. The primacy of economics in politics was already clear to him as a boy, as was the importance of hard work and determination. He threw himself into his times, as it were. Only after he retired did he have time for himself; but even then his academic interests were about what we may call "economic engineering".

I wish I could mention in a word what the essence of his thinking was. What "-ism" would suffice? Socialism? Elitism? Statism? Modern Neo-Confucianism? Asian Nationalism? Utilitarianism? Economism? Pragmatism?

To all, I have to answer both "Yes" and "No". He did show affinity to all these approaches, some more than others, but his basic tendency was always "achievement-orientated". Economism does connote a practical approach, but only if understood in a sense broader than mere concern with money matters. Pragmatism describes his thinking as well. Sun Zi, the militarist he admired most, was definitely a pragmatist. But I fear the term is useful by virtue of its vague and accommodative nature. Pragmatism is about means, not ends.

Perhaps it is because we are dealing with someone who lived in a time when ideologies reigned that we try to summarize his thoughts and actions. That is really not a fruitful undertaking. In lieu of a label — in lieu of ideology — he thought in informed and practical terms. He succeeded in what he set out to do, and he made Singapore succeed.

Dr Goh wished for results, the foremost of which was economic growth. For that to occur, national stability and security was imperative, and that required shrewd institutional manipulation of global capitalism and judicious control over macro-economic factors. Since time was a luxury new states do not have, state participation in economic growth was vital, and in conjunction with market capitalism if policies were to be effective. Competition forces people to excel, which meant that welfare measures had to be eyed with suspicion, and traditional economic mindsets had to be transformed. After Singapore had gained stability and security, and the national economic and state finances had found solidity, the government shifted its attention to education and moral upbringing. In the case of Dr Goh and in Singapore policies in general, we witness a strong appreciation of Confucianism by the late 1970s which went beyond the interest in ancient generals like Sun Zi and Wu Qi. The search for an integrated way of thought that would encourage economic competitiveness, enhance patriotism and develop high-minded and cultivated citizens pointed towards an old solution. Confucianism — or at least Legalist Confucianism — became an attraction, not only for its capacity to strengthen the country, but also for its ability to provide moral guidance as well.

In a profound sense, therefore, the chapters in Section Two chart major aspects of nation building in Singapore considered as a former English colony in Asia with a Chinese-majority. The apparent holism that we end up with is thus the sum of the stages telescoped in time, through which the country — and Dr Goh — travelled over a half century.

Ooi Kee Beng
ISEAS, Singapore
14 June 2010

PART ONE

The Civil Servant

Chapter 1

PRE-WAR WRITINGS

He who has ambition will do his best in order to satisfy himself. He will stick to his work and see that he is the best man that ever has done that work. Our ambition must be to make ourselves useful to our country, our people and ourselves.

— Goh Keng Swee, 12 years old
("My Ambitions", in *ACS Magazine*, 1931)

As 1918 drew to a close, old and once-powerful empires in Europe and Asia Minor were drawing their last breath. Unbeknownst to victors such as the British, their empires too would not survive the Great War for long. New states were replacing them, and over the recently begun century more would emerge in all parts of the world. In East Asia, most significantly, China was still mired in the confusion caused by the fresh collapse of its millennia-old dynastic system. Japan, on the other hand, was moving from victory to victory, modernizing impressively and filling the power vacuum left by Europe's misfortunes.

On 6 October of that eventful and chaotic year, Goh Keng Swee was born to Goh Leng Inn and Tan Swee Eng in the historic town of Malacca on the Malay Peninsula.

Leng Inn was "an upright, frugal and hardworking" Methodist who in his bachelor days worked as a teacher at Singapore's Anglo-Chinese School. Swee Eng was a Peranakan like Leng Inn, and belonged to the affluent Tan family of Malacca. The couple were to have five children — two boys and three girls.

Goh Keng Swee was only two years old when his family moved to Singapore, where he attended the Anglo-Chinese Primary School in 1927–1932, and the Anglo-Chinese Secondary School in 1933–1936.* He showed a talent for music, playing the piano and learning the accordion on his own.

Since the Goh family lived far from town on the Pasir Panjang Rubber Estate, the children relied on a chartered bus for transport to school. This they shared with the children of Leng Inn's closest friend, Kwa Siew Tee, who lived down the road from them. Siew Tee's daughter, Geok Choo, would later become Mrs Lee Kuan Yew.

Goh Keng Swee maintained a soft spot for the Anglo-Chinese School throughout his life and became a member of the ACS Old Boys Association on leaving the school (ACS Vol. XII 1939: 78). Years later, when he was Deputy Prime Minister and Minister of Education, he participated publicly in criticism of "student-snobs at ACS" (*ST* 25 May 1980).

The Anglo-Chinese School was established in 1886 shortly after the first Methodist Church was set up on Coleman Street by W.F. Oldham, with help from new friends he had made in

---

* Tan Cheng Loke, founder of the Malayan Chinese Association, was Swee Eng's first cousin. Cheng Loke's son, Siew Sin, later Finance Minister of Malaysia, was therefore Goh's second cousin.

The *Peranakan* are also known as Baba and Nyonya. They are an urban hybrid born of centuries of cultural interaction between Chinese and Malays.

Many details about Goh's early life are unless otherwise stated extracted from Tan Siok Sun's *Goh Keng Swee: A Portrait*.

Singapore's China Town. Both Chinese and English were taught to the first batch of 13 Chinese boys, but English apparently became the sole medium of instruction immediately after that. Within a year, the school had over a hundred students. The education the school provided was undoubtedly popular, and the student body grew to 624 members by 1896. That year, however, controversy over missionary activities caused registration to drop by almost 20%. Relations between the church and the Chinese community seemed to have quickly mended after that. A Secondary Level school was started in 1928 on newly bought land at Cairnhill, after land on Oldham Lane proved unable to support a big building. The *ACS Magazine* itself began publication only in 1929, after its predecessor, the *ACS Journal* had failed to survive an attempt to turn it into a collective organ for the Anglo-Chinese School in Penang, Ipoh and Singapore (Lee 1936: 29–32).

Goh demonstrated early in life a talent, if not a need, for writing. At the age of 13, he won a consolation prize of Five Straits Dollars in a newspaper competition. The paper had published a limerick without its punch line, requesting that competitors provided it. It read:

> *A planter cried out in affliction,*
> *"If only they'd give me restriction,*
> *It might end all my woes,*
> *But as everyone knows,*
> ....

"Restriction" here referred to curbs on the planting of new rubber trees. Goh's concluding submission was: *It's only a planter's conviction.* The winning entry was, *Some want it — some don't — hence the friction,* submitted by a J.A.L. Simmons from the Department of Statistics (*ST* 6 March 1932).

Goh published a couple of noteworthy short pieces in the school magazine, the first of which was written before he had turned thirteen years of age. The second was written four years later. Since both are extremely short, they are reproduced here in their entirety.

My Ambitions (1931)

Anybody who wants to prosper in this world must have an ambition. Ambition comes from a thought or when we get enthusiastic we determine to carry out our thought. He who has an ambition will do his best in order to satisfy himself. He will stick to his work and see that he is the best man that ever has done that work. Our ambition must be to make ourselves useful to our country, our people and ourselves. To be ambitious we must have determination so that we may never slack or shirk in our work.

My ambition is to become an engineer. China needs engineers, scientists, inventors and sailors badly. She has not a respectable navy and air force and so to have these things she needs people to produce them, and keep them going. So China needs soldiers, sailors and airmen to help her become one of the best nations in the world. She needs useful men, and for me engineering is the thing.

This early document, though only two paragraphs long, is fascinating for a variety of reasons. First, we see a boy who is certainly more philosophical than his age would coax us to expect. Not only does he show conviction that ambition is critical to success, he wishes to persuade others of that as well. Doing one's best and having staying power depend on the person already having an adequate idea that expresses a concrete ambition. Second, this ambition goes beyond itself and has ethical goals, namely serve "our country, our people and ourselves". At the risk of reading too much into a 12-year-old's words, there is here a hint that he professes "enlightened self-interest" and does not stress contradictions between social benefit and individual satisfaction. Third, this boy, who would later become one of the most successful economists in the world, identified engineering as the field into which he should venture. He chooses this because his country needs engineers. Fourth — and this reminds us of the general absence of Malayan nationalism in pre-war times and of how the looming struggle in China to find a place in the world overshadowed any nascent nationalism in Southeast Asia — the country that the boy imagines as his, is not Britain or Malaya or Singapore, but China.

One may be excused at this point for inquisitiveness into the emotional significance of Goh's involvement late in life in China's Dengist experiments. This point is discussed in the final chapter.

The complexity of political identification among Chinese in Malaya in those days was reflected in the activities of the Malayan Kuomintang (KMT). Its branches exerted great influence in Chinese vernacular schools; for example, its leaders were the ones responsible for the founding of the Anglo-Chinese Girls' School in June 1913. The Malayan Kuomintang consistently raised huge funds throughout Malaya for Sun Yat-sen's attempts to topple the Qing Dynasty. Massive memorial services were held in Singapore in his honour following his death in 1925. When the party, led by Chiang Kaishek, managed to unify China in 1928, a great surge of nationalism welled up in Chinese communities throughout the world (Yong & McKenna 1990: 30, 39–42, 79). Staggered and harsh Japanese encroachment into Mainland China also acted as a consistent stimulant for Chinese nationalistic sentiments throughout the *Nanyang* (the maritime region south of China). This was evident in September 1931 when the Japanese infantry invaded Manchuria.

Ineffectively banned by the British in October 1925, the Kuomintang was able to function until the arrival in February 1930 of the former Governor of Hong Kong, Cecil Clementi. In his position of Governor of the Straits Settlements and High Commissioner of the Federated Malay States (FMS), Clementi immediately unleashed a crackdown on the Malayan Kuomintang. Between February and July 1930, he "strengthened punitive measures against all avenues of perceived Chinese nationalism and against the KMT in particular". In order to limit Chinese nationalism, he worked "to increase the standing and practical position of the Malays and Malay rulers in relation to the position of the Chinese population". The larger picture was the British policy to decentralize control over the peninsula in order to standardize the complicated colonial administration, which was given to internal struggles between the High Commissioner and the Chief Secretary of the Federated Malay States. The goal was to decentralize and standardize the colonies in order for control to be exerted more rationally and effectively (*ibid.* 138–39).

This was the mood of the times; British standing in Malayan Chinese eyes was at a new low, and a battery of measures limiting Chinese immigration from China and other regions in Southeast Asia, constraining the Chinese press and affecting Chinese education were being implemented. We can only speculate how this affected young Goh and his family, but it would be quite unlikely for this well-connected and well-educated family to have been ignorant of or disinterested in these impressive changes.

Where China's place in Goh's imagination was concerned, author and long-term Southeast Asian correspondent for *The Observer*, Dennis Bloodworth (1919–2005), had this to say in April 1982 (CORD Bloodworth p. 43):

> Goh had an intense desire to know more about China; interested
> in Chinese culture and history from the outside since he was

English-educated. And later on, he was trying to read Chinese classical works which I think he found very trying.

Whichever the case, *Sun Zi's Art of War* would be one of Goh's most cited books, alongside Adam Smith and John Maynard Keynes.

Wanted — A Playing Field (1935)

When our Geographical Society excursionists went up the FMS they noted that every school worth glancing at had an extensive playing field embellished with at least a pair of goal posts. All the schools, the large ones I mean, make us most envious. Think of it. They have acres of playing fields!

For many years now our school, which is one of the leading ones in this Island, has not a football field to boast of. At Cairnhill there is only one badminton court and one volleyball court. It is true that Oldham Hall field is more or less always available but, considering that the homes of most of our students are miles away from that place, there is not very much use made of it. Besides, the playing fields of a school should really adjoin the school.

We are, of course, grateful to the Y.M.C.A. and to St. Andrew's School for the occasional use of their grounds, but it is deplorable that we should depend on outside institutions for our games facilities.

We are also in need of a science laboratory and a gymnasium.

We hope that all these needs will be supplied in the not distant future.

In 1935, Goh, now nearing the end of his time at the Anglo-Chinese School, wrote this short piece to take the school authorities to task for having neglected the sorry lack of playing fields. This last reminder would have been a sore point for the reputable school. For good measure, he threw in the pressing need for "a science laboratory and a gymnasium".

Again, at the risk of reading too much into Goh's words, the two short pieces, taken together, nevertheless suggest a writer given to terse prose, who goes straight to the point, who seems concerned about the situation of the world, and who is geared towards changing that situation.

After graduating second in his class in the Senior Cambridge Examinations and receiving a prize for English, Goh continued his schooling at Raffles College, from which he received a Class II Diploma in Arts in March 1939, with Special Distinction in Economics. He was the only one to receive that high grade that year (*ST* 29 June 1936; 24 March 1939; 26 May 1940).

His penchant for economic thinking is firmly registered through the fact that he served successively as secretary, vice-president and then president of Raffles College Economics Society. His schooldays also coincided with the Great Depression, and the fall in rubber prices hit his family's rubber plantations to the point where his father, as manager of a rubber estate, had a hard time making ends meet.

His roommates at Raffles included Lim Kim San and Hon Sui Sen (Tan 2007: 34, 36, 204). All three were freshmen in 1936 but while Lim was in Arts with Goh, Hon was in Science (RCM 1937). Amazingly, these three would later take turns at being the Finance Minister of Singapore between 1959 and 1983. Lim became the first chairman of the Housing and Development Board (HDB) in 1960, and took the Ministry of Finance after Singapore's separation from Malaysia in August 1965, when Goh went over to the newly formed Ministry of the Interior and Defence. When Lim got married on 24 February 1940, Goh acted as his best man (*ST* 25 Feb 1940).

Hon was awarded a scholarship to Raffles for being top-scoring student at Penang's St Xavier's Institution. He became the first chairman of the Economic Development Board (EDB) in

1961, and left it to start the Development Bank of Singapore (DBS) in 1968. It was he who was brought in to succeed Goh — who was moving to the Ministry of Defence — as Finance Minister in 1970, where he remained until his untimely death on 14 October 1983 (Hon 1984; *ST* 21 June 1936).

Later in life, Hon reminisced to his daughter Joan about Goh "breezing through exams without much effort".

> Oh, Dr Goh, of course, has always been very good. I mean that, even in those days, he was an economist and he was quite a bright student. And of course, he was a good writer even in those days. He used to make fun of economics. As...if you want to go to sleep, just read Marshall, or something like that. But I think people had respect for Dr Goh, even in those days (Hon 1984: 39–40).

Joan Hon in turn remembers Goh admitting to her that he was one of the few students who did read Alfred Marshall's classic from cover to cover but without understanding it (*ibid*: 40). Marshall (1842–1924) authored *Principles of Economics*, the textbook that for generations influenced scholarly thinking about political science and economics. First published in 1890, it went in defence of the deductive method used by the dominant economist of the nineteenth century, David Ricardo (Wagner 1891).

General Theory of Employment, Interest and Money, the classic written by John Maynard Keynes, was published in 1936, the year Goh went to Raffles. He ploughed through it hungrily, reading it at least three times from cover to cover. Although he was fascinated by it, he found certain flaws in it. The issue of inflation, he thought, was consciously concealed by Keynes through his coinage of "wage units". Worse than that, Keynes failed to take account of foreign trade. Incidentally, this defect would make Keynesianism unsuitable in Goh's eyes for use in little Singapore (Goh 1991). Other books that Goh is known to have studied at this time include the writings of John Locke, Thomas Hobbes' *Leviathan* and Thomas Aquinas' *Summa Theologica*. These failed to captivate him. What did absorb his interest were the works of Bertrand Russell (Tan 2007: 37).

Maurice Baker, who would later become Professor of English at the University of Singapore and also Singapore's High Commissioner to Malaysia in 1969–1971, was a junior by a couple of years to Goh, Lim and Hon at Raffles College. He remembers those days vividly (*Oral History*, Reel 2):

> [Goh] had a tremendous reputation. [...] Even in his final year, Silcock used him to tutor his first year students, which very rarely happens. He was exceptionally good in Economics. In my view, he is an economic genius. [...] I got to know Goh Keng Swee well only in London later, not in Raffles College. He was quite aloof. The thing about Keng Swee is that he has got no time for small talk. Every discussion with him is a serious discussion. He wants to get things done. He doesn't waste time talking about nothing in particular just to be pleasant to people. He remains aloof. He is usually aloof until you got to know him.

In fact, Prof. T.H. Silcock (1910–1984) joined the Department of Economics only in 1938, during Goh's last year at Raffles. Unfortunately, an earlier teacher in economics, Ralph Arakie, had committed suicide, which gave Goh no choice other than to study economics on his own. He seemed nevertheless an active student, sub-editing the *Raffles College Magazine* in 1937 and representing his school in cricket and tennis in 1938, as he had done at the Anglo-Chinese School (*ST* 22 April 1935; 1 Feb 1937). He also played cricket and hockey for the YMCA (*ST* 19 Sept 1932; 13 June 1936). Apparently, he never took to cricket.

His contributions to the *Raffles College Magazine* were somewhat limited, and included two poems — "A Paradox" and "College Personalities". The only lengthy article he ever wrote for the periodical was titled "Capitalism versus Socialism".

THE POEMS
A PARADOX (1937)
&
COLLEGE PERSONALITIES (1938)

"A Paradox" is a short poem apparently portraying a young mind confounded by Reason's helplessness in the face of fleeting Beauty. It is written as rough octameter, rhymed but with a stunted first line:

A Paradox
You baffle me...
Beyond the probe of the searchlight
Of cold logic, like some ethereal being
Fluttering in the depths of the night
A fleeting glance at beauty draws
Fervid attempts to locate substantiality
Which then dissolves in reason's jaws
And leaves behind blank perplexity

The following year, Goh published a longer and much less sombre ode to school life and to his schoolmates in the same magazine.

College Personalities
Pardon me if I wax too romantic;
It's just an escape from economics,
Which leads us to think of things pedantic,
And make[s] us miss much of life's comics.

Let's forget Mr. Keynes' Liquidity-preference,
And Alfred Marshall's representative firm,
And proceed with all due deference
To neglect them the rest of the term.

Let's switch on a running commentary
On the people around us who are distinctive;
Even though the pleasure afforded is momentary,
Yet the urge to gossip is instinctive.
The Olympians may object to such a game:
So apologies now to their noble entities.
But it is the price they have to pay for fame —
To amuse the whims of us nonentities.

It is right that we begin with Hercules,
Who is, at least, theoretically strong.
His friends know too well what a mule is,
"Stiff in opinions, always in the wrong."
His moon face beams on all and sundry,
When he achieves his heart's desire;
But when argument with him goes thund'ry,
Oh well, it's best for us to retire.

Typhoon's traits are peculiar and many;
Of pet theories he has an infinite number
On everything on earth, real or uncanny,
Which when expounded (God help!) send us to slumber.
Nothing* his poise in feminine society,
Cynics unkindly placate their grouse
By dubbing him a name of great notoriety
In ancient classics and in Mickey Mouse.

---

* This may be a typing error. "Noting" seems more appropriate here than "Nothing".

In this world of ours with all its badness,
More friends like Tock Tai we should seek.
He never knows a moment's sadness,
Except during the examination week.
His sporting prowess attract[s] great attention,
Though of late he's grown rotunder.
One weakness in him, I'd like to mention —
His singing splits our ear-drums asunder.

The great Lord Khaidu now demands attention:
So quiet all round if you please!
Experience he has of wide extension,
On which, during his hours of ease,
He will discourse without a halt
To many a long suffering disciple,
They all take it with two ounces of salt,
And in politeness their yawns they stifle.

No commentary on college lights would be complete
Without mention made of Donald Lim.
For the title 'Robert Taylor' many beaux compete, *
But all throw down the sponge to him.
His tactics win the day with the ladies,,
Whether at tea, meetings, dinner or dance.
A common appeal that should be made is
"Oh, Robert, won't you please give us a chance?"

An end must now come to this tattling,
With apologies for any omission.

---

* Robert Taylor (1911–1969) was a major Hollywood actor who was especially active in the late 1930s. He was known as "The Man with the Perfect Profile" (see *IMDB*).

My conscience within me is rattling:
To-morrow's the day for my essay's submission;
And I haven't as yet been able to start.
I hear Mr. Keynes' voice calling;
So hence, vain! Deluding joys — depart!
Shades of Ricardo! Isn't life appalling?
                                    — (RCM 1938).

The jovial cheekiness evident in this poem is not found in Goh's later writings.* For that alone, this early piece is worth contemplating. What lingers after a reading of these lines is the impression of an elated and passionate schoolboy full of recognized promise, enchanted by his odd school pals and excited about school life in pre-war Singapore. Due to the high probability of getting it wrong, no attempt shall be made here to identify the caricatured characters he lampoons in this ode other than to suggest that "Donald Lim" is probably Lim Kim San, a young man known for having a way with the ladies.

CAPITALISM VERSUS SOCIALISM (1938)

Goh wrote "Capitalism versus Socialism" in 1938, and published it that Trinity Term (April–June) in the *Raffles College Magazine* (Vol. VIII No. 1), the same number that included his cheery poem, "College Personalities". It is safe to say that the title of this, his first serious article on economics, was a deliberate play by the young man on the title of the book by A.C. Pigou (1877–1959) which came out a year earlier, called *Socialism vs. Capitalism*.

---

* One rare example of this impish side of him appeared in a speech he gave at the opening of the Jurong Bird Park on 4 January 1971. Another light-hearted speech was given at the inauguration of school councils on 22 February 1981.

Pigou was Alfred Marshall's star pupil, and succeeded the latter as Professor of Political Economy at Cambridge University in 1908, a position he held for 35 years, until 1943. Through works such as *Wealth and Welfare* (1912) and *The Economics of Welfare* (1920), Pigou exerted great influence over the discipline during the first third of the 20th century, personifying the "Cambridge Neoclassicals" who defended what became known as "Marshallian orthodoxy". His major contribution to the discipline was in welfare economics (CEE).

One of Pigou's greatest intellectual opponents was John Maynard Keynes (1883–1946), a close friend whom he had earlier financed from his own pocket to study probability theory. Poignantly, Keynesian thought came to overshadow effectively Pigou's own teachings from the 1930s onwards.

Pigou's most influential work was *The Economics of Welfare* (1920). In it, Pigou developed Marshall's concept of externalities, which are the costs imposed or benefits conferred on others that are not accounted for by the person who creates these costs or benefits. Pigou argued that negative externalities (costs imposed) should be offset by a tax, while positive externalities should be offset by a subsidy. Pigou's analysis was widely accepted until the early 1960s, when Ronald Coase showed that taxes and subsidies are not necessary if the partners in the transaction — that is, the people affected by the externality and the people who cause it — can bargain over the transaction. Pigou's reliance on taxes and subsidies was further undercut by public choice economists who observed that governments can and do fail, sometimes more spectacularly than markets (Encyclopaedia Brittanica).

Interestingly, Pigou's concepts of positive and negative externalities — operationally remedied through what are today known as Pigovian taxes and subsidies — have regained popularity in the 21st century, especially in environmental economics.

Graduating as he did in the late 1930s, Goh was strongly aware of these disputes in economic theory, just as his lecturers, such as Silcock, would have been. Indeed, not only did Goh play on the title of Pigou's *Socialism Versus Capitalism*, he also adopted to a large extent the book's structure in writing his essay.

The struggle between capitalism and socialism — and fascism — was heating up in Europe. Adolf Hitler's successive annexation of bits of central Europe was in full swing. Nazi designs to attain Sudetenland from Czechoslovakia were being formed on the heels of the Third Reich's *Anschluss* to incorporate Austria into Greater Germany on 12 March 1938. Just a few months earlier, on 6 November 1937, the Axis Powers had officially come into being when Italy finally joined the Anti-Comintern (Communist International) Pact that was founded a year earlier between Germany and Japan.

After Josef Stalin (1878–1953) enforced radical industrialization and agricultural policies in the late 1920s and throughout the 1930s, a conception of socialism — some would more readily say "Stalinism" — had come into being which claimed to be realizing key ideals of Marxism-Leninism.

In comparing capitalism with socialism, therefore, the 20-year-old Goh wisely chose in his nine-page article to avoid "ethical and political issues", and decided instead to concentrate on "the economic point of view". Tellingly, he defined "the world economy outside Soviet Russia" as a capitalist economy.

Capitalism, in his understanding, was about economic structures made up of "individually-owned industries". Such a system was characterized by two economic classes. These were "the capitalist-owners or entrepreneurs who assume[d] control over their units of industry" and "workers, employed by entrepreneurs and given wages in exchange for the labour they put in, but divorced from any ownership or control of the business".

Socialism, he postulated, did not rely on profits to motivate economic activity. Instead, "the State, or rather the Central controlling body of the State", was the major actor. Owning practically all industries, its job was to direct resources towards maximizing social welfare (pp. 41–42).

Before comparing the two systems, however, Goh postulated that the essence of economic activity, as seen most clearly in a primitive society, was "man's efforts to satisfy his wants with existing stocks of scarce economic goods". His wants were met directly through his own efforts, without an exchange of goods. Modern systems, on the other hand, were extremely complex and could not but be exchange economies.

Goh identified this process of exchange as a fruitful approach to adopt for comparing the two systems. This process was characterized in the capitalist system by (1) "freedom among consumers to buy [...] commodities on the market according to their preferences" and (2) "freedom of action among producers to meet the demands of consumers, the intensity and direction of which [were] indicated by the state of the price system". This interaction between supply and demand, Goh argued here in line with classic economic theory, decided price levels and dictated "the direction and volume of production".

Socialism rejected this price system and sought to replace it through central regulations and planning instead. A discussion about how such a price system could be instituted satisfactorily would have required much technical analysis. Goh avoided doing that and merely posited that "the technical difficulties attending the construction of such a system and the practical difficulties of administration etc., must be immense".

Goh then limited his study to four specific areas: (1) distribution of wealth; (2) unemployment in capitalist society; (3) technical productive efficiency and; (4) difficulties and dangers of central planning. These were clearly based on themes highlighted in Pigou's book. Goh summarized six of Pigou's themes into the four mentioned here. Only the discussion on "The Rate of Interest" was left out. Interestingly, Pigou ended his analysis by giving considerably more marks to Socialism than the young Goh did.

It was where income differences were concerned that "the socialist attack on capitalism [was] most withering and most justified", claimed Goh. Lacking data for Malaya — or Singapore for that matter — he used British figures to exemplify the great disparity in wealth that capitalism fostered. In 1936, the top 12% in Britain actually cornered 42% of the national income (pp. 43–44).

Not only was this tendency in capitalism a moral problem, social welfare also suffered because economic resources were "directed towards satisfying the whims of the rich — in building palaces, luxury yachts etc. — while a multitude of the poor [remained] ill nourished, badly clothed and housed."

> The tendency if unchecked will progress cumulatively through time; wealth, when invested in industries will increase wealth; while the poverty of a set of people will result in increased poverty in their children who have been originally handicapped" (p. 45).

At the same time, advanced capitalist countries had at their disposal an arsenal of measures that could be used to reduce income inequality. This was undeniable in Franklin Roosevelt's successful Keynesian New Deal that had been implemented in the United States since the early 1930s, and through the peaking of Scandinavian Social Democracy in the historic signing in Sweden in late 1938 of the *Saltsjöbaden* Agreement between Capital, Labour and State.

Goh reasoned that capitalism did possess the means by which it could "reduce the evils of inequality of distribution". The socialist ideal of perfect equality of wealth distribution, on the other hand, was not viable since it would "destroy the incentive of profits and social distinction" (p. 45). He also rejected the common claim that a close approximation to the socialist ideal would be good enough, "owing to the different propensities of individuals to dispose of their income, some making better use of their incomes than others".

The constant reoccurrence of high unemployment was of course another weakness of capitalism, one that socialism claimed it could resolve through the state assignment of jobs. "Frictional unemployment", which was of a temporary nature and which resulted from delays in changing jobs, was common to all systems. What needed solving was "abnormal unemployment", which arose through the very nature of capitalism itself.

Here, Goh provides a short presentation of the trade cycle to which capitalism was prone. This bears repeating at length to showcase the balanced and concise style of reasoning that he had already developed early in his life.

> The two fundamental features of capitalism which allow serious disequilibrium to take its course cumulatively through time may be re-stated: (1) The profit incentive in capitalistic economic activity; (2) The competitive individual ownership of factors of production. These give rise to a peculiar constellation of decisions, which by their reactions and repercussions on each other make possible a cumulative tendency towards disequilibrium in the economic system. Individual entrepreneurs make their decisions to produce greater or lesser quantities in

one line of production or another on basis of the state of prices in the market, with a view to making the greatest profits if possible, or undergoing the least possible losses if not. Thus a fair state of prices conduces great activity in production owing to excessive optimism among entrepreneurs. The capitalistic structure is such that although individual entrepreneurs act with little anticipation of the action of other entrepreneurs, [...] individual actions [have] repercussions on each other; increased productivity say in one line of production say, the motor industry, will stimulate production in many other industries — tin, steel, iron, rubber etc. — with the result that the forces in one direction will act cumulatively until a certain point at which a turn towards the reverse will take place when it becomes obvious that consumption lags behind production. The cumulative tendency is further accentuated on the courses of wages and level of employment — both being higher in the 'booms' thereby allowing greater production to take place with a greater possibility of consumption; while lower wages and greater unemployment increases the downward tendency by the reduction in purchasing power (p. 46).

The system's tendency to swing too much in one direction and then in the other could not but lead to great economic wastage. The way Goh saw it, capitalism tended to generate an occasional paradox — "poverty in the midst of plenty". Such a system, he reasoned, should rightly be "subjected to severe criticism". Socialism's claims of solving these fluctuations were on the other hand highly exaggerated. Here, Goh mentioned Keynes as one of the many modern economists trying to limit these excessive swings. The major innovations that had been tried with some success were in the areas of (1) public investment policy, which sought to create employment and increase purchasing power during a slump; (2) monetary policy, where the central banking system controlled the volume of credit and interest rates; and (3) budgetary control, which counter-intuitively involved overspending during a slump and under-spending during a boom to cover the foregoing deficit (p. 47).

Where technical productive efficiency was concerned, Goh claimed that the results of his comparison of the two systems were inconclusive. A reading of his analysis unquestionably shows, however, that he held strong doubts that the supposed enthusiasm of socialist planners and workers could be superior to the profit-seeking instincts encouraged by capitalism. Goh was highly sceptical of socialism's central planning mechanisms to function adequately given the "infinite kinds of goods required to satisfy the complicated wants of a civilized population". This dilemma was made worse by the "extreme difficulty of obtaining a satisfactory price system", and by the fact that "any centralization of control [lent] itself to abuse". He ventured that, "the catastrophic trade depressions of Capitalism [were] perhaps preferred to one of Stalin's occasional 'purges'" (p. 49).

His conclusion was that although capitalism had grave weaknesses, socialism as a remedy was "dangerous". Furthermore, the latter was unnecessary since the nature of capitalism allowed for its own remedies.

In scrutinizing this early work, one must stay cognizant of the fact that it was a piece written for a school magazine, and that the student was still one year away from graduation. What is important, however, is not necessarily what he thought but how he thought, and how he approached his subject. Goh was already showing at this tender age a strong propensity to be systematic in his thinking, clarifying matters one idea at a time.

Not one to waste words, Goh's narrative from 1938 blended opinions and referential facts fairly smoothly, moving straight to the point, adopting relevant generalizations along the way, and ending with clear conclusions. This was, one could say, a schoolbook example of academic writing. It is not hard to see why Silcock awarded Goh a Special Distinction a year later when it was time for the young man to leave Raffles College.

Considering the pragmatic thinker that he was in later years, it is fascinating that he ended his first academic publication with the following line:

> Above all this essay attempts to prove that the attainment of the 'ideal system' does not depend so much on the form and structure of the system as on the intelligence, energy and sympathy with which the affairs of the system are conducted (p. 50).

His command of the English language at this point was already impressive, with due consideration being given for hasty editing. Incidentally, the official sub-editor for that issue of the school magazine was Goh himself. Whatever room there may have been for improvement in his academic style was elegantly and undeniably filled by the time he produced his next publication — *The Economic Front from a Malayan Point of View* — two years later.

THE ECONOMIC FRONT FROM A MALAYAN POINT OF VIEW (1940)

Goh graduated from Raffles just as the British Empire went to war with Germany in 1939. He joined the newly created War Tax Department, but apparently did not excel particularly well at tax collection. What he managed to do successfully was court a spirited member of the office's secretarial pool, Alice Woon (Tan 2007: 38). The two married in 1942.

He retained his attachment to Raffles through tutoring under Silcock at the Department of Economics (*ST* 26 May 1940), and becoming a member of the alumni body, The Stamford Club. It was while working for the Tax Office that he published his first booklet *The Economic Front from a Malayan Point of View*. It won him considerable coverage in the Press.

Only a few days after the publication was introduced in *The Straits Times* on 20 and 21 May 1940, *The Onlooker* column in the same paper carried a short but significant review of it (*ST* 20, 21, 26 May 1940).

> An interesting pointer to the part that Raffles College will one day play in the life of Malaya was given last week. It was the publication of a pamphlet on the economic aspect of the war by Mr Goh Keng Swee, who has recently graduated in the economics department of the college.
>
> Since the outbreak of the war, professors and lecturers of the college have on several occasions been before the microphone and have given interesting and informative talks on various aspects of the great conflict that is now raging. But these views have been presented by men trained in British universities and with a definitely European background. Mr Goh Keng Swee's views are noteworthy not only for their clarity of thought but because they are presented with an essentially Malayan background (*ST* 26 May 1940).

The fact mentioned earlier that Goh, Lim and Hon — men destined to be major actors in the history of Malaya — were roommates at Raffles testifies poignantly to the point about the central role the college was playing. What was of further historical interest was the contemporary rarity of a strongly Malayan point of view on late colonial and wartime economics. For that alone, Goh's booklet is worth serious consideration.

A year earlier, on 18 January 1939, Goh had made his
presidential address to the college's Economic Society, which
was titled "The Economic Reconstruction of Germany" (*Annual
Report* 1938–39). This subject appears substantially as Chapter II
in his three-chapter booklet. That earlier address may not have
survived, although the school magazine carried the following
report of the occasion:

> The Speaker gave a brief survey of the German economy before
> the Nazi Regime and attributed the peculiarities of the present
> structure to the political influence of the economic policy in a
> depleted country (RCM 1939 Vol IX: 62)

The introduction to *The Economic Front* was written by Silcock,
Goh's former teacher and long-time head of the Economics
Department. Silcock would much later in life when comparing
Goh to Lim Kim San and Lee Kuan Yew — who studied economics
only briefly at Raffles — say this of his star pupil (Silcock 1985:
315–16):

> Goh Keng Swee is the one of the three who is clearly a
> professional economist with a strong sense of commitment to
> the subject as a subject. He is not, however, an orthodox
> economist; he believes strongly that skill in economists, at least
> in relation to economic development, is based on a deep
> appreciation of Adam Smith and Ricardo and other economists
> of the nineteenth century. He has very limited regard for advice
> based on detailed and quantitative assessment of the precise
> value of economic parameters. While he might consider that,
> in a highly developed market economy, these could be useful,
> he appears to attach less importance to their use in the areas of
> international trade and finance even in the industrial world,
> than some other development economists.

Where Hon Sui Sen was concerned, Silcock humbly proclaimed
that his department "could probably claim little credit for his

training except to have given a slight initial impetus in that direction". Hon's development into an economist of distinction, Silcock gracefully admitted, came from his later training in the United Kingdom and the World Bank and not from Raffles College as such (Silcock 1985: 70).

In his introduction to Goh's 40-page booklet, Silcock expressed a worry that life going on as usual in Malaya despite the war in Europe would "dull" the memories of Malayans. There was nothing noble in the mere making of money at times such as those that they were living in. The contribution that Malayans had consciously to make to the war effort went beyond that. As suggested in Goh's book, they should make an effort to "grow food on spare garden land; consume less goods from non-sterling countries; [and] cut out all wasteful expenditure". Even if no money were saved at the individual level, savings made on foreign exchange and precious resources should be valued (p. 5).

Goh provided in the preface his own elaborate reasons for writing *The Economic Front*. This was done in impressive fashion, especially for a 22-year-old. He noted that in the First World War, the economic factor was not given due consideration by the warring sides because of the expectation that the conflict would be short and also because of the dominance of liberal views on economic matters held by the British government and the public at that time. As a result, "no government mobilization of industrial and financial resources was introduced during the early phases [of the war]". The official control exercised later in that war was small when compared to measures already undertaken by the Allies in the recently initiated Second World War, not to mention the "extreme measures that had been in operation in Nazi Germany for the past six years".

Goh's intention was to use "non-technical language" to describe how the free economies of the Empire and of France had been adapted for war in order for resources to be efficiently used "even when this necessarily involved a curtailment of individual freedom to some extent"; to compare Allied economic power to Germany's; and to explain the role that Malaya's economy would play in the war effort (p. 7).

A comparison between this booklet and "Capitalism versus Socialism", which was written about two years earlier, reveals a dramatic development in Goh's style. Although both are tightly constructed, the author of the later work commands a confidence that is not obvious in the earlier work. More strikingly, *Economic Front* sees a pioneering Goh in virgin territory, exploring the literature and the data available and trying to make manifest a scholarly Malaya-centrism that had not existed until then.

He started off by systematically explaining what the fundamental arrangement in a peace-time economy looks like, largely based on classical theory *a la* Ricardo. In an ideally free economy, "customers are free to buy what they like and producers to produce and sell those things that offer greatest attraction to them". The going price for goods acts as a confident guide for the producer in judging consumer preferences.

> Market prices of goods relative to their costs of production are the basis on which producers decide to increase, decrease or maintain production depending on whether profits and losses are being incurred (p. 9).

Excessive profits trigger automatic correction "by tempting existing producers to increase output and new producers to enter these fields". Losses are on the other hand a strong indication of sub-optimal resource use, with production being consequently lowered and further investments repelled.

Goh conceded that recent history had shown that this guiding mechanism for price-setting and investment subjected the world economy to "occasional severe trade depressions". However, he brushed off criticism against this basic theory and the global structure it supported, stating that no one had proven "conclusively" that other systems — ostensibly meaning authoritarian ones — would give better results, or that the present system could not remedy itself.

At this point, Goh made the argument that war conditions injected a new and critical criterion into the equation, which was that the use of the existing resources of a country must be geared towards "ultimate victory".

A society at war must control its economy for three reasons at least, according to Goh. The state must first of all handle the expensive business of providing "equipment, maintenance and enlargement of the fighting forces", after which it must maintain the health of its population through adequate supplies of various necessities. Goh's third reason was especially interesting in that it reveals the combative and strategic mind in which it was conceived. This final point was that the state must prevent the enemy from achieving the above two aims "as far as possible by means of military action". Strengthening oneself involves weakening the enemy.

The means of control at the disposal of the central political power were not few in number, Goh claimed. Britain had by then intervened in the economy through the issue of new capital, the redistribution of labour between various industries, and the management of raw material use. As many as 22,000 workers had been withdrawn from the army to service the industrial sector. The result sought from concentrating capital, labour and raw materials on military production was the maximization of war goods output at the lowest possible cost.

Lowest possible costs in the production of goods considered most essential for sustaining the war effort were achieved by official limitation of demand for the means of production coming from industries producing less essential goods.

Goh also suggested that the cost of accruing finances for the war be kept low by limiting the new capital that private industries were allowed to attract. In a free market, the government competes for capital by offering attractive — and costly — rates of interest. Wartime control would assure government access to huge amounts of savings, and at low cost.

During a war, the country's productive capacity in general has to be optimized. To what extent this can be done before the output of non-essential goods is affected depends on the availability of unused resources; the supply of additional raw materials; and the possibility of increasing the aggregate volume of public savings.

> When the resources — land, labour and capital — are fully employed, any increase in the production of war commodities can only be achieved if there is a corresponding decrease in less essential output, and this necessarily involves an increase in the savings of the nation, or an increase in taxation, or both, to reduce consumption (p. 12).

Goh drew the conclusion that consumption in a wartime economy threatens the production of essential goods by increasing the demand on consumer goods, thus increasing their price or their supply, or both. What is needed therefore are savings: "An act of saving is an act of not spending".

Not only do savings divert resources away from the production of consumer goods towards war products, they also stabilize the prices of scarce and basic consumer goods. More importantly, they constitute a reservoir of funds that the government can draw upon, which in turn keeps interest rates low.

After presenting these "essential points of a war economy", Goh then considered the "real conditions" of this economy by allowing for the effects of foreign trade.

Balance of trade, he reasoned, depends on the favourable inflow of foreign money through exports being used up for the payment of imports. Both visible and invisible items are involved. Goods constitute the former, while the latter includes payments for "shipping services, banking, insurance speculation, flights of 'refugee' money", etc. (p. 14). A currency's stability depends therefore on total imports being equal to total exports. For the state to have some control over this precarious balance, at least in the short term, a strong foreign exchange reserve is required.

A war economy involves an abnormally sharp increase in the import of raw material for production, as well as in war items such as munitions and planes. Since this tends to destabilize the home currency, some degree of control over foreign trade in general must be exercised.

Capital flight to safer countries, or what Goh called "refugee money", was another phenomenon that needed curbing. Such movements had been the cause of several crises since the First World War, according to him. Elaborate machinery for control of foreign trade and currency exchange was needed if the strength of the currency was to be maintained during the present war. More specifically, such control served four aims (p. 15):

1. Strengthening of gold and foreign exchange resources "by calling in privately-held amounts of these, and preventing flights of 'refugee money' held by residents";
2. Cutting down on the import of luxury and unessential goods for more effective use of import capacity;
3. Prohibiting the export of essential goods; and
4. Encouraging export trade in order to expand import capacity.

Goh felt that Great Britain and France had applied these measures, but needed to take "drastic steps" to stimulate her export trade, including preferential treatment to export industries, subsidies, trade agreements and, possibly, "the use of a specially depreciated currency". Rationing did not seem a desirable method to him.

The British in particular were commended for the new functions given to existent ministries at the outbreak of war and for the creation of new bodies. These included a ministry for controlling shipping and a Ministry of Economic Warfare, which was tasked with weakening the German economy through blockade.

In summation, Goh referred to the highly influential economist Francis Ysidro Edgeworth's maxim that "resources for war are to be obtained by abstention from ordinary consumption", declaring that the economic modifications he was suggesting stemmed from that doctrine (Edgeworth 1925, cited on p. 16).

After presenting his basic reasoning for adapting the economy for war, Goh moved to a study of the enemy. He had over the preceding months been strongly interested in the construction of Germany's post-First-World-War economy. The extreme conditions under which Germany laboured, promised pickings for comparative analysis. Goh's point of departure was that while Germany's money income had increased due to rearmament activity, goods production had not been able to match consumer needs:

> If we were to select one word only to describe expressively the development of the Nazi economy, the word "shortage" would come in most aptly. [...] The general shortage of economic resources — capital, gold and foreign exchange, and labour (since 1938) — together with the great strain imposed on the system by huge rearmament projects explain all the unique features of the Nazi economy — the rigid control of capital issues, foreign exchange, wages, prices of certain goods, heavy taxation and a public debt so high that the actual figure was kept secret to prevent a collapse of confidence (p. 17).

Most significantly, the depleted state in which Germany found itself did not allow for taxation and orthodox borrowing to fuel its militarisation programme. What the government had to resort to was credit-creation through the *Reichsbank*. Such a move was potentially highly inflationary. However, in the beginning, the large number of unemployed being put to work absorbed that tendency. Once technical full employment was reached, the deficit incurred in rearming was offset through what Goh called "international brigandage". The war machine already created could subsequently be used as a threat that effectively won Germany new territories. Given how economic resurrection under the Nazis was constructed, international conflict became inevitable. And thus, the present war began, with the invasion of Poland.

> By entering on this War, the Nazis saved themselves the task of disentangling their economic system, because this War will provide them with the shortest cut to inevitable ruin (p. 18).

Goh then went on to discuss the potential for growth in the cases of both the Allies and the Nazis. In building its war machine, Germany put its population under great strain; and once the war started, "her economic position deteriorated as a result of the Economic War waged on her" (p. 23). Indeed, the Allies were in a good relative position. Goh claimed that "because of the preponderating superiority of the Allies in respect of economic and financial resources, governmental control need not amount to the setting up of a rigid totalitarian state, such as we find in Germany" (pp. 16–17). By Goh's reckoning, Germany came out short in comparison with the Allies.

Yet, when the conflict finally did develop into a full-scale war, its outcome was not as certain as the figures suggested. To his credit, Goh realized that his study of the political economic situation was important — "economic forces are our great ally". But in the end, he said, "wars are won and lost on the battlefields".

Poignantly, on 10 May 1940, just when he was putting the final touches to his book, something momentous that Goh had not taken into full account took place. He had imagined, as most did, that Britain and her continental allies would hold up against the might of Germany's badly stretched economy and its military forces.

But on that day, however, the Nazis began their invasion of the Low Countries and crucially engaged the harassed Allied armies throughout that month. The miraculous evacuation at Dunkirk by the British took place during the last week of May, and Paris itself fell to Hitler on 14 June. On that score at least, Goh's mention of French economic preparedness for the war was painfully optimistic.

The economic trend was until then definitely moving in favour of the Allies. This was almost certainly sufficient reason for Hitler to move quickly from economic competition to full military engagement. Goh had thought that the Allies, having so far managed the economic front well, would "be steadily increasing the efficiency of their fighting forces, and victory will ultimately be theirs". The invasion of Western Europe certainly changed the equation for the next five years.

Be that as it may, his argument for a concerted mobilizing of economic resources — at least in colonial Malaya — gained added significance in light of the concurrent fall of Europe, and with Britain now huddling down to endure long-term German bombardment.

In Chapter III of the booklet, Goh described the Malayan economy of 1940 as he saw it, and in the process provided an understanding of the global colonial economic structure of which Malaya was such an integral part. This is of great interest in many ways, given how rarely such analyses were carried out by local and locally trained economists; and how central a role Goh would later play in differentiating Singapore's political economic structure from that of other states.

What Malaya was contributing, and could contribute, to the war effort, in Goh's view, was "almost wholly economic". This was nevertheless "immense, incomparably more valuable than any military help we can give, *e.g.* by sending volunteers" (pp. 24–25).

Malaya's economy was an "open" one dominated by the export of rubber and tin. Its major markets were the highly industrialized countries, supplying all in all 41% of the world's rubber and 37% of its tin. These were even more important to Malaya itself, making up as they did as much as 73.4% of her gross exports.

Dependence on export markets put the economy at the full mercy of global vacillations, especially in peace time. For example, Goh noted — movingly, given how his own family suffered from it — that in 1932, during the Great Depression, rubber prices fell badly, and exports that year to the United States, for example, was only 20% of what it would reach in 1937. During a war, one had to consider the fact that these industries were a huge source of critical foreign reserves. Much of Malaya's exports went to the United States, the payment for which either flowed to London or were used to settle British imports from the United States. In that way, they buttressed the British war economy to no mean extent.

The importance of the Malayan economy to Britain at this time was clearly evident from the fact that Malaya was the biggest exporter to the United States in 1937 outside of the American Dollar bloc, outranking even Britain and Japan. If the dollar bloc was included, Malaya ranked second only to Canada. However, since the British colony imported little from the United States, its favourable trade balance with that country was far better than that of any other country in the world. Needless to say, rubber and tin accounted for most of this, making up as much as 97% of Malaya's total exports.

Other export industries in Malaya, though expanding, held less significance to the war effort because their markets were largely within the sterling commonwealth. Palm oil, pineapple, copra and coconut oil were exported mainly to countries like Canada, British India, Britain and a few other European countries. Interestingly, on the eve of the Pacific War, all of British Malaya's iron ore exports went to Imperial Japan.

Just as importantly, Malaya, especially Singapore and Penang, facilitated the entrepot trade for the whole Southeast Asian region. However, new channels of collection and distribution had badly reduced this trade in the Straits Settlements over the preceding 25 years. Recapturing this trade was difficult, Goh thought, as any attempt to exert currency exchange control over this trade would be in a war situation.

Where imports into Malaya were concerned, available statistics were harder to interpret since so much of the economy was based on the entrepot trade. However, it seemed common knowledge that the bulk of the goods consumed in Malaya had to be imported. At this point in his presentation, Goh again focused on the special conditions of war which altered the economic policy that would reasonably apply in times of peace.

It has been suggested that Malaya should develop greater self-sufficiency, especially as regards her food supplies. From the purely economic point of view, there is little to recommend in the rigorous pursuit of self-sufficiency, as a peace time measure, if the free workings of economic laws ordain otherwise. The trade of a country will have to be obstructed by tariffs; subsidies will have to be given to certain privileged industries; and the burden of these ultimately fall on the home consumer (in the form of higher prices) and on the taxpayers (p. 28).

War conditions should "overrule purely economic considerations", Goh reasoned. Since independence of foreign manufactured goods was obviously not possible for Malaya, "the problem [was] narrowed down to the production of her own essential foodstuffs" (p. 29). Having narrowed Malayan contributions to the warring empire down to the gift of American dollars, Goh sought to identify likely leakages to this crucial cache.

> The payment for imports of foodstuffs absorbs a fairly considerable proportion of foreign exchange, and with the need to economize the use of foreign exchange for ordinary purposes, attempts to reduce our dependence on foreign supplies of food stuffs are consistent with our general war efforts. The urgency to grow more food is even more real now than a few years ago when there appeared to be a possibility of war breaking out here, because, whereas the policy of growing more food at that time was at best an insurance against the cutting off [of] our food supplies in the event of a Far Eastern war, now the growing of food is an essential item in our war programme (p. 29).

Rice production was of major interest. More specifically, it was the relationship between locally grown rice and imported rice that was significant. Unlike in other rice-growing regions, the many smallholders in Malaya had the choice of tending to rubber or producing rice. Should the price of rubber rocket, then rice production would fall as a result and supply would have to be complemented by imports. These had to be paid for with foreign currencies. The price of tin also played a major role in this equation. Should tin and/or rubber prices go up, immigration from India and China would increase to provide the extra labour needed by the larger plantations and mines. Immigrants would also be attracted by work opportunities in the growing cities. This increase in population would raise the demand for imported rice even further, leading to more leakage of foreign currency out of the colony.

This correlation between tin and rubber prices and rice production had held true before 1933. Since that year, however, rising rubber and tin prices were actually accompanied by rising rice production. This apparent contradiction, he ventured, was due to restrictions on new planting of rubber and on successful irrigation schemes in rice-planting areas. But what was noteworthy was that the proportion of local rice production in relation to import volume for the 1930s did diminish nevertheless.

Another leakage of foreign exchange was in the remittances sent to China and India by immigrants. This had increased tremendously in the case of China after the Japanese invasion of China on 7 July 1937.

Dividends and profits transferred to Britain by Malayan companies incorporated there and by private British investors were another factor affecting Malaya's foreign exchange. The government had also been investing increasing amounts of budget surpluses in sterling securities.

In summation, Britain's European war had resulted in the immediate mobilization of the Malayan economy. The regulations had been tweaked occasionally, but the basic aims had remained unchanged (p. 33). These were (1) Exchange control; (2) Restriction and prohibition of certain imports; (3) Restriction on certain exports; (4) Control of capital issues, and; (5) Fixing of maximum prices for certain foodstuffs and engineering stores.

As Goh had argued, the economic front in the war was very much about the sterling being able to maintain a steady exchange rate with foreign currencies, especially the American Dollar. This depended on the combined balance in foreign trade of all the sterling countries remaining beneficial to the Empire.

> Malaya, for instance, by having large favourable balances of trade with foreign countries, will enable Great Britain to increase her purchases of planes, munitions, etc. to that extent from foreign countries without running the risk of a currency depreciation (p. 34).

Realizing the complexity of the subject he was examining, Goh decided to study exchange control according to three aspirations evident in the Defence (Finance) Regulations of 1939 and 1940. These were (1) the conservation of resources; (2) the disposal of foreign exchange; and (3) the receipt of foreign exchange.

To conserve resources for the war effort, gold, foreign currencies and securities that were privately owned had to be sold at market price to authorized dealers unless special permission was obtained beforehand. No money of any form could be exported from Malaya to non-sterling countries, and sometimes not even to sterling countries, while money and securities being taken out by travellers had to be declared at the point of exit.

Imports from non-sterling countries were also strongly controlled to reduce the expenditure of precious foreign exchange. Well aware of the loopholes that existed in payment procedures for exports, the Controller of Foreign Exchange closely supervised these through banks and other means. The fact that the entrepot trade was so important to Malaya meant that such control had to balance between closing loopholes and strangling businesses. The collaboration of most parties was therefore necessary.

Aside from the need for foreign exchange control, imports and exports also had to be regulated for strategic reasons. Where Malaya was concerned, the general ban on the export of raw materials such as copper, lead and zinc did not apply since its products, such as tin and rubber, were largely meant for export. Instead, the controls were mainly to safeguard reserves and to ensure that these products did not find their way to the enemy.

Since Malaya's role in the war against Hitler was to supply London with as much foreign exchange as possible, imports from outside the sterling region had to be restricted. This was being done through various regulations put in place already at the outbreak of war. All in all, the import of 76 articles was controlled, while over 200 items were banned. Due to the entrepot trade, however, certain exemptions had had to be allowed.

The regulations were of a general nature, and were applicable throughout the empire. As such, the control of capital issues was not as relevant to Malaya as it was to Britain itself.

We thus had a situation where, although trade in tin and rubber boomed, the expected subsequent increase in the supply of imported non-essentials in response to increased demand had to be curbed. Inflation was bound to result from such a course of action, and that was the reason why regulations for fixing the maximal price of these goods were hammered in place.

However, Goh realized the complexity of the market for the numerous non-essential items, and warned that any rigid regimentation of the economy to make such measures viable would bring greater disadvantages than benefits. On this point, therefore, he disagreed with the British regime of price control, advocating instead that "prices must be left to be determined by the forces of supply and demand" (p. 38). What he suggested instead was for Malayans to increase their savings. If local demand for non-essentials, despite the flourishing rubber and tin market, was curtailed in this way, the curb in supply would not lead to higher prices, and foreign exchange would not be affected.

Supposing as Goh did that Malaya would not be drawn into the war directly, the increase in savings would enable Malayans to subscribe heavily to war loans, thus keeping the latter's rates of interest low.

In conclusion, Goh's analysis of the Malayan economic front led him to suggest that Malayans (1) decrease imports from non-sterling countries and grow more food themselves; (2) decrease their general expenditure and avoid hoarding and "panic buying", both of which would "cause acute and unnecessary dislocation in the market"; (3) make contributions to the so-called Patriotic Fund, and; (4) bear with fortitude the discomforts of the war. These sufferings were "trivial when compared to the hardships suffered by those fighting against Nazism for our common cause, so that we all may continue to enjoy freedom, justice and security" (p. 39).

The concern for salient details and the rationality that the newly graduated Goh exhibited in writing this, his first book, is impressive, revealing a mind that seemed to seek out factor after possible factor and then presenting in lucid form the parameters thus distinguished, resulting in the end in a formidable exposé of the subject under study.

A striking point about this publication is the "Malayan point of view" provocatively embedded in the title. The deeper significance of this perspective lay in how Goh considered Malaya as an economy in its own right, and studied its trade and financial relations to the rest of the world — despite the express aim of aiding Britain's war economy — in a Malaya-centric manner. This makes the booklet a highly interesting historical document where the emergence of Malaya as a socio-economic, and not merely political, entity is concerned. As will be shown later, Goh's contribution towards socio-economic awareness among Malayans about their approaching nationhood continued unabated in the 1950s.

Be that as it may, the young Goh, in studying the management of the war's economic front by the British colonial regime, showed great appreciation for the rationale behind the moves, the speed with which these were made, and the elasticity with which these allowed for adjustments to changing situations.

What the reader catches a glimpse of in this booklet is an able young author applying basic concepts of economics which he had learned in school, but adapting them in an intelligent manner onto a clearly defined context. Goh's reasoning was put across in a lucid manner, and one may be lured into thinking it a simple one. But what this work potentially suggests of his style of economics was at least three things. First, Goh exhibited a structural mode of thought that focuses on the economic behaviour of social forces. Second, he presented the prerequisites for a certain situation only to show how policy has to change when that situation is compromised at a basic level. Although subscribing to the classic understanding of supply and demand, Goh thought that the underlying value of survival where the socio-economic entity in question, in this case the colonial outpost of Malaya, is concerned, must be allowed to influence economic policy in a decisive manner. This view reveals a readiness to manipulate from on-high the basic price mechanism and the economic behaviour of society when society's survival seems at stake. Third, the idea of war as a disorientating factor may be widened to include other situations where covert conflict or overwhelming competition is involved. This modification of the ideal case does not only inject the macro-economist into the equation but also elevates his role enormously without pushing him towards socialism.

The pre-war period promises some understanding of the traits that came to characterize Goh's brand of economic strategizing. Of special significance is the fact that (1) his lecturers were largely trained in classic English economics; (2) his academic learning of economics was carried out during the Great Depression and when the worst war in human history was brewing; and (3) he as a young man put extra effort into studying the unique case of the depleted economy of Germany in the 1930s.

One can perhaps argue that by this point in his life, Goh had already become cognizant of the constraints that theoretical thought, no matter how useful, must place even on a mind bent on practical action. Furthermore, economics seemed to appear to him already as an arena of necessary competition that covered other aspects of human life, where success depended on relative advantages.

The period was a formative one for Goh, both with regards to his political consciousness and his understanding of macro-economics. This would become even more obvious in the choice of subjects he would write about in the post-war years.

He went on to join the Straits Settlements Volunteer Force (SSVF) in January 1942, just a month before the Japanese launched their full-scale and successful attack on Singapore. The Force consisted of few non-British, but had an infantry consisting only of Chinese — the E Company. Eurasians such as Edmund William Barker, who would later become Minister of Law, were placed in the Machine-Gun Company.

The Signals Company to which Goh was attached was initially located at the Chinese High School on Bukit Timah Road, but moved to Beach Road just before Singapore fell. He took part in the burning of official documents at Fort Canning a few days before the docks were bombed. The British finally surrendered on 15 February, exactly seven days after the Japanese began their attack on Fortress Singapore (*ST* 23/11/47; Tan 2007: 41–42). Goh was arrested along with all other surviving members of the Force, but was released along with other Indians and Chinese. Many were not that lucky (CORD Baker: p. 20).

Goh was soon recalled to work at the Japanese Tax Office. The pay was meagre, and he managed to supplement his income by selling cigarettes. The family soon moved from Pasir Panjang to 119 Bideford Road, a two-storey terrace house. On 6 October that year, the 24-year-old Goh married Alice Woon, who was seven years younger than he was, at the Kampong Kapor Methodist Church. A son, Kian Chee, was born to them on 24 January 1944.

Goh soon became uneasy about having his family in Singapore. He suspected that an all-out Allied attempt to regain Malaya would devastate the island, and so, he moved them to Malacca. As things turned out, the bombing of Hiroshima and Nagasaki in early August 1945 precipitated the sudden surrender of the Japanese throughout the Far East. His worst fears of an impended house-to-house battle in Singapore were not realized, and the family quickly returned to Singapore (Tan 2007: 43–46).

Chapter 2

SOCIAL SURVEYS AND POLITICS

Our social revolution is not brought about by violence. It is the result of the impact of history.

— Goh Keng Swee
("The Social Revolution in Malaya", 1959)

In June 1946, soon after the Labour Party in Great Britain came to power, a Social Welfare Department was established in Singapore. This body, where Goh worked after returning with his family from Malacca following the fall of Japan, was initially concerned with distributing money to the post-war poor, and providing food for the destitute.

A committee was later formed at the department for the express purpose of conducting a first-ever social survey to determine the conditions under which Singaporeans were living. Goh was made supervisor for the project. Monie Sundram, an old schoolmate from the Anglo-Chinese School and Supervisor of Public Assistance at the department, who later became a lawyer; and Goh's old teacher, Silcock, were also involved in it (*ACS Magazine* Vol. XVII 1948: 48).

As reported in *The Straits Times*, the initial survey involving 500 households carried out in July/August that year revealed "the terrible state of overcrowding in Singapore homes, and the amazing diversity of family structure — ranging from a single man to a family of over 25 making up a household" (*ST* 23/11/47). The response in the survey was good, with only 16 refusals among the 500. This was partly due to the chosen tactic of avoiding questions on household incomes. The fear was that public suspicion that such information would be used for tax assessment would affect the participation rate (Department of Social Welfare 1947: 20).

Goh, with Sundram as secretary, took charge of the project's detailed planning and the training of staff, which included directing the Social Survey Group at Raffles College during the 1947–48 academic year (*Annual Report* 1947–48; Singapore Department of Social Welfare 1947: 21–22). About 100 students helped out in the survey. Half of these were from Raffles College's Economics Department, while the rest came from King Edward VII's College of Medicine, and Saint Andrew's School. (*ST* 23/11/47). In recalling these matters years later, Silcock thought the project a major event for the school, and certainly for Goh.

> The Singapore Social Survey was a critical event in the development of the Department of Economics. It established Goh Keng Swee's reputation as a professional economist; it involved students of the department for the first time in published research which was recognized as significant far beyond Malaya; and it introduced the whole department to the conditions of life of many in Singapore of whom they had hitherto been hardly aware (Silcock 1985: 97).

A SOCIAL SURVEY OF SINGAPORE (1947)

The Department of Social Welfare published the final report as *A Social Survey of Singapore* on 11 November 1948, almost two years after the project started (*ST* 11/11/48). By that time, Goh was already in London.

The report noted that Silcock had requested that Goh's contribution "be expressly acknowledged and commented", and that the Department "unreservedly endorses this tribute".

> Most of the spade-[work] at the planning stages, the whole conduct of the pilot and pre-testing surveys, the training of enumerators, the organization of the final survey, and most of the preparation of this report were carried out by Mr. Goh Keng Swee, a member of the staff of the Department of Social Welfare (Singapore Department of Social Welfare 1947: 5)

The fact that Goh was credited therein for the initial planning, the pre-testing surveys, the training of enumerators, the main survey and even the final report, makes it highly likely that the elaborate structure of the survey was largely his design. One of his innovations concerned the identification of "the household" as the basic unit of investigation. A household was defined as "a group of persons who eat together or share in common housekeeping expenditure". This was decided for practical as much as scientific reasons, Singapore social conditions being highly complex, and a list of houses compiled in May 1947 for population census purposes being available.

Since Singapore's population was "less homogenous than others", it was decided that a larger sample than normal would be needed. By picking one of 30 households from the census list over municipal Singapore's six wards, a sample of 5,000 was achieved. This procedure attained a high degree of correspondence to census figures, with regards to both ethnic and population distribution between different districts. This spoke well for its feasibility. Where Europeans were concerned, the difference between the survey and census was clearly greater. According to the report, this was due to more refusals among Europeans to participate in the survey.

Goh thought it better to avoid questions about income in order to minimize refusals. The trade-off was that the scope of the survey was somewhat diminished (*ibid.* 7–11, 19–20). Be that as it may, the final report was ground-breaking, not only for being the first of its kind ever done for Singapore — or perhaps the region — but for the imposing assortment of raw data collected. The preparation for the survey was impressive from all accounts, both in the technical structure of the survey and also in the tutoring of the young enumerators. Among this last group of helpers were names like Kwa Geok Choo (later Mrs Lee Kuan Yew), Ungku Aziz (later vice-chancellor of the University of Malaya), and Wan Abdul Hamid (later prominently and notoriously involved in the leftist movement among Malayan students in England) (*ibid.* 21).

The tables supplied in the report range from expected ones such as "Percentage of household overcrowding in dwellings of different unit-sizes" to more surprising schemas such as "Percentage frequency of numbers of returns to homeland by duration of stay in Malaya".

Of special interest is the note that since Singapore did not have free universal schooling, data about child education was especially informative and attention had therefore to be paid to it. However, a look through the contents and the survey structure shows that the importance of education as a parameter in the data analysis is somewhat understated in the introduction. The issue of child education forms a substantial and significant part of the findings (see "More boys than girls in schools" in *ST* 11 Nov 1948).

Silcock wrote an opinion piece titled "Is there a conscience in Singapore" in *The Straits Times* when the report was published.

He noted how its "cold, factual and moderate prose" told a tale of "squalor, ignorance and degradation [...] to shock and shame any who live here and who are content to let these things be" (*ST* 11 November 1948).

It is hard not to assume that this thorough two-year study of municipal Singapore provided Goh — who was a central figure in the project — with intimate knowledge about the urban population and the harsh socio-economic conditions and political uncertainty under which this ethnically diverse society laboured. It is almost certain that the fieldwork and analysis involved in this project augmented his growing interest in politics.

It also encouraged him to further his studies in research techniques. Where better than the London School of Economics? The famous social survey that he was to lead in 1953–1954 — *Urban Incomes & Housing* — has to be understood in many ways as a continuation of his earlier survey, but done by a mature colonial civil servant and experienced academician.

Soon after the war, Goh rented a two-storey bungalow in Wee Nam Road, and moved his family there. He was by then a consummate chess player, and his team matches were often mentioned in *The Straits Times*, sometimes with him as member of the Singapore Chess Club. He would continue playing the game competitively and triumphantly during his stay in London in 1948–1951 (*ST* 10/4/46; 7/5/46; 14/6/47; 14/8/47).

Goh certainly did have contact with leading members of Singapore's first indigenous party, the Malayan Democratic Union (MDU). This was partly because his old friend from Raffles College, Eu Chooi Yip, lived close by and was party secretary, and partly because his wife Alice was working at the Singapore Co-operative Store set up by party founder Lim Kean Chye, a Cambridge-trained lawyer from Penang. Beer drinking was a common social event for the young men. Incidentally, Goh and Eu were the two men whom Silcock considered his best students (Yeo 1973: 95).

There is no evidence, despite a passing mention to that effect by Gerald De Cruz in a taped interview carried out years later, that Goh was ever a member of the MDU. De Cruz was a journalist who had joined the MDU after the war only to be disillusioned with communism following a trip to Czechoslovakia (see CORD: de Cruz).

The immediate post-war political situation in Malaya was very unsettled. Days before the fall of Malaya in 1942, the British had tried to maximize popular support by recognizing all political parties and groups. This of course included the Kuomintang (KMT) and the Malayan Communist Party (MCP). The fight against a common enemy in 1942–1945 encouraged the post-war British Military Administration established in September 1945 after the British returned to be more charitable where Chinese politics were concerned (Yong & McKenna 1990: 195).

The new Labour government in Britain under Clement Atlee, in keeping with plans forged during the war, went ahead with the establishment of the Malayan Union on 1 April 1946. This merged the Federated Malay States, the Unfederated Malay States and the Straits Settlements excepting Singapore into one administrative unit within which liberal citizenship rights were to be granted to non-Malays. The Malay elite and the sultans were roused into protest to form the United Malays National Organisation (UMNO) on 11 May 1946.

The following two years were thus a time of strategic negotiations and frantic manoeuvres on all sides. While the shaken British sat down with the Malay elite to discuss the Federation of Malaya that would succeed the ill-fated Union on 1 February 1948, other parties worked to strengthen their roles in the new political terrain.

The KMT managed to revive its post-war organization in the wake of several visiting missions from the mother party in China, which was fighting the Chinese Communist Party (CCP) in the civil war that broke out in June 1946. An Overseas Department was founded in Singapore in December that year to garner support for the KMT on the Mainland. This body allowed for a new generation of non-communist leaders within the Chinese community to join the party. By the time the British decided to ban the KMT — in May 1949 in Singapore and in August 1949 in Malaya — many of these had moved to the Malayan Chinese Association (MCA). The MCA was formed with British prompting in February that year (Yong & McKenna 1990: 200–202, 205, 217–20).

Post-war class struggles began with a general strike on 29 January 1946, which saw as many as 150,000 participating in Singapore alone. A demonstration planned for 15 February by the MCP-controlled General Labour Union (GLU) to celebrate the MCP "taking over" four years previous to the day when the British had so ignobly surrendered to the Japanese, was disallowed. A stand-off between demonstrators and the authorities on 14 February saw police opening fire and killing two rioters.

The reason usually advanced for why the MCP did not take to arms earlier than they did was that its secretary-general, Lai Tek, was in fact a British agent. This idea is corroborated in Chin Peng's book *My Side of History*. Lai Tek disappeared for good in February 1947.

Throughout that year, as many as 300 strikes were held. In June 1948, the British implemented strict rules on the unions. In response, the communists abandoned their tactic of "peaceful agitation", and took to arms. The British declared a state of emergency in the Federation on 18 June, and in Singapore on 23 June. The MCP was banned on 23 July (Clutterbuck 1973:

50–70, 168). Incidentally, the adoption of violent means by the MCP at this time coincided with the Asia Youth Conference held in February 1948. The many Asian communist parties that attended it were in effect urged to return home and seize power "by any means" (Clutterbuck 1973: 56).

When the Malayan Democratic Union was dissolved, Lim Kean Chye escaped to China and Eu Chooi Yip went into hiding. Goh had decided by this time to sharpen his skills in statistics, and had managed to secure a Colonial Development Welfare Fund scholarship to the London School of Economics (LSE) (*ST* 10/9/48).

In Europe, the Berlin Airlift was in full flight, with Allied air forces moving supplies into the city in response to the Berlin Blockade that Josef Stalin began to place around the city on 24 June 1948. This challenge to western control of West Berlin would end in failure for Stalin only after an entire year, on 11 May 1949.

Goh thus left behind a Malaya that was now involved in the Cold War, and embarked on the SS Carthage on 9 September 1948 to a Europe embroiled in that same global conflict. Also on board but travelling separately were his school mate Monie Sundram, a fellow scholarship winner who was to study at the Inns of Court School of Law; Maurice Baker, later professor of English at the University of Singapore and also High Commissioner to India and Malaysia; and Queen's scholar E.W. Barker, later Singapore's Minister of Law (*ST* 9/9/48; 10/9/48). Among passengers that the ocean liner picked up in Penang before traversing the Indian Ocean was Tan Boon Teik, later Singapore's long-term attorney-general.

Alice managed to join Goh only in March the following year, after which the couple rented a room in North London. Their son Kian Chee stayed in Singapore under the care of his paternal grandmother (Tan 52–61).

In late August 1949, Goh went with several Malayans including Maurice Baker, Fred Arulanandum, Dennis Lee, the younger brother of Lee Kuan Yew, and Lee Kip Lin, a relative of Goh's, to Budapest to attend the Second World Festival of Youth and Students. Reportedly, 10,400 young people from 82 countries participated. This was a biannual event organized by the "left-wing, anti-fascist" World Federation of Youth and Students, a body formed in London in 1945 and then headquartered in Budapest (Tan pp. 61–62; SIEN p. 91; CORD — Baker 31).

China was on the brink of falling to Mao Zedong at this time, and the CCP made a strong presence in Budapest, as did the newly independent Indonesia. Goh and his group inadvertently became the Malayan contingent, and were cheered through the stadium, possibly mistaken for representatives of the guerrilla movement that had recently taken to arms in Malaya.

> [We were] about a dozen fellows not knowing very much what it was all about, but rather enjoying the scene; knowing we were thoroughly frauds. We were fraudulent. We had never fought a day against the British, but nevertheless, you couldn't disillusion [the crowd] (CORD — Baker 31–32).

Baker was approached by Lim Hong Bee and offered a scholarship to Moscow. Tempted as he was, Baker nevertheless decided to listen to his friends, especially Goh, "who was as usual the most sober of the lot", and refused the offer. Be that as it may, Goh was impressed by the sight of so many emerging nations marching and advocating anti-colonialism and disarmament, He apparently told Lee Kip Lin that they should "start a movement" when they returned home to Singapore.

Baker recorded for the Singapore National Archives on 14 April 1993 his impressions of Goh during their days together in London, when both of them started the Malayan Forum to discuss political matters and to interest Malayan students in events back home. As Baker remembers it, the manifest political apathy amongst Malayan students in London was the reason why the Forum was founded. The lack of political interest by Malayan students was a common complaint in the 1950s (see T.H. Tan's article in *Suara Merdeka* April–June 1954, for example).

Six students — Abdul Razak Hussein, Mohamed Sopiee Sheik Ibrahim, Philip Hoalim Jr, Fred Arulanandum, Maurice Baker and Goh Keng Swee — got together at Razak's flat, and started the Forum. Who exactly founded the Forum is sometimes a matter of controversy, and other sources do not even include Razak among them (Tan 2007: 64). Philip Hoalim Jr was a founder of the recently dissolved Malayan Democratic Union; Mohamed Sopiee would go on to help establish and be chairman of the Pan-Malayan Labour Party established in June 1952; and Arulanandum would join the non-communal Independence of Malaya Party founded by Onn Ja'afar in September 1951 (Cheah 1973; *ST* 23 Jan 1954). Baker remembers that Goh did not wish to be president of the Forum, hating leadership roles as he did: "But we forced him to take over because we were very busy. So he did. He did eventually. He was the Chairman" (CORD Baker 34, 53–57). Mohamed Sopiee was the secretary in the Forum's first committee.

> [Keng Swee] is a background man. He's a very poor speaker, very thoughtful, profound thinker who never has any time for ordinary conversation. [...] He's a perfect committee man. I think he's the thinker from whom the ideas come. But I think he wants somebody else to project the ideas for him. [...] Once he told me that the problem with Kuan Yew is, he hasn't got an ounce of sentiment in him. But in fact, this is also true of Keng Swee. He's very practical and down to earth, a fascinating

character. [...] His brain is almost of genius quality I should think (*ibid* 34, 53–57).

Goh however felt on the whole that they were a rather "ineffectual study group", but one thing that left a deep impression on him from discussions with Malay members was that the communal problem was going to be a difficult one for Malaya to solve in the future (Tan 2007: 64).

REVIEW OF *KAKEMONO: A SKETCH BOOK OF POST-WAR JAPAN* (1950)

The Forum also published the magazine *Suara Merdeka*, partly in retaliation against *The Malayan Monitor*, a pamphlet started by Lim Hong Bee, a Queen's scholar who was an avowed communist. Lim was also the first secretary-general of the MDU (GDC folio 2; Press release 8 November 1947).

In Vol. 1 No. 1 of the magazine, published in November 1950, Goh surprisingly contributed a review of popular columnist and travel writer Honor Tracy's (1913–1989) first book, *Kakemono: A Sketch Book of Post-War Japan* (*Suara Merdeka* 1950: 14–15). Tracy worked for the British Ministry of Information as a specialist on Japan during the war before becoming a travel writer and columnist for major English newspapers (Flint 1989). A *kakemono* is a Japanese vertical wall picture or calligraphy mounted on a roller, and would in this context more or less conjure the idea of a tapestry. Tracy shares her impressions of Japan in the years after the war, and largely expresses her admiration of Japanese character and culture. This bemuses Goh somewhat, since his experience of the Japanese during the occupation was jarringly different.

Sometimes, indeed, I find it difficult to identify the people whom she so highly and so sincerely extols, with the drunken unkempt brutes who used to stagger past my house on their

way to the military brothels. And yet her estimation is probably
justified. For in his own social environment, in which he is
subject to the normal civilising restraints, the Japanese would
obviously behave quite differently from the way he did when
he donned the mantel of liberator of mankind. In this, I suppose,
he is not very much different from other liberators of mankind.

Aside from the enjoyment he obviously drew from reading Tracy's
"excellent prose style", one has reason to suppose that Goh
decided to review the book after observing some reversal in the
demilitarization of Japan in light of the outbreak of the Korean
War that was raging even as he wrote. Just five years after the end
of the Pacific War, Japan was evolving into a potential ally in the
eyes of the American occupiers. The militarists were "beginning
to take fresh heart", Goh ventured.

He took issue with Tracy's argument that the Americans were
putting the Japanese through "a cruel humiliation" and that
they should not seek to remake "one of the most civilised races
on earth to its own bizarre pattern".

> There are excellent reasons for wanting to re-model the Japanese
> way of thinking, and the American experiment is by no means
> uncalled for, even though the results, in detail, turn out to be
> different from the experimenter's anticipation. A people who so
> fanatically believed in their divine origin and their manifest
> destiny clearly need some drastic overhaul of their ideas before
> they will cease to be a menace to their neighbours.

With his interest in politics on the rise, Goh sought to make full
use of the intellectual atmosphere at LSE, attending numerous
lectures outside requirement. The most prominent lecturer he
remembered from that period was Harold Laski who was known
for giving exciting talks on Marxism. Others included Professor

Lionel Robbins the economist and Professor R.G.D. Allen the statistician.

Goh also grew to know Archibald Fenner Brockway (1888– 1988), and even once campaigned successfully for him in the Eton and Slough constituency. Brockway was chairman of the Movement for Colonial Freedom (Tan 2007: 60).

All in all, Goh stayed three years at LSE, putting much more effort into his studies than he had done at Raffles. He remained on campus during vacations, going daily to the library. And so, when he graduated in June 1951, it was as a Bachelor of Science (Economics) with First-Class Honours. His hard work paid off so well that he was also awarded the William Farr Prize "for proficiency and merit in the special subject of statistics". To top it off, he was granted a scholarship for doctorate studies. This he successfully asked to be deferred for several years.

URBAN INCOMES & HOUSING 1953–54 (1956)

Goh and his wife left for home that autumn. He returned to the Research Section of the Social Welfare Department as Assistant Secretary, and in December that year was chosen to lead two researchers from his section and a group of 70 volunteers from the University of Malaya in a pilot health survey titled "Pilot Study of Illnesses". Goh explained then that once the questions had been tested and approved, a proper survey involving about 6,000 respondents would be carried out and the results would be used to guide future social welfare work (*ST* 15/12/51).

The first draft of this pilot study report was completed in April 1952. The project had been carried out in what was termed "the slum areas of the city" (*ST* 10 April 1952). Due to a lack of funds, however, the major survey on "sicknesses and resultant financial difficulties" was "postponed indefinitely" (*ST* 2 Oct 1952).

Six weeks after the cancellation was made public, *The Straits Times* reported that Goh was among 31 local men appointed to jobs in the colony's higher services under a recently started scheme to bring Asians into top positions within the service. Goh now became Assistant Director of Social Welfare (*ST* 12/11/52).

More administrative clout for Goh would have accompanied this promotion. Instead of a health survey, the Department immediately planned a huge study of the urban working class, which was carried out between late 1953 and the first half of 1954. Goh headed this project, which involved 6,804 household respondents — as many as had been earmarked for the one shelved a year earlier. The focus now shifted from the sickly to the poverty-stricken. More specifically, Goh's new survey sought to map the living and housing conditions of those with a monthly income below $400. This apparently represented 82% of Singaporeans at that time.

This new project — titled "The Survey of Family Living Conditions" — amounted in an important sense to "taking the bull by the horns" and showed greater confidence on the part of Goh in his own abilities as a researcher. The 1947 survey had tiptoed around the issue of income, with the excuse that questions on incomes would raise the number of refusals significantly.

The final report of this later and highly significant survey was officially released as *Urban Incomes & Housing: A Report on the Social Survey of Singapore, 1953–54*, on 1 February 1956. This time around, Goh led his new team straight into the social fray, structuring the survey questions around specific details not only about housing conditions, but more importantly around income and outlay. He explicitly stated that there was a common bias among researchers that Singaporeans were "naturally suspicious by disposition towards any enquiry conducted by the Government, particularly an enquiry into personal incomes".

The experience of his team, he also stated, proved this to be groundless and only a lowly 2% of those approached refused to grant an interview.

> The public will co-operate in voluntary enquiries of this kind provided certain safeguards are taken — of these, the most important are that the objects of the survey should be carefully explained to people and that the interviewers who meet them should be carefully selected and well trained for the work.

Goh also argued competently for his sample size. Aside from the obvious economic considerations, he said that questioning only 4% of the chosen population may mean running the risk that the group may not be totally representative, but the small size had the advantage of allowing a small group of interviewers to be properly trained. Sampling error in a small survey was therefore more than compensated for by the minimizing of badly collected information through the higher level of efficiency attained by competent interviewers.

Also of interest was Goh's continued reliance on "household" as the basic unit of investigation. The 1947 survey defined a household as "a group of persons who eat together or share in house-keeping expenditure" (p. 27). But in 1953, this concept is changed for essential reasons. A household was redefined as "a group of persons living together and sharing a common housekeeping expenditure". Unlike the earlier survey, the new one sought to capture data about low-income persons. Should the old definition be used, then groups of "shop assistants living and messing together" could be subsumed under the household of their employer who would be making more than $400 a month, and thus fall outside the purview of the survey (p. 28).

One of the aims of the 1953–1954 survey was to relate earnings to the number of dependants, be these living with the wage-earner in Singapore or not. The definition effectively increased the proportion of single-person households living in Singapore, giving that group "undue weight" (p. 29). In effect, the groups surveyed were manual and low-end clerical workers. What the project uncovered was that only 27% of the worker population lived under conditions that were "not overcrowded". Another 22% lived "overcrowded but not acutely" and a fifth were found to be in "acutely overcrowded" conditions. Most shockingly, as many as every fourth person lived in what Goh termed simply as a "space" (Table 4.13 and 4.14, p. 79). This "space" was either "a hired wooden bunk or a camp bed in a shop or on a pavement" (*ST* 2 Feb 1956).

What was most shocking were the data showing how bad living conditions actually were for so many Singaporeans. Goh had systematically determined what the minimum requirements were for sustaining even a low standard of living. These included "minimum amounts of the cheapest foods to supply adequate quantities of essential nutrients", and of clothing and footwear. After deducting rental, facility and transport costs, as many as 20% of families comprising 25% of the survey population fell below this minimum level. A third of all children covered by the survey belonged in this extreme group. Just as appalling was that half of the wage-earners in those destitute households — which were generally larger than the average — actually worked full-time. They were simply not being paid enough.

As with the 1947 investigation, giving a proper summary of the 1953–1954 survey here would be too outsized an undertaking. This was an observation already made by commentators when the report first appeared, one of whom likened it to "reviewing an encyclopaedia" (Wells 1956: 60). What was undeniable, however, was that the later study had a great impact, not only in the reporting of the day, but also among academicians. The significance of the survey is best realized through contemporary responses to it.

The Straits Times underlined four points of unique interest in the report. For one thing, it was shown to be untrue that Singaporeans were suspicious of inquiries conducted by the government; the participation rate was an enviable 98%. It was also revealed that the belief that Chinese families clung together was not well-founded; the survey found very few multi-generational households. Third, as much as 43% of interviewees were illiterate. Lastly, divorces were most common among better educated women (*ST* 2 Feb 1956).

Another commentary in the same newspaper, by "Cynicus", notes the following:

> One of the surprises of this survey is the extent to which Singapore is still a city of immigrants. Only one-third of the heads of these 6,000 households were born in Singapore or the Federation, a proportion which apparently can be accepted as true for the Colony as a whole (*ST* 4 Feb 1956).

One of the findings was that immigrants in general were more willing to work than the local-born. Among men above 60 years of age, three-quarters of those locally born were no longer working, compared to only one-quarter among immigrants.

Interestingly, S. Rajaratnam, who was then editorial writer for *The Straits Times* and who would later become Singapore's first Foreign Minister, also had salient observations to make about Goh's report. Firstly, he proposed that the interviewers would have met with more unwilling respondents if the survey had been done on Singaporeans earning more than $400 a month. After a reminder that poverty was a rather subjective experience, and thus hinting that Goh's "bare existence" technical definition was somewhat overly quantitative in nature, Rajaratnam chose to highlight the finding that immigrant groups were "the most economically depressed". Indonesians were the most poverty-stricken, followed by Chinese, with Indians immigrants marginally above them. When households as earning units were considered, Chinese immigrants moved above the Indians, with the Indonesians still remaining the poorest.

Among the local-born, this ethnic ranking was repeated. Chinese households were less poor compared to Indian and Malay households, in that order. The advantage the Chinese had was the dependence on two incomes. Although only 12% of women in Singapore worked, every fourth immigrant Chinese woman and every fifth local-born Chinese woman were wage-earners. Only 10% of Malay women did the same, while the corresponding figure for Indian women was negligible.

Contributions from relatives were substantial, especially among the Chinese, particularly the immigrants. About 20% of households did spare time work to get by. As many as 15% were actually self-employed, often earning a low income pedalling trishaws or hawking. Chinese and Indian immigrants were more inclined to be self-employed than their local-born counterparts.

Despite hard work, the urban poor could not pull themselves out of poverty, being engaged in occupations that did not pay enough. One income supplement was the sub-letting of rooms to others — renting out "space". A large share of incomes was received in kind of one type or another (*ST* 15 Feb 1956). Rajaratnam concluded:

> Mr Goh has, as a social scientist, given us, for the first time, a detailed analysis of the nature of poverty. Legislators and politicians would do well to consider what possible impact their oratory could have on the large group of citizens preoccupied with the all-absorbing task of trying to keep their noses above the poverty line.

A short review of the report was carried in the June 1956 issue of the *Malayan Economic Review*. Written by A.F. Wells, it acknowledged the significance of the research as "the most comprehensive sociological investigation made in the Colony to date". The difficulty of doing a social survey in Singapore, Wells noted, was evident in the discussion on methods in Chapter One of the report.

Indeed, Goh's presentation of the scope and method that he used, though tersely formulated, testifies suitably to his penchant for adapting theoretical concepts to epistemological practicalities.

Findings that interested Wells included data on household types. It was found, for example, that the man-wife-children household was very common; that two-thirds of households consisted of four or less persons; that Hokkiens tended to have parents and relatives living with the couple more than other Chinese groups; and that over a third of all households were single-person ones, with Malayalees being overrepresented in that group (Wells pp. 60–61).

One impact of the survey which went beyond mere social work can be noted in James Puthucheary's *Ownership and Control in the Malayan Economy*, written in jail after Puthucheary was arrested in a crackdown on leftist elements by Singapore's chief minister Lim Yew Hock in 1956. It was published soon after his release in June 1959.

Ownership was declared a pioneering piece of work by later scholars such as K.S. Jomo, and perhaps had a lasting impact through its influence on the conceptualization of Malaysia's affirmative action programme, the New Economic Policy, that was put in place in 1970 (Puthucheary 1960: 186; Ooi 2006: 216). The exact nature of this influence, however, is not clear, especially given the way the NEP actually played itself out. Only the unlikely release of official papers about discussions surrounding the creation of the NEP will illuminate the matter satisfactorily.

Goh's contribution to *Ownership* came partly through his visits to Puthucheary at Changi Prison Camp, during which the latter "picked his brain quite shamelessly" (Puthucheary viii). But more concretely, Puthucheary — locked in a prison without a library and relying on friends and his fiancée Mavis to bring him the latest relevant literature — used Goh's survey report to argue that "facts about poverty do not fit easily into communal moulds" (p. 175).

Puthucheary noted the survey revealed that "the percentage of Chinese households suffering from extreme poverty was more than twice that of Malay households in Singapore" (p. 178). Indeed, what he considered of great value in Goh's report was ignored in the NEP as practised especially during the administration of Mahathir Mohamed. Mahathir did his best to create a group of Malay capitalists in the belief that this would somehow solve economic disparity between ethnic groups. Puthucheary's conclusion was the opposite.

> So the Goh Keng Swee Report provides the short answer to those who think in communal terms and insist that "the Malays are poor, the Chinese are rich". And those who think that the economic position of the Malays can be improved by creating a few Malay capitalists, thus making a few Malays well-to-do, will have to think again (p. 179).

Working as a top civil servant under colonial masters was a sore point for Goh. Years later, his old friend and colleague, S. Rajaratnam, would remember that he "resented being ruled by aliens, Europeans" (Chew 1996: 154). Goh's postponed scholarship now beckoned, and he left the exciting but testy situation in Singapore for London in August 1954, immediately after completing the project. He would not return until 5 November two years hence. He was therefore not in Singapore when the survey report was officially released on 1 February 1956; and he did not go down in history as one of those present at the founding of the People's Action Party (PAP) on 21 November 1954.

But even before leaving for England, Goh's political activism had become undeniable. A close rapport had developed in London between him and personalities such as Lee Kuan Yew, Kenneth Michael Byrne and Toh Chin Chye. Byrne and Goh — both civil servants — founded the Council of Joint Action (CJA) in 1952 which they then used — with Lee's help — to protest against glaring disparities in benefits between local and British civil servants. Similar activities in alliance with union movements and the University of Malaya Socialist Club provided the experience and the network that culminated with the founding of the PAP (Chew 1996: 145; Yap, Lim & Leong 2009: 32–35; Tan pp. 68–69; Yeo 1973: 118).

In London, Goh immediately involved himself with the student crowd there, and was elected the president of the Malayan Students' Union of Great Britain. This fact was proudly proclaimed back home by the ACS Old Boys' Association in the *Anglo-Chinese School Magazine* (ACS 1955: 149). As president, he also headed the editorial board of the newly started *Bulletin of the Malayan Students' Union*, the first number of which was published in February 1955. It was estimated at that time that there were about 1,300 Malayan students in Britain, a quarter of whom lived in the London area (*Bulletin* 1955).

In his "pledge" as president, Goh promised a host of activities. He suggested that sub-committees be formed for each type of activity, be these concerts, debates or film shows. For this to work, he called on Malayans to adopt the voluntarism that was so obvious among British students at that time, not least at LSE (*Bulletin* p. 8).

> I do not believe that we have less initiative or organising ability than our British colleagues. The real reason lies in a difference in psychological attitudes. Malayans are more diffident and less inclined to push themselves forward....We should try to overcome this diffidence and develop a more aggressive attitude in life. This, after all, is the way to get on in the world! And there's nothing like re-orienting your minds when you're here.

Goh had since his schooldays shown a propensity to lead despite his reputation of being a less than appealing speaker. He wrote engagingly, however, and the tightness of his ideas tended to impress the reader far better than his oratory skills could ever hope to do the crowd. As evidence of this, in the same issue of the bulletin, the full-length version of a letter written by him to *The Straits Times* in Singapore can be found. On learning that the Johore government was discontinuing a scholarship given to Wan Abdul Hamid as punishment for the latter's disregard of a ban on travel across the Iron Curtain and was ordering him to return home, Goh decided to argue his case publicly. (The same newspaper had reported on this on 24 December 1954.) Wan Hamid was defying an order to go home and was planning to finish his studies, purportedly so as not to let hard work go to waste. He was also in danger of losing his position in the Johore civil service.

Taking the newspaper to task for a leader titled "Reddening the Student" for exaggerating "the influence of the extreme left" on Malayan students, Goh reminded the paper that the political sympathies of the average Malayan student lay "somewhere to the right of the Conservative Party". This was to be expected since most Malayan students were either "Government scholars or sons of the very wealthy, neither of whom [were] distinguished for radicalism of political opinion". His main point however, lay elsewhere.

> The Malayan in Britain quickly settles down to the normal
> routine and takes for granted the academic freedoms of British
> University life. In such an atmosphere, the rigid codes of
> behaviour and the dogmatic beliefs generally accepted in Malaya
> appear to him a trifle absurd. After about two years' stay, Malaya
> seems to be a far away place where all sorts of incredible things
> happen. This isn't an intellectual pose however much it may
> appear to be so to people at home; it is the natural effect of the
> environment on the person.

This letter was published almost unchanged in the newspaper on
8 February 1955. Of special interest is the fact that Goh was at
this time arguing the case — in vain as it turned out — for a man
who was very much at the centre of the extreme leftist group that
had gained control over the Malayan Forum that Goh himself
had founded during his earlier stint in London.

Wan Hamid had become chairman of the Forum in October
1953, with John Eber as secretary, ousting in the process Toh
Chin Chye who had succeeded Goh as chairman in 1951. Wan
Hamid and Eber were brothers-in-law by virtue of being married
to sisters (Tan p. 76; *ST* 17 Nov 1953).

Goh soon found his own position as president of the Malayan
Students' Union untenable, with the pro-communists forming a
strong pressure group within the organization. He resigned in
mid-1955, and was soon preparing a coup against Eber, Wan
Hamid and their supporters (Tan p. 76).

In January 1956, the Malayan Students' Union of Great Britain
held its general meeting at which Eber and Wan Hamid were
voted out of office. The following month, the conflict moved on
to the Malayan Forum. After succeeding in calling for a vote of
no-confidence against the Forum committee, Goh's group
prepared themselves to nullify the tactic that Eber's group was
known for in such situations, which was to extend the meeting

by dragging speeches until less committed members lost patience and left before allowing the vote. Although many did indeed leave early during the three-hour meeting, the motion against the committee managed nevertheless to secure 66 votes against 38, with 18 abstentions. The new chairman was M. Tharmalingam and the new secretary was Hedwig Arazoo. Wan Hamid managed to stay on as a committee member (*ST* 15 Feb 1956).

During the preceding debate, Tharmalingam had taken Eber's group to task for attacks published in *Suara Merdeka* against Tunku Abdul Rahman and David Marshall, the chief ministers of the Malayan Federation and Singapore respectively.

The views expressed in the magazine, Tharmalingam argued, were in no way representative of what the common Malayan student in the United Kingdom felt (*ST* 15 Feb 1956). Aside from calling these two leaders "colonial stooges", the publication had jibed that the Tunku was "Bourne's messenger boy" (*ST* 15 Feb 1956). Lieutenant-General Sir Geoffrey K. Bourne was Director of Operations in charge of Emergency activities in Malaya at this time.

The Tunku was incidentally in London in early 1956 at the head of an eight-man delegation. His negotiations with the British on independence for the federation between 18 January and 6 February proved highly successful, allowing for independence to be granted to Malaya by 31 August 1957 (Ooi 2006: 76).

The editorial in the December 1955 issue of *Suara Merdeka* had evaluated Marshall as a "pro-colonialist" whose "anti-communism" was more comprehensible as a position against uncompromising nationalism. David Marshall had been in London earlier that month, and had refused an invitation to speak to the Forum, citing his "unfortunate experience" with Wan Hamid a year earlier, when Marshall had given a talk to the Forum.

You then promised me that you would show me your report of
my talk which would be published in the Forum magazine. Not
only did you not keep your promise, but the report, in my
honest opinion, was malicious and dishonest.

Wan Hamid denied that such was the case, and retaliated by
reprinting his piece in the following issue of the *Suara Merdeka*
(*Suara Merdeka* 1955: 9).

Goh continued working diligently at his doctoral dissertation
despite his involvement in student politics and his support of the
nascent PAP back home. His supervisors were Professors R.G.D.
Allen and H.S. Booker. In September 1956, he submitted his highly
technical PhD thesis for review (Tan p. 77; *ST* 6 Nov 1956).

TECHNIQUES OF NATIONAL INCOME ESTIMATION IN UNDERDEVELOPED TERRITORIES, WITH SPECIAL REFERENCE TO ASIA AND AFRICA (1956)

Goh's doctoral achievement was a highly technical one, but
nevertheless, it brought to the fore many of his persistent interests.
Firstly, he maintained his focus on the Malayan economy, but
now in a comparative context. Furthermore, the ongoing switch
by most countries from war economics back to peace economics
convinced him that "national income estimates gave the essential
landmarks for guidance of policy".

However, the supplementary role that most underdeveloped
countries played in the world war, and their low level of
industrialization, meant that their post-war concerns were more
about raising production than changing economic footing. What
they did have to do, given the recent acquisition of independence,
was to intervene in the economy more than colonial governments
had done before in order to accelerate economic growth rates
beyond population growth rates. To carry out the planning

required, underdeveloped countries had to, some for the first time, decide on ways of estimating what their national income should be. This appears to be the functional backdrop for Goh's concern with an apparently technical subject, and explains what would otherwise have been an uncharacteristically ineffectual use of time and energy on his part.

No proper review of this work seems in existence — a testimony to how technical and academic it was to the popular eye. One short comment can be found in *Doctoral Dissertations on Hong Kong 1900–1997* though.

> [The work is a] critical analysis of the methods that were in use during the early 1950s to estimate national income within the Third World. Goh concluded that the prevailing method of aggregating factor income was inappropriate for the countries of Asia and Africa including Hong Kong particularly because it did not adequately estimate the value of gross and net agricultural products. Using Malaya as a case study, he showed how more satisfactory techniques of estimation could be applied to available data (Shulman & Shulman 2001: 127)

A fair and detailed analysis of Goh's 385-page dissertation will require more expertise than I can master. However, several important factors are worth reiterating nevertheless. The project provided Goh with a chance to widen his grasp of global economic dynamics and fortuitously equipped him with further technical knowledge useful in the key role he was later to play in creating the financial institutions of independent Singapore. Surely, the thought stimulated by the writing of a thesis on the finer points of estimating national income and expenditure, and how one often cannot tell one from the other, would stand anyone in good stead, especially if one's later job is to regulate national budgets.

Perhaps just as significantly, the project made him acutely aware that concepts developed in the West were not always suitable for application in underdeveloped countries. This insight was already expressed in 1940 when he wrote *The Economic Front*. The question is, how does one strategize against such pervasive bias? This was — and is — a common quandary for non-Western scholars in all disciplines. To be sure, being an economist, Goh tended more to contrast industrialized economies with underdeveloped countries than Western with non-Western countries.

He agreed that national income estimates in industrialized economies related easily to modern — or Keynesian — macroeconomic terms. But in countries not predominantly populated by wage-earners, the concepts for generating these estimates would have to be very different. Significantly, Goh drew inspiration on this point from M. Mukherjee's "The Technique of Social Accounting in the Pre-Industrial Economy", a conference paper that had been published in 1954 (Mukherjee 1954). As Goh noted, the problem had recently been occupying the minds of a long list of Indian scholars.

The challenge went beyond the mere discussing of procedures adopted for these estimates. What was required was a critical examination of notions "derived from Western theory and practice". Goh's job was "to study the validity of such concepts when applied to a different kind of economy". Naturally, what he was taking issue with were concepts and procedures generally accepted in the 1950s, especially by Western economists.

Concerns about measurability tended to lead to the exclusion of a wide range of activities. In general, services rendered or received outside market conditions would not count. The same was true of illegal activities. Expediency and not principle decided what was in and what was not in.

An example of how extra-market factors chosen for national income estimation carried hugely different significance depending on the developmental level of the country in question was that of subsistence output. In Western countries, this had limited implications. But in underdeveloped countries, the self-consumption of farmer products, for instance, was substantial in relation to the national income. Thus, most experts seemed to agree that this should be included. At the same time, its inclusion would highlight several difficulties. The mere estimation of the output, given logistical challenges alone, is quite a challenge. Communication problems had to be overcome as well. Evaluation of the products was not without serious problems, and these varied from one underdeveloped country to another and from one culture to the next.

One factor that held greater significance for underdeveloped countries than for developed ones was that of nationality and residency. Whose income should be included, and whose not? Income generated by foreign capital, along with high-earning foreigners, put greater pressure on underdeveloped countries to decide on the issue.

REVIEW OF THE COST OF LIVING IN HONG KONG (1957)

Goh returned to Singapore on 5 November 1956, and was awarded his doctorate two weeks later, on 22 November (Tan p. 77; *ST* 6 Nov 1956).

Within two months after coming back to Singapore, Goh, now Assistant Director at the Social Welfare Department (Research) had teamed up again with his old colleague Kenny Byrne, who was now Acting Deputy Secretary at the Ministry of Commerce, and with L. C. Goh, the Deputy Secretary of Higher Education, in a move designed to grab public attention and to embarrass the colonial establishment. Byrne was secretary of the Senior Officers Association.

All three were in the running for nine permanent secretary positions, but decided to declare publicly that they wished the pay scale at that level to be cut before they would fill the spots. Goh described the "reduction in top-level wages" as inevitable and "part of a trend towards an egalitarian society" (*ST* 5 January 1957).

In April 1957, the one-year-old *Malayan Economic Review* published by the Malayan Economic Society of the University of Malaya carried a short review by Goh of Edward Szczepanik's *The Cost of Living in Hong Kong*. The latter was a 25-page booklet published the previous year. Goh, just ending a very successful and exciting stint in London wrote academically on the subject and was more concerned with statistical method than anything else. He pointed out serious issues of reliability in the "recall method" used by the author in his survey on family expenditures, in contradistinction to a record-keeping method. However, the consistency in the results of two referenced studies that had relied on relatively small samples prompted him to conclude with a salient point that probably stemmed from his frugal nature and his affection for efficacy.

> Why take large samples if you get adequate results with small samples? While it is true the Hong Kong experiments are not conclusive in that random sampling methods were not used, it is nevertheless a disturbing thought that, in studies of family expenditure to derive weights for price indexes, the relation between sample size and sampling error has not been adequately investigated. It may well be that such an investigation should show that increasing the size of samples beyond a certain stage would merely be throwing money down the drain since any increase in precision gained thereby would have no practical value in increasing the precision of the final overall retail index.

ENTREPRENEURSHIP IN A PLURAL ECONOMY (1957)

On 27 September 1957, Goh, as vice-president of the Malayan Economic Society, addressed the group's annual general meeting. T. H. Silcock, who as president should have been the speaker for the day, was on leave. Goh's subject was "Entrepreneurship in a Plural Society" through which he sought to highlight the great importance the "general climate of opinion" held for economic development even in a society where entrepreneurship was a cultural norm. He extrapolated that private investments and public investments had separate roles to play.

This speech was significant in several ways, one of which was that it showed Goh in nation-building mode, exactly three years before the Economic Development Board (EDB) that was already emerging in his mind was finally established to direct Singapore's post-colonial development, and the Jurong wilderness was tamed and tarred to attract investors (Cheong 1993: 8).

Extra importance has to be given to this 1957 speech — published in *The Malayan Economic Review* the following year — since it was presented to the economist community just four weeks after Malaya had gained independence (and on the eve of self-rule for Singapore). Just as significantly, this was also when Goh was known to be paying visits to James Puthucheary in jail. Puthucheary had been arrested a year earlier, and would be released only in 1959. During his internment, he wrote *Ownership and Control*, a pioneering work on capitalism in colonial Malaya, for which he thanked Goh for the latter's contribution.

> Many parts of the book owe a lot to my friend and party colleague Dr Goh Keng Swee, who put his brilliant analytical mind at my disposal during the many visits he paid me in jail. (Puthucheary 1959: viii)

One can indeed see a common direction in these two works, and as mentioned earlier, Puthucheary did make good use of data from Goh's *Urban Incomes and Housing*. But while the younger man wished to present exploitation and poverty as class problems and not communal problems, Goh approached the matter in a less ideological way through the use of the term "entrepreneurship" to capture the communal difference in the ability to participate in the modern economy.

In Puthucheary's book, while the processes of unbalanced ownership and control were laid out in some detail, the solution was not discussed at any length and was simply expressed in the following manner: "Development must be such that it will overflow into the countryside and solve the poverty of the Malays" (Puthucheary p. 180).

Goh's solution was more concerned with practicality than ideology. Malaya, he stated, was a fortunate place when compared to other nations newly granted independence in having a special resource that was often taken for granted, namely "an entrepreneur class which [was] both extensive in numbers and high in quality". In states where entrepreneurs were lacking, the "cry for industrialisation is loud and can hardly be resisted". With few exceptions, state-initiated industrialization took place under this pressure and turned out to be extremely costly failures.

In what was surely a premature conclusion, not only because he was speaking very shortly after Malaya had gained full independence but also in light of the central developmental role that gigantic government-linked companies would be created to play in both Malaya and Singapore, he claimed that entrepreneurial resourcefulness and ability would discourage the governments of both "to embark on such a hazardous operation as going into business".

He predicted that post-colonial Malaya and Singapore would experience an orthodox pattern of development where governments would seek to provide basic social and infrastructural goods and services, after which investments from the private sector would follow. However, it soon became evident that he was no classical liberal. The relationship between the public sector and private investments was a complex one. Though not inherently antagonistic towards each other, the fact that savings were limited did imply a zero-sum game at some point. More importantly, private plans were decided by individual concerns and could only be coordinated after the fact.

> Where private plans have been brought into fruition, it is the general process of competition in a free market that determines which plans are sound and may survive, and which are unsound and have to be scrapped. The total volume of private investment which is planned is the result of decisions made at numerous points in response to economic and other stimuli operating within the system. It is this complex of stimuli which would determine both the aggregate level of private investments and the directions through which these investments would flow.

We observe here a return of the idea Goh entertained as a student exactly 20 years earlier when writing *Capitalism versus Socialism*. Back then, he discussed the cyclical mechanism within capitalism which repeatedly misguided investments and wasted resources and caused crises to recur. Enormous and targeted state spending to stimulate job creation, as proposed by Keynes, was the pre-war answer to this unfortunate defect in the economic system.

Just as interestingly, a widened use of "plans" was introduced in his talk in a way that would boost analytical comparability between public activity on one hand and private investment on the other, increasing symmetry in their relationship.

The state could remove "bottlenecks" to growth by providing goods and services to aid industry; but more significantly, Goh advanced the idea that "by maintaining economic activity at a higher level than would otherwise be the case, [the state helped] to provide a general climate of prosperity which would add to the confidence of private investors". The Keynesian idea was extended beyond economic factors to focus on the importance of "the general climate of opinion" and Goh discussed whether that was conducive to "the psychological atmosphere under which private investment plans [were] made and decisions to embark on private expansion [were] arrived at".

This innovation was Goh's attempt to locate the general statements he had been making in the specific sociological situation that post-colonial Malaya found itself in. To assist him in this, he adopted J.S. Furnivall's concept of "plural society", considering it a perfect way of describing the state of entrepreneurship in Malayan society. This term denotes a society "comprising two or more elements of social level which live side by side, yet without mingling in one political unit", and which functions through the imposition of an external force.

For Malaya, this external force was being withdrawn to be replaced by local forces. Economic differentiation between the ethnic groups was bound to be the major issue with the removal of the former masters from the equation. As Goh had learned from discussions with Malay members of the Malayan Forum in the late 1940s, the issue of inter-ethnic relations was going to be a serious one in the years ahead.

As he saw it, the plural society in Malaya was marked by the differentiation between "the Malays who [did] not form the entrepreneur class to any significant degree", and the "non-Malays from whom the entrepreneur class [had] almost exclusively been recruited". This was an unusual arrangement, to say the least, which challenged the Marxist claims that the government of a capitalist economy was merely doing the bourgeoisie's bidding.

> The dangers of the situation are fairly obvious. There is a possibility, even a probability, that measures will be taken through political action to redress the disparity in wealth between the components of a plural society. The anxiety which is felt in some quarters is that these measures may be such as to leave a country poorer for a while though a greater measure of equality may be achieved within it.

Dismissing the idea that a spontaneous increase in entrepreneurship among Malays was possible, Goh concentrated on "inducing the growth of Malay entrepreneurship by appropriate governmental measures". Two issues concerned him: the efficacy of such measures on the disadvantaged group and the effect on the country's general economic well-being.

His basic perspective was that "the best test devised by society for the selection of its entrepreneurs [was] by proved achievement in free competition with all other contestants". Any policy denying this "test" ran the risk of achieving unintended and unwanted results, and in the long run, of subverting the entrepreneurial quality of the country.

> The process of modifying competition to serve particular ends is therefore fraught with danger. At best, it can produce entrepreneurs of a lesser calibre who can survive only within the protected walls of state regulations. At worst, it would lead to the creation not of an entrepreneur class but of a rentier class whose contributions to the management of business are nominal and whose role in affairs depends on the possession of special

privileges. In such situations much activity will consist not of entrepreneurship but of spivvery.*

The consuming public would be the one to bear the burden stemming from the reduction in business efficiency "in the form of higher cost and prices and inferior output of goods and services".

Instead of trying by risky means to create a Malay entrepreneur class, Goh instead suggested a measure that would admittedly not change the plural societal structure of Malaya in the short term. His solution — still premature because of the infancy of the country and the smallness of economic units — was to "foster the growth of a managerial class among the Malays". Things were made more difficult by the fact that the best brains were being recruited into the civil service:

> In future, when economic activity is undertaken more by
> corporate organisations and less by family units, and when the
> supply of trained personnel increases, there may be greater
> opportunities for the creation of a Malay managerial class.

Without going further into particulars, Goh argued that the way to go was to concentrate on general rural development and on "the improvement of standards of living for everybody in the rural areas rather than to try, by artificial means, to contrive prosperity for a few". Acknowledging that some endeavours — most significantly the work of the Federal Land Development

---

* A *spiv* is a colloquial expression for "a man, typically flashily dressed, engaging in small-time trade in illicit or stolen goods" (Times-Chambers). "Spivvery" is uncommonly used outside England and was almost definitely a term Goh had picked up in London.

Authority (Felda) — were already underway, he nevertheless felt that "the place of rural development in relation to the wider scheme of things might not have been given its due appreciation".

> It is in the field of rural development that Malay economic enterprise and managerial skills may best be developed and has the greatest chance of success. And they may develop not necessarily through institutions appropriate to urban trade and industry but through special institutions yet to be created.

Felda was a statutory body that had its first meeting on 8 August 1956, during which it was declared that it would not concern itself with marginal projects, and would instead "give opportunities to those who [had] initiative, rather than charity to those who [had not]". Its accepted motto was "The best land for the best people" (Shamsul & Perera 1977: 5).

Goh opined that with his solution, the existing economic division would no doubt remain but predicted that "artificial measures to remedy it [would] not meet with success" anyway. Rural development, however, would be a better bet in the long run, he felt, helping the country transcend the division between economic power and political authority. In fact, the more he thought about it, the more he felt that the urgency for rural development was great.

> With the emergence of a prosperous rural sector, of which the Malays form the majority, many of the handicaps which now serve to restrain their economic progress will disappear. Educational standards will certainly increase and with it a greater awareness of events outside of their own circumscribed world; also larger incomes would mean a greater ability to accumulate capital. With rising standards of living and improved standards of education, it will be far easier for rural people to move into the urban industrial world and lay down their stakes there.

On 17 December 1957, Goh, now Acting Director of the Social Welfare Department, made it publicly known that a thorough investigation into the living conditions of farmers and their methods of production was in the works. A pilot study started four months earlier had just been completed, and the year-long main survey would commence in January 1958 (*ST* 18 December 1957).

It is highly likely that this initiative was an expression of Goh's realization that he needed to complement his earlier studies on housing and urban poverty with a better understanding of rural economic conditions. However, things were moving fast, for the Federation of Malaya, for Singapore, for the PAP, and for Goh himself. His ideas about the importance of rural development to the inter-ethnic peace and the future of national economics appear not to have been developed further. In his discussions about China in the 1980s and 1990s, however, rural development in the form of town and village enterprises did figure prominently, and excited him significantly.

On 20 December 1957, then Singapore Chief Minister Lim Yew Hock told the State Assembly that an economic research unit would soon be set up under Goh as part of the process of Malayanization that was being heatedly discussed at that time (*ST* 21 December 1957). By May 1958, Goh had indeed taken over from Dr F.C. Benham, who was retiring as economic adviser to the Singapore Government (*ST* 26 May 1958).

Lim had carried out a crackdown on left-wingers on 18 September 1956, arresting seven prominent leaders. This provided the PAP with the opportunity in the coming electoral campaign of popularly promising their release should the party be victorious. With the movement towards self-rule for Singapore accelerating, Goh's strong ties to the PAP put him at an impasse. His impressive career as top civil servant and Singapore's most noted social researcher was coming to an end. In August that year, he resigned as director of the Social and Economic Research Division in the Chief Minister's Office, and joined the party he had helped conceive, four years after it was founded.

Elections were around the corner. Soon after leaving the civil service, Goh gave a talk to students at Nanyang University. It was titled after his doctoral thesis: "Estimating the National Incomes of Underdeveloped Countries" (ST 12 September 1958).

> Malayan society is complicated. It has not been developed over several hundred years by intellectuals and scholars as in other countries. [...] Our society is not uniform. It comprises groups with different standards, different philosophies.

He believed that the airing of grievances in moderation was necessary, but "no group should adopt an aggressive attitude likely to provoke hostility among the others". A self-governing Singapore had a big role to play in creating a Malayan outlook to overshadow ethnic consciousness.

This would nevertheless take three generations to accomplish, he thought. Not only was undivided loyalty to be fostered among the people, each ethnic group had to have the opportunity to enjoy democratic benefits. The latter would assure inter-racial harmony within which the second generation, through education, could develop new attitudes of loyalty towards the new country. This was crucial.

> The present school system is all wrong. Boys and girls are not being taught loyalty to Malaya. [...] Text books should be written for Malayans by Malayans. The present books were written by Englishmen for English children. By the time Malayan boys and girls leave school they are intellectually timid. [...]We must develop literature, music and drama in the new Malaya.

> We have little art for a modern, self-respecting nation (*ST* 12 September 1958).

During question time, he called for the formation of a common market encompassing the Federation, Singapore, Brunei and Sumatra. This was necessary for economic growth and as a long-term measure to offset the post-war record-breaking population increase.

His talk, given so soon after he left government service, clearly marked the beginning of a new period in his life. While he did make political speeches when in London, his image back in Singapore had largely remained that of a top civil servant and researcher until this point in time. His style of writing also changed to reflect his new public image as politician and would-be nation-builder. The strict academic style of writing that he had been using so far would become somewhat rarer after 1958, and especially after the PAP gained power in 1959, his articles would inevitably express the political exigency and practical urgency that suffused his later years. Be that as it may, Goh's later speeches and writings are known for a heaviness that was only partly due to bad delivery. His need to state facts and present step-by-step reasoning stayed with him throughout his career.

OUR ECONOMIC FUTURE (1958)

One of the first pieces that Goh wrote for *Petir*, the PAP party magazine, was published in its 4th anniversary issue in 1958. Crafting an article for the masses evidently cramped his style. It starts out with a series of factual statements with little literary quality, which are punctuated by regular rhetorical questions, suggesting that it was conceived as a speech. Only after the first page in this three-page piece does Goh's prose relax into something more reminiscent of his earlier writings. The point Goh made on the eve of general elections, and on the eve of self-government for Singapore, was that Singapore and the Federation of Malaya must merge: "A thorough-going socialist transformation of our society is possible only when we have merged with the Federation". This may be contrary to the thinking of "some people in the Federation", but would benefit both territories.

What Singapore had going for it despite many constraints were the availability of capital waiting for the right inducement; the access to large markets in neighbouring areas; and the presence of industrious and skilled workers. But for economic growth to accelerate, two conditions had to be fulfilled: industrial peace and political stability. These could be achieved by something he termed "a socialist government". What he considered the foundations of this "socialist society" stemmed from historic practicality. For example, he was convinced that Singapore could not move towards socialism alone because it was a free port economy "whose principal livelihood [depended] on international trade".

> It should be possible to initiate socially owned factories but this must be done largely within the framework of free competition. [...] Whether, in the long run, industrialisation in Singapore will be carried out principally by private enterprise or principally by socially owned enterprises depends on which of these two forms of economic organisation is the more efficient. This is a matter which cannot be determined by dogma or theory; it is something to be tested by actual experience.

Goh's main concern was with giving maximum encouragement to the private sector to establish new factories. Socialism would come through "a limited redistribution of wealth through social welfare policy".

Welfare measures require money; such money comes from taxation; adequate taxation comes from steady and continuous economic expansion; such growth depends on private enterprise and investment; and these, in the final analysis, require political stability and industrial peace. This process sufficiently sums up Goh's concept of "the temporary phase of Singapore's political evolution".

Further insights into Goh's thoughts about socialism can be gleaned from a newspaper report on a forum on "Socialism in Asia" held at the University of Malaya on 1 December 1958 at which he spoke (*ST* 2 December 1958). If Malaya were to fail, he warned the student crowd, it would be in the coming decade. Socialism, he reasoned, was hampered in Asian countries by the lack of "a stable ruling elite". This flaw in turn was aggravated by "the widespread misconception among Asian political leaders of democracy". He saw no inconsistency between democratic government and the governing of a country by a ruling elite.* Finally, there were difficulties in saliently defining the word "Asian".

> We think we are Asians, but we are by no means typical of Asia. The Asians are the peasants who grow rice in the river valleys of the continent. And so, any change that can be thought of must be deliberately thought out for them.

---

* Significantly, Goh would establish The Pyramid Club in early 1963. This club formalized The Establishment that he thought vital to stable government. More than that, it offered a space where English-educated politicians and civil servants could build ties with the Chinese-educated business community. Goh's sources of inspiration for this initiative were apparently The Athenaeum Club and the Traveller's Club of London, as well as the Oxford and Cambridge Club. In a memorandum to Lee Kuan Yew written on 19 March that year, he proposed that membership to this elite organization be restricted "to those who participate in making important policy decisions in the State of Singapore as well as those who are responsible for directing implementation" (Chew 2005: 34–40).

OUR ECONOMIC POLICY (1959)

Two months before the elections, Goh spoke at a mass rally at Dhoby Ghaut in the city. That speech contained his basic ideas about Singapore's economic situation, and was included in the PAP's booklet *The Tasks Ahead*, published in May 1959 not long before polling day. His delivery that day was probably characteristically lacking in excitement, but as a printed document, the reasoning he expressed appears very thorough.

Starting with a warning that the growing population would soon mean high unemployment, he advised little Singapore to quickly expand her manufacturing industries. The island's enviable location, the available capital waiting to be put to optimal use, the huge surrounding markets, and its "hardworking, resourceful and enterprising people" were its main advantages.

But it was in his symmetric listing that day of the island's disadvantages that we detect his brilliance and his practical mindset. Despite Singapore's fortunate location, he said, the free entry of foreign goods made it extremely risky for local capital to go into manufacturing. Local industries would take too long to reach full efficiency. Secondly, as long as import duties had to be paid on goods going into the Federation, investors would prefer to establish factories in Johor than in Singapore. He also realized that not only was the general technological skill level among Singaporeans not up to standard, training facilities were "grossly inadequate" (Goh 1959a: 21). Lastly, he noted that "too much of the business and banking brains of Singapore [were] orientated towards trade and not towards industry". All these had to change.

To achieve that, Goh contended, a common market comprising of the Federation of Malaya and Singapore was necessary. While the Federation could lift import duties for goods from Singapore, it would be offered joint control of the port in Singapore. This would take place within an economic union where a coordinated development programme that benefited both could be implemented. Getting rid of unnecessary competition would keep price levels low, while making the investment climate more stable and predictable in both territories would attract capital. Investment opportunities would increase naturally with the creation of such a union.

> The establishment of a common tariff-free market within the framework of a larger economic union based on a co-ordinated development programme is the only way whereby both territories can find answers to their pressing economic problems. It would be foolish in the extreme for one territory to take temporary advantage of the other for this would set off a chain reaction of reprisals and counter-reprisals which will lead to the ruin of both territories.

Goh would remain strongly convinced of the correctness of this analysis, and the subsequent failure to reach agreement on a common market with his counterpart in Kuala Lumpur, his second cousin Tan Siew Sin, was a pivotal reason for the separation of Singapore from Malaysia in August 1965 (Chew 1996).

The encouraging of educational opportunities in science, engineering and technical skills and managerial proficiency had to occur alongside efforts to motivate industrial capital. Waiting for one to enhance the other would not work, according to Goh. Interestingly, he also harped back to something he thought in the early 1950s was one reason why the communists could gain broad support among the masses, and that was that persons educated in vernacular schools had limited prospects under the colonial regime. Successful training and educational programmes in a post-colonial Singapore would lead to "a tremendous release of human energy and skill which [were] now being held back in frustration".

Further evidence of his originality is found in his assertion that although foreign capital was welcome, it was local capital presently lying idle or placed in foreign lands that would play the major role in developing Singapore.

> There are no benevolent foreigners knocking around the world, anxious to discharge these duties and responsibilities which are rightly our own. Let us not face the economic problems in the era of freedom with the mental attitudes appropriate to colonial servitude. Let us never forget that self-government is not possible without self-reliance. This is true both in politics as well as in economics.

This distrust of external powers was evident later in Goh's efforts after Singapore's separation from Malaysia to lay the foundations for a strong defence force.

In the 1959 campaign speech, we see very little that would pass for socialism in its normal sense. What concerned Goh most was what he later agreed was a basic tenet in his political thought — the primacy of economic growth in the building of a new nation (Chew 1996: 169). He also took the opportunity to announce plans for the formation of a well-financed Economic Development Board (EDB), whose responsibility was to make general economic plans, appraise and develop individual projects, and coordinate technical training programmes with industrial expansion.

The abovementioned board was established on 1 August 1961. Goh, by then Minister of Finance, appointed his old schoolmates from Raffles College, Hon Sui Sen and Lim Kim San, as the board's chairman and deputy chairman, respectively (*Report* 1962: 1).

Goh ran successfully as the PAP candidate for the Kreta Ayer constituency on 30 May 1959, winning 9,313 of the 14,173 votes. He would retain that constituency for the rest of his political career. The PAP as a whole did exceedingly well in the elections, securing 43 of the 51 seats available (Tan 82–83).

Writing in the party organ, *Petir*, Goh discussed his victory in a piece titled "My Election". Kreta Ayer, situated right in the middle of China Town, was home to 30,000 and was the most densely populated constituency on the island. Goh suffered great demands on his time being chairman of the party's Mass Meeting Committee, and Kreta Ayer was chosen as the seat for him because it was a compact place and would not put too much extra strain on him. His committee's job was to arrange mass rallies and street corner meetings. During the campaign, as many as 12 mass meetings per evening and 40 per week were organized. The mass meeting was, in his words, "one of our most powerful campaign instruments" (Goh 1960a: 4).

Goh was immediately made Minister of Finance after the elections (Morais 1963: LVII). The party's triumph meant that its leaders now had a real chance at preparing the self-governing colony for full independence. But at this time, the most promising way for that to happen seemed to be through a merger with the relatively stable two-year-old Federation of Malaya.

However, an official announcement about such a solution would not be made for two years yet, and Malayan Premier Tunku Abdul Rahman could not be coaxed by the British into making a public commitment for merger until early 1961.

Along the way, the inherent conflict within the PAP between Lee's faction and its left wing had to be settled. For the time being, however, the PAP kept its campaign promise and released leftist leaders that Lim Yew Hock had imprisoned. The British objected strongly and put pressure on the Malayan Federation's representative in the Security Council of Singapore, External Affairs Minister Dr Ismail Abdul Rahman, to do the same. Ismail's conclusion was that Lee had read the situation correctly:

> It was to no avail because Lee Kuan Yew knew that having won the elections by a large majority, he now held the whip in his hand while the British and ourselves were not prepared for a showdown (IAR, Drifting c15).

Incidentally, it was Ismail who decided that contacts with Lee and Goh within the Security Council would be easier if they played golf together. In the process, the two Singaporeans became skilled at the game (IAR, Drifting c16).

THE SOCIAL REVOLUTION IN MALAYA (1959)

Despite Goh's inherent practical sense and his long experience in the civil service, becoming the minister in charge of the purse strings of a self-governing Singapore and being central to its development plans could not but bring a new urgency to his ideas. His speech, titled "The Social Revolution in Malaya" and delivered to the Malayan Forum in London on 20 September 1959, just five months after he was elected, was an attempt to summarize the colonial past; justify the political activism he was party to; and face Malaya's major problems as he saw them (Goh 1959h: 27–30). Most significantly, he presented the historical context within which the election of the PAP should be understood.

With young Malayan students as his target audience, it was perhaps in its place for Goh's speech to utilize dramatic terms and adopt a wide historical purview within which to evaluate recent events. Goh simplified Malaya's history into three parts.

A social revolution, he ventured, was one that had profound effects on the social structure and the lifestyles of common folk.

Revolutions did take place regularly throughout the region, but these tended to be what were generally known as "palace revolutions". Armies move in and replace one leader with another, and no profound social changes need to follow.

> Our social revolution is not brought about by violence. It is the result of the impact of history. Stamford Raffles started our social revolution. Before Raffles, Malaya was a traditional society: people earned their living by fishing, hunting, rice-growing, etc. Generally, there was not the slightest trend of western civilization. At the time Raffles came to Malaya, the West was just beginning to change from the traditional society to the industrial stage. Singapore was then just a trading out-post. Merchants found Singapore a better place for trade than most other places. (Goh 1959b: 27)

Being a global-minded economist, especially after his work on his recent doctoral project, the next important stage to Goh's mind of the country's social revolution was the introduction of the rubber tree into Malaya.

> There was no inducement before rubber plantation for investment in Malaya. After rubber was introduced, there was a tremendous investment of British capital in Malaya and the opening up of the Malay Peninsula started (p. 28).

Most importantly, this new industry needed manual labour. With the local inhabitants not willing to leave the villages, labour had to be brought in from southern China and southern India. The available supply of such labour from territories that were under the influence of the British made this industry possible. The tremendous growth in migrant population became a serious worry for the Malays. Their lack of participation in what was part of a globally fuelled industry left them relatively poorer, especially when the traditional economy was gradually subsumed under the new one. In response to this worry, the British introduced immigration control in 1931–1932.

Interestingly, Goh saw the Japanese invasion as the third stage in the Malayan social revolution, in which the status of the British was destroyed.

> [The British] ruled by prestige. The old show of their heroism disappeared in two months and after that it was quite impossible for the British to re-establish their predominance. (p. 29)

There is an understandable Singapore-centrism in Goh's rendition of the peninsula's history, biased further not only by the economic teachings of the day, but, by the fact that these chosen stages — as he pointed out — were all initiated by foreigners, with Singapore as the major venue for those interventions.

In truth, Goh was simplifying history to explain a practical and poignant point, which was that "the future political development of the country could depend on how we resolve the conflict between the indigenous and the immigrant sections of the population" (p. 29). The aim of his speech becomes obvious at the end. He was calling on the English-educated group — which his audience in London certainly was — to rise to the occasion. Being victims of a history authored by foreigners, Malayans had inherited an unholy mix of ethnicities and were saddled with the impossible task of creating a homogenous nation from it.

> The English-educated group are the only group that transcends all racial barriers, all living together, largely sharing the same values, mixing with one another very freely and establishing confidence. [...] But never imagine that in performing this role

they can preserve all the rights and privileges which they enjoyed in the past. If they are prepared to make the necessary sacrifice, I think, they will have a vital role to play because they are the only group in Malaya where members of the various races come into contact. I do not offer you an easy solution. The problem cannot be solved by one political party or an individual (p. 29).

The political considerations that underlined Goh's reasoning in 1959 act as a reminder that his situation, both as a thinker on, and participant in, Malayan history, was greatly changing.

Given his stature as intellectual and social researcher, now greatly enhanced by his standing within the ruling party in Singapore, he was in a position to plan and build the economy and bring many insights to bear on the future of Malaya. As Goh's own writings suggest, this was an ambition that had slowly grown within him, and it is highly probable that his observation that the Japanese invasion destroyed British prestige for good in Malayan eyes was in fact a generalization of his own experience. Up to that point in his life, his writings were not clearly political in nature and did not venture into fields he did not master.

Speeches, by their very nature, need to be treated as being essentially different from articles written with academic pretensions. But Goh remained a man who practically always wrote his own speeches and who was never known to entertain frivolous ideas. His interest in politics became evident only after the war, and was openly expressed only during his first sojourn in London.

Throughout the 1950s, Goh was able to use his reputation as a promising student and his privileged position in the civil service to gather information about the socio-political situation in Singapore, to widen his own views on Malaya's political economy, to foster ties with left-leaning political activists, and to prepare for a post-colonial reality.

PART TWO

The Nation Builder

Chapter 3

PRACTICABLE ECONOMICS

Practitioners need to be innovative in grappling with tasks of a third world economy. The book of rules tells you very little, and precedents borrowed from advanced countries have a nasty habit of coming apart in your hands.

— Goh Keng Swee, 6 June 1977

Arranging Goh Keng Swee's works in a chronological fashion as I have done in Section One allows for an easy contextualization of his thoughts and his works within his life experiences and within the general history of Malaya and Singapore.

From here onwards, the presentation of his writings has to take a new form. To the extent possible, I rely on a thematic arrangement and the included works are chosen for their substance, their representativeness of his thoughts and their significance in helping us understand the man and his ideas.

Although his speeches given as a minister, either of Finance, Defence or Education, or as Deputy Prime Minister of Singapore (which he was from 1980 to 1984), were formal affairs in a sense, a surprising number of his writings after 1959 are so substantial in content that they make the job of filtering his thoughts quite a daunting task. The three collections of his speeches and writings which were published between 1972 and 1995 are without much accompanying analysis, either by him or by editors.

The wealth of information and solid reasoning found in Goh's speeches and talks after 1959 is a powerful testimony to the depth of his participation in, and the breadth of his influence on, Singapore's nation building. In that important sense, his life and thoughts amount to a rare study of post-colonial reality in Southeast Asia and the Third World.

One shortcoming in the chosen approach of analysing Goh's own words is that the social being is not properly captured. Quotes about him are therefore provided here and there, as has been done in Section One. The following two citations, for example, grant a glimpse of the civil servant turned national visionary. The first is from one who worked under him and the other from one who worked with him.

> Dr Goh was a gruff, short-tempered person who, though he had a fine economist's brain, liked to play bully, especially with senior civil servants like myself. (De Cruz, in *Rojak Rebel* 1993: 192)

Gerald De Cruz was one of many young Malayan activists in the post-war period who were attracted to Communism. He became disillusioned after some visits behind the Iron Curtain, and was brought back to Singapore to work under David Marshall.

Albert Winsemius, the Dutch economic adviser to the government in the early years, remembered Goh as a "goal-getter", but one with "a playful mind" that "jumps from one thing to the other".

> Once he grasps [a point,] he will push it through; carry it through to the end. Then it becomes boring for him and he's

looking around for something else. And when it was over, he
tackles something else. (CORD Winsemius pp. 25–26)

It is not the aim of the following sections to convince the reader
of Goh's enormous role in building Singapore. He or she probably
does not need any convincing. In any case, there exist numerous
texts testifying to his great importance, not forgetting the volumes
written by Lee Kuan Yew, in which Goh is often mentioned.
Others include works like *Leaders of Singapore* (1996); the two
well-written chapters on him in *Lee's Lieutenants* (1999); *Goh
Keng Swee and Southeast Asian Governance* (2004); *Goh Keng Swee:
A Portrait* (2007); and most recently, *Men in White* (2009).

All will agree that the history of Singapore cannot be told
without constant reference to Goh. Since this book tries to view
matters through his writings, it cannot amount to a typical
narration of the country's history. Such an undertaking is better
left to professional historians and to a later date when official
and private papers are more easily accessible.

For now, what the later parts of this volume attempt to do is
to highlight the comprehensive reach of Goh's thinking and
actions. The issues overlap, naturally, and the writings selected
for analysis cannot claim to cover all essential aspects of his
thinking. It is nevertheless hoped that a deep impression of his
approach to life and his understanding of human society can be
gained from a thorough study of his words.

THIS IS HOW YOUR MONEY IS SPENT (1960)

Proclaiming that "a government is judged not so much by its
expressions of good intentions but by its concrete achievements
in the way of economic prosperity and public welfare", Goh
presented his second budget to the Legislative Assembly on
29 September 1960. The first one had come too soon after the

1959 elections to provide clear ideas about how he imagined Singapore's development to go. Technical details will be avoided here, but suffice to say that Goh's attention was very much focused on regional economies, and on the situation in superpower economies. He noted that the past year had shown trade expansion, a rise in industrial output and personal consumption, and improvements in business confidence, worker conditions and public services.

The American economy was slowing, but not to an extent that worried him. India and China were each in their own way executing national development plans. Goh's highest praise was saved for the Japanese, who had ploughed back as much as 25% of the national income for economic expansion. Their industrial output had consequently jumped by 29% in 1959, and with prices remaining steady and foreign reserves increasing at the same time.

Where Malaya was concerned, Goh's worries were about negotiations on common market provisions, and with the fact that five separate polities — the Federation of Malaya, Singapore, Brunei, North Borneo and Sarawak — now participated in one currency. He wished to maintain that arrangement, for "without a firm financial base of a sound currency, no underdeveloped region can hope to tackle the immense problems of economic development" (Goh 1960b: 5). A trade agreement with the Soekarno administration in Jakarta was also of grave concern to Goh at this time.

Singapore figures were reassuring, but industrial expansion, though proceeding as before, was unsatisfactory in Goh's eyes. With the new political situation and Singapore's population explosion, the rate of industrial growth had to be doubled or even tripled for progress to be effective. A team under Albert Winsemius sent by the United Nations Technical Assistance

Administration was already in place, writing a report on methods of industrial expansion for Singapore.

Referring to the two articles he had published in *Petir* in 1958 and 1959 as statements that guaranteed security for foreign capital and that dismissed the nationalization of means of production, Goh announced that the PAP's socialist government "would not merely bring about equality of opportunities between groups and classes" but also "expand opportunities for all to exercise their abilities to the full for the benefit of society" (*ibid.* p. 15). The first was almost certainly a nod to the strong socialist sentiments existent among PAP supporters at this time, while the latter clearly stemmed from his wish to remove the career limits that Singaporeans not educated in English continued to suffer from.

SOME PROBLEMS OF INDUSTRIALISATION IN SINGAPORE (1963)

The government in Kuala Lumpur used the Internal Security Act against 50 persons in mid-December 1962, and Operation Cold Store was launched in Singapore on 2 February against the leftist Barisan Sosialis, with 111 arrests being made. These were tense times. Ethnic tensions were high, and Indonesian President Soekarno was threatening serious repercussions should the proposed Federation of Malaysia be carried through.

Between 2 and 12 January 1963, Goh made six appearances on radio to speak on "Some Problems of Industrialisation in Singapore". The formation of the Federation of Malaysia was in the works, and the results of a referendum on the merger had gone in favour of the PAP and against the Barisan Sosialis formed in August 1961 after left-wingers split from the mother party over the proposal to join the Federation.

The radio talks were meant for the average English-speaking Singaporean, and were therefore couched in relatively simple terms. In introducing the setting for Singapore's economy, Goh used the coming of age of post-war baby boomers as his point of departure. The only way of overcoming the impending unemployment, he contended, was to accelerate the already rising rate of industrial expansion. The founding of the Federation of Malaysia later that year would improve the situation drastically, and the economic and political isolation that had hampered economic growth would end.

His first task was to hold discussions with international experts, and to recruit "very able people from overseas, and from Singapore and from Malaya as well". Now placed within the Economic Development Board (EDB), these people were studying what types of industries would be most appropriate for Singapore (Goh 1963: 2). A range of factories had over the previous two years been set up to provide about 3,500 jobs at four industrial sites — Redhill, Tanglin Halt, Bendemeer and Kampong Ampat. At the same time, a huge industrial estate was being prepared in Jurong.

In the second talk, Goh argued that Singapore had to depend on manufacturers from overseas for much of the "pioneering work". These already had the technical know-how and the necessary experience. Singapore's advantages were "our central geographical position, our banking services, our port, our stable currency, easy exchange control regulations, ample supplies of power and water, cheap land, low building cost", and easy loan conditions from the EDB. But beyond that, the foreign investor would worry about "management-labour relations" and market size. Goh explained that market size was a major concern because of the need for investments in costly machines. Advantages of scale were needed for these machines to produce in quantities large enough to push costs down to a competitive level.

Goh discussed import-substitution industrialization in the third talk, asserting that the lack of local capital could be surmounted through joint ventures between local and foreign manufacturers. The bigger problem was the fact that some products would be selling at a higher price than similar imported products. For these selected products, then, import duties would have to be imposed to allow local factories to grow. Since the advantages of scale would be more obvious the bigger the protected market was, a common market that would grow to cover the whole of the Federation of Malaysia would be the most rational solution. Exempting goods central to the entrepot trade would help preserve that chunk of the economy, and work towards those ends had already started with the formation of the Tariff Advisory Commission Ordinance in July 1962.

In the fourth and fifth parts of the radio series, Goh spoke on the controversial issue of labour troubles, and attacked unions associated with Barisan Sosialis. He named several examples where union actions had caused factories to suffer losses or to close down.

> The government intends to set up a Commission of Inquiry to go into all these matters and expose the scandalous state of affairs in some of our factories. Intense indignation at the misdeeds of these dangerous anti-social elements is certain, once the facts are known. So when the time comes to take action to curb them, the general public and workers in particular will say, "And about time too" (Goh 1963: 12–13).

Goh was greatly concerned with newly started pioneer industries, and how union strikes and wage demands affected them. The reason why unions in post-war Britain and Holland were so supportive in rebuilding those countries, he argued, was because "their leaders were not dedicated to outside interests" and they "placed loyalty to their country before loyalty to an ideology", unlike parts of Singapore's trade union movement (Goh 1963: 15).

He wished for five-year wage agreements for the pioneer industries, and for disputes to be settled through negotiations and arbitration. To accomplish that, he convinced Devan Nair, the secretary-general of the National Trades Union Congress, to form the Pioneer Industries Union as the organization for workers in those industries. He also asked that training opportunities be made available to those workers. Finally, he recommended that Singapore's union movement study the role of its counterparts in Scandinavia and Holland, where "organised labour, employer and Government jointly bear certain responsibilities in economic policy" (*ibid.* p. 17).

In a style reminiscent of *The Economic Front*, the booklet he wrote in 1940, he ended this series of talks by asking "everyone" to assist in the national project of industrialization by buying local products. Other measures included the sending of 30 to 40 of the country's best students to choice universities abroad for special training in science and technology. This number would increase with the years, and on their return, these young men and women would function as "the core of our engineers and technicians". He also asked the following of his fellow citizens:

1. Workers and their trade unions had to "calculate the effects of whatever action they take on industrial growth", and realize that their "real employer" was "the overseas customer";
2. Those with higher income should put their surplus into industrial shares, and civil servants should be free to do the same;
3. Businessmen should adjust to changes to the free port status,

and also take greater interest in industrial development and not only in trading. Joint ventures with eager foreign manufacturers would allow for an inflow of industrial know-how into the country, with help from the EDB.

Of great practical consequence to Singapore's industrialization and Housing Development Board projects was the creation in 1963 of the Public Utilities Board. This board took over the supply of power, water and gas from the defunct city council. Its main responsibilities were to plan for the future, increase generating capacities, and secure supplies (Goh 1976a: 83). It was also to expand water reservoirs, build power plants and supply the increasing number of households with electricity, water and gas (*ST* 13 Oct 1970).

The founding of the Federation of Malaysia is largely seen today as a successful collective move by the British in their withdrawal from their colonies, the Malayan government which had been triumphant in fighting the Malayan Communist Party, and the PAP government in Singapore which had been facing powerful challenges from the Barisan Sosialis. For Goh, at least, the economic advantages to be gained from the merging of all the British-controlled territories were just as important as the political stability that he hoped the new federation would bring. The two were inseparable to him. This reasoning was obvious in his speeches made before 16 September 1963, and in his actions after that date. Negotiations for a common market, however, were failing badly.

Goh did not show much support for PAP initiatives such as its entry into Malaysia's general elections in 1964 and the forming of the Malaysian Solidarity Convention with several opposition parties on 9 May 1965, (Lau 1998: 258; Chew 1996: 142–49). But when relations between Kuala Lumpur and Singapore began sliding from dreadful to dangerous, Goh took upon himself to work for a separation, and kept it secret from the British as well as certain members of the Singapore Cabinet who were deeply involved in PAP ventures on the peninsular mainland (Lau pp. 258–65: Chew p. 147). "Rajaratnam's histrionics" was also upsetting Goh (Dee 465).

Apparently playing his role as Minister of Finance to the hilt, Goh mentioned to Australia's representative in Singapore, William Beale Pritchard, just five days before the separation that "Singapore might just as well be out of Malaysia if Kuala Lumpur was not going to co-operate economically". He feared that [the PAP leaders] would all be "butchered", and after Lee Kuan Yew's "moment of anguish" in signing the document for separation on Monday, 9 August 1965, Goh confided in Pritchard about "the long haul ahead and the need for hard work" with "none of the nonsense of the last six months". As a further sign of how frenzied and insecure the political situation had become by July that year, Goh, being perhaps the Singaporean leader least emotional about Malaysia, remarked further to Pritchard that "Lee would be kept under control" (Dee 2005: 464–68).

Australia's High Commissioner to Kuala Lumpur, Tom Critchley, a close friend of Malaysian Internal Affairs Minister Dr Ismail Abdul Rahman, wrote home to Canberra on 12 August to say that the latter had repeatedly described Goh, Razak and Eddie Barker — Singapore's Law Minister — as the "architects" of the separation (Dee p. 479).

> I agree that Barker was more a draughtsman than an architect, but I am satisfied that Goh played a big part in the settlement and this is confirmed by Razak. Razak has explained Goh's change of portfolio [to Defence] as a move that will enable him to work more closely with the Malaysian Government than if his responsibilities were in the economic field where the sharpest controversies will arise.

However, Critchley soon took the view that "personally, I think [Lee and Goh] were cooperating closely" (Dee p. 490). He wrote that according to Tan Siew Sin, Goh had raised the separation at a meeting on July 15 at which Tan was present and then had a second meeting with the Malaysians on 20 July at which Tan was not present. Ismail had confided in Critchley that Goh had already signed the agreement — drafted by Barker — on 5 August (*ibid.* pp. 497–98). In a telegram to British Premier Harold Wilson sent two weeks later on 23 August, Lee Kuan Yew explained:

> The difficulty was not the Tunku but Tan Siew Sin, Tunku's Finance Minister who hates my party because he fears that my colleagues and I would displace him and his party as co-partners with the Tunku's party. On 6th August he threatened Singapore with economic sanctions which may include the cutting off of our water consumption (CRO 1965: 59).

On the day of separation, the Finance portfolio was handed over to Goh's old schoolmate Lim Kim San while he took over the Ministry of Interior and Defence, apparently feeling that priority had to be given to Singapore's physical safety. The Indonesian threat was still very real. Two other possible reasons for this switch were firstly that relations with the Malaysians at that point would be better handled personally by Goh as head of the Ministry of Interior and Defence — not as Minister of Finance, given how bad relations with Tan Siew Sin had become, and as an old friend of Razak. Secondly, deteriorating relations between major personalities within the PAP could be better managed if Goh did not stay on at the Finance Ministry with its necessary and constant involvement in the work of all other ministries.

As Lee Kuan Yew pointed out later, there was a more personal reason for the switch in portfolios. Lim, besides being a practical man, was someone who "could work closely with Keng Swee without friction, thus allowing Keng Swee to contribute informally to policies on finance" (Lee 2000: 23).

The day after the separation, the British High Commission reported to the Commonwealth Relations Office that Lee was "still worried about solidarity of PAP Cabinet, particularly Toh and Rajaratnam".

> They and other ministers whose homes were in Malaya had been brought to sign separation agreement only by great efforts. It was negation of first article in PAP's original constitution which called for re-integration of Singapore and Malaya and there was still risk they would abandon Goh Keng Swee and himself as men of no principle for advocating [separation]. [...] Goh had from outset been contemptuous of do or die attitude taken by Rajaratnam and others, and [had been] strong advocate of separation agreement; others had been explicitly prepared to see Goh resign until worked on by Lee himself (CRO 1965: 155–57).

The PAP leadership managed nevertheless to stay sufficiently united during these critical times. Over the next two years, Goh, as Minister of Interior and Defence, rushed through the establishment of the Singapore Armed Forces, the implementation of National Service and the founding of the Singapore Air Force. By August 1967, he was back at his Finance post.

TWO YEARS OF ECONOMIC PROGRESS (1967)

On 5 December, just four months after returning to the Ministry of Finance, Goh gave his budget speech for the coming year to Parliament. This was published by the Ministry of Culture as *Two Years of Economic Progress*.

The Cold War was far from chilly in the mid-1960s when Singapore became independent — incidentally doing that twice, first on 31 August 1963 and then on 9 August 1965. Changes throughout East Asia worked strangely in Singapore's favour.

The increasing power of General Suharto following his crackdown in 1965 on the 30 September Movement signalled the beginning of the end of Indonesia's war of attrition against the Federation. This quickly allowed for rapid improvements in economic relations between Singapore and Jakarta.

At the same time, the Vietnam War intensified, raising American and South Vietnamese demand for petroleum and petroleum products from Singapore.

Further north, Chairman Mao Zedong's struggle against his own party saw the Cultural Revolution accelerate beyond his own control, with demonstrations and Maoist violence spilling into Hong Kong, convincing many factories there to move to Singapore. On 7 September 1967, Goh told newsmen that as many as 300 investment proposals from Hong Kong industrialists had recently been received by the Economic Development Board (EDB). Two months after that, he would reveal that 86 of them had committed themselves to investments in Singapore amounting to $49 million (*ST* 3 Nov 1967). This huge inflow of capital led the EDB to launch a "crash programme" to build factories in various estates to meet this demand.

Obviously, these three scenarios all brought advantages to Singapore. However, the doubling of petroleum-based exports to South Vietnam did not excite Goh as much as trade with Indonesia or the immigration of Hong Kong factories did. His conviction was that the country had to industrialize broadly, and trade with South Vietnam brought narrow favours only to refineries and the tanker industry. On the other hand, the export of manufactures to Indonesia held much greater promise for the industrialization of the country, as did the immigration of Hong Kong factories.

The building of factories had had to be speeded up in Kallang and Jurong to meet this demand.

Aside from the fast-growing population, a new threat to Singapore's economic future came in the form of the British military withdrawal from the region. Tens of thousands of new jobs had to be created to replace those that would be lost, and extra expenditure generated to compensate the cut in British spending.*

What was not mentioned in Goh's budget speech was Britain's surprise decision to devalue the sterling by 14% on 18 November. A press statement released on 23 November announced that Singapore's Cabinet had unanimously decided not to devalue its own currency. The reason given was that although the government had been diversifying its reserves since July 1966, it did not wish to make any hasty move that would weaken the sterling further. This was especially important when British aid had been promised in sterling as compensation for losses expected to be incurred by the military withdrawal from the island (CRO 2-AED 72/701/2).

Goh also presented figures to show that rural occupations had fallen by 25% over ten years while the number of workers in the manufacturing sector had grown by 56%. Commercial activities had not generated any new jobs over the same period. The construction industry may have grown, but this was a sector that relied on growth in other sectors.

The big picture, according to Goh, was that past efforts, though commendable, had not accomplished enough. One sector worth developing for the future, he suggested, was tourism. Industrial growth remained his "principal weapon". However, it

---

* For the 1968 budget, Goh was counting on the British pulling out in stages over the coming seven years. Worse was to come, however. It was soon learned that the withdrawal would be completed — and not halved, as he had been led to believe — by December 1971. This issue is discussed more thoroughly below.

was time to move to a new phase where that was concerned, away from the first "shoes and ships and sealing wax" phase when all industries were welcome. Through the EDB, "a deliberate selection of those kinds of industries which [had] the greatest potential for long term growth" had to be made. Selecting was one thing, but getting the selected industries to come was another. Incentives such as tax exemptions were needed. But more than that, the government would have to actively foster selected industries. The most promising for the moment, he ventured, were the engineering and metal fabrication industries. These were labour intensive and required a wide range of substantial skills, and had strong "inter-industry" linkages that would encourage activities in a host of related industries.

Goh's strategy for economic growth had now clearly moved from import substitution to export orientation. More than that, after working out the right things to produce and how to create the right climate for investors, he went on to envisage a central body that would deal with the marketing of Singapore products, whose activities would go beyond mere market research, product displays or the dissemination of information. He imagined that "this policy may result in far reaching re-arrangements in the structure and pattern of our international trade today" (*ibid.* p. 26).

The British withdrawal brought a new urgency to Singapore's development, Goh stated. This required the government to involve itself even more in direct investments, infrastructure creation, and building training institutes.

> All this means that substantially larger funds must be allocated to building up our economic sinews than had been the case in past years, and it cannot be said that the Government had been niggardly in providing these funds.

The speech is striking in the same way many of his earlier speeches and writings on the economy were. This one is however a thorough one that provides a clear idea of what Goh saw as the major problems facing Singapore two years after independence. His ability to present the big economic picture was certainly enviable. Few of the problems he presented — and these were almost always placed in relation to each other — were without an accompanying attempt at a solution.

News came soon after this speech that the military withdrawal would be completed by 1971, and not 1975. Fiery public disappointment from the Singapore side was underlined by a visit to London by Lee Kuan Yew and Goh, where they lobbied for a postponement via television. The British made a small compromise, postponing the final date from March to December 1971.

During his final stint as Finance Minister, Goh directed the establishment in 1968 of the Institute of Southeast Asian Studies (ISEAS) as a unique centre for regional research, and the Jurong Bird Park, which was finally completed in January 1971. In his own constituency of Kreta Ayer, he supported the building of a permanent stage for Cantonese opera. The project — the Kreta Ayer People's Theatre — was officially opened on 24 March 1969 (Tan 177).

In August 1970, when Goh returned to the Ministry of Defence (now split from the Ministry of Home Affairs), his old Raffles College classmate Hon Sui Sen (1916–1983) replaced him on his recommendation as Minister of Finance. Hon had been the first chairman of the EDB (1961–1968) and also chairman of the Development Bank of Singapore (1968–1970), besides being permanent secretary at the Ministry until 1966.

Giving up responsibility for the country's economics allowed Goh to focus his considerable energy on various other aspects of nation building. Nevertheless, his approach to issues remained — to use his own phrase — "achievement-orientated" (Goh 1971b: 17). He continued to write and speak on economic issues, but clearly, he now had the luxury to be more circumspect.

Although his influence on economic policy was considerable, he would in later years complain that too much public credit had been given to him — and not to Hon — for Singapore's economic success. He blamed this on the fact that he had written extensively on the subject.

> Too often, we have seen governments floundering because the policies they prescribed were beyond the competence of the machinery to carry them out. This never happened to Singapore under Mr Hon's direction [...] Singapore is fortunate to have had a man of Mr Hon's calibre in charge of the economy. (Cheong 1993: 8)

The key economic adviser to the PAP in the early years, the Dutchman Albert Winsemius later summed up his impressions from working with Goh, Hon and Lee Kuan Yew in the following fashion:

> But almost from the very beginning, [Lee] was working towards his vision in a determined way, towards a goal which he would pursue to the end. [...] If you make a list of things which Dr Goh started with fantasy, it's enormous; it ranges from Jurong Town to the Symphony Orchestra. [...] Mr Hon Sui Sen is a beautiful complement of the two. Quiet, a lot of experience, no rash actions, listens, when a decision is taken, it is a decision, and soon after it, it is being done. So the three together was a most amazing trio and very pleasant to work with. (CORD Winsemius pp. 25–26)

TALK AT *SEMINAR ON MODERNISATION IN SOUTHEAST ASIA* (1971)

On 13 January 1971, Goh was asked to officiate at the opening of the Seminar on Modernisation in Southeast Asia organised by the Institute of Southeast Asian Studies (ISEAS). He took the opportunity to air his dislike for economists, political scientists and sociologists who were "interested in developing a consistent, logical and self-contained set of principles within its own domain with but scant regard and superficial understanding of knowledge in other disciplines". Economists, for example, had by and large ignored Gunnar Myrdal's call in his classic *Asian Drama* for the explicit study of non-economic factors in search of "a new set of economic principles applicable to the situation in less developed countries". This concern echoes the analytical approach used by the young Goh himself in *The Economic Front* from 1940, when he adapted economic principles to the unique situation of a Singapore at peace whose colonial master was at war.

Just as he had argued in "The Social Revolution in Malaya" in 1959, he perceived modernization in the region to have begun with the arrival of the Europeans. It all started therefore with Vasco Da Gama entering Calicut harbour in May 1498 (six years after Christopher Columbus failed to get to India by sailing west from Spain and arriving at the Bahamas instead).

Until the middle of the 18th century, however, relations were largely commercial in nature, and it was with the increasing pace of industrialization in Europe that the drive for empire grew strong. The impetus now moved from south Europe to west Europe.

The goods to be produced in the colonies were decided increasingly by the Europeans and large-scale plantations and new mines were opened to serve the European market. Investments increased in size and infrastructures grew to accommodate the business networks, emanating from ports into the hinterland.

To ensure steady production and distribution, law and order had to be kept and contracts had to be enforced. This led to the establishment of administrative and legal systems in the region. In order to populate the lower ranks of these systems, an educational structure was put in place to train locals for service in the colonial administration. As certain locals began benefiting from the economic growth, parents began wishing for their children to gain better education at institutions of learning in the metropolitan capitals.

> So we see the seeds of modernisation planted during this age of colonisation in three principal fields. The first was in the establishment of plantations and mines supported by modern communication system — seaports, railways, transportation, telegraph — leading to the growth of cities; Second, the introduction of modern administrative and legal systems; Third, the introduction and development of modern education systems.

This simplified and seemingly rosy understanding of colonial socio-economics is certainly Malaya-centric, Malaya having been the most lucrative and stable of European colonies in the region. But the point is clear. Industrialization in the region had always been Eurocentric, and the colonies developed in ways that best served London, Amsterdam and Paris. Development was not a priority.

What this also meant was that development only reached as far into the hinterland as suited the Europeans, and where possible, colonial governments refrained from "upsetting the traditional social structure and reduced interference with local customs and institutions to the barest minimum".

It is this legacy, which has gained definitive salience after independence, that Goh wished to highlight: "But whereas colonial authorities, in general, had little reason to disturb the traditional order of things outside the modern money exchange economy, the local ruling elite [after independence] were exposed to considerable pressure to improve the well-being of all their citizens, for those in the cities as well as those in the countryside".

That had been the point of departure for economic planning in the post-colonial world. As Goh saw it, Asian development economists generally realized that scarcity made it wise to avoid distributing resources to all sectors evenly, and "preferred the strategy of encouraging the leading sector to the strategy of balanced growth". In most cases, this "leading sector" was identified as the manufacturing industry.

> In short, industry would modernise and enrich. The general raising of the technological level of the countries, the spread of modern systems of production and management, all these, in the calculations of the planners, would not only generate economic growth but also help to bring about a rapid transformation of social attitudes, more consistent with the needs of modernising societies.

To offset the inherited imbalance where the colonies supplied raw materials and acted as the market for finished goods at the same time, their next conclusion was to produce these finished goods themselves, and with the raw materials that they had been exporting. Import substitution became the common path towards development. It appeased national demands for genuine independence, and made economic sense to the national economists. And yet, in almost all cases, it failed to work. Tongue in cheek, he stated:

> The exceptions were those laggard countries which, while paying lip service to this policy, in practice did little to implement it.

Instead of saving foreign exchange, this strategy led to increased foreign debt. External public debt had braked and was reversing development in many countries. While acknowledging a variety of factors that had worked against this development policy, including pure bad luck, Goh advocated that the logic was nevertheless flawed in the first place. While the rationale aspired to cut foreign interests down to size, it actually could not. First, import substitution required heavy investments in machinery and equipment that had to be imported from overseas. This disadvantage was worst in capital-intensive industries such as steel production, oil refineries, and other "basic industries", and yet these were the ones to which planners were fatally attracted. Second, local demand for import-substituting goods was usually low. In order to right this weakness, governments began either protecting certain firms through high tariffs and encouraging monopolies or providing subsidies. The final result was that these locally produced goods ended up being more expensive than earlier imported versions. Goh did not mention that they also tended to end up being of lower quality.

Success in business in such a milieu would depend on "obtaining official permits and licences more than on efficient production and management", paving the way for corruption. The overall picture got more depressing the wider a perspective one took. What was more harmful, Goh claimed, were the non-economic effects of this damage-control route to development. The original goal was after all to spread new technologies and "new social attitudes appropriate to modern societies".

> These include respect for hard work, innovation, a meritocratic system of personnel selection and advancement, continuous striving for greater efficiency, in short, achievement-orientation.

In his basic reasoning, Goh show a deep discomfort with systemic and systematic interference in the free exchange of goods and foreign exchange. As with protectionist measures and subsidies, a bad imbalance in foreign exchange earnings tended to lead to controls through a system of permits.

The result of this is that the government became the sole arbiter of what goods may be imported, who may import them, in what amounts and under what conditions. This control endowed governments with the power of patronage of immeasurably greater range and variety than were possessed by the wealthiest monarchs of ancient civilizations.

> In a modern national economy, such power in the hands of the state would lead to abuse "such as strengthening the bond of loyalty and cohesion in the rank of the governing party or creating short-term economic euphoria have obvious appeals.

Although these occurred in advanced countries as well, such "departures from financial rectitude" in fragile developing countries put severe strains on the system. In order to protect their position, leaders tended to "depart from rational economic policies".

> Once things go wrong, events in the economic, social and political fields interact in a cumulative way. Unless arrested at some stage, the process reduces the whole system into a pathological condition.

Goh would later build on this idea about how undesirable state control of economic processes was when lecturing on *Business Morality in Less Developed Countries* in 1979.

After pointing out the dangers involved in favouring the manufacturing sector, he nevertheless proclaimed it to be a sound one, given certain conditions. What these countries should have done was to focus, not on import substitution but on export-oriented industries instead. They should also have developed their raw material industries despite "the taint of colonialism". Other possibilities were tourism money, a lucrative and new source of foreign exchange, and the discovery of oil.*

---

* Incidentally, it was his early recognition of tourism as a major channel for foreign exchange inflow that gave Goh the idea in 1968 to develop Pulau Blakang Mati into a holiday resort. In the process, the island was renamed Sentosa for branding purposes (Tan p. 177).

Creating wealth in this day and age, Goh felt, was "a simple process". What was difficult was creating a stable political system, especially in cases where the first steps in economic development had gone wrong.

Economic development, he reasoned, had a continuity that was not matched in the political arena. Colonial economics functioned under a strong political power. The break in political stability that the gaining of independence amounted to was what posed a big challenge for Asian governments today.

Modernizing traditional man directly, he felt to be wrong. The process must occur in the cities, "for it is here that the transformation is taking place and the interaction between old cultural systems and values and new ones takes on their most acute form".

Goh rounded up his formidable presentation of the history and the challenge of modernization in Asia with expressions of distinct disappointment in the social sciences, but not in themselves as such, but in the detachment of their approaches and conclusions from the reality of Asian life. This, he claimed, was due to the fact that they were derived from Western teaching institutions: "As a result, the Asian intellectual is often a confused person and the process of education can be a traumatic experience".

> I suspect that it is this lack of comprehension of contemporary social processes, this absence of adequate preparation which should have been given in school, that contributes to the fragility of political institutions in the new states, especially those which are based on democratic elections. And unless we prepare the young adequately, it is unlikely that we shall achieve that durability and resilience of political institutions which have to underpin the economic development effort.

This concern with education would later lead Goh to accept the Education portfolio in 1979. His single-mindedness regarding

Singapore nation building was obvious, and his career since 1959 had been about putting in place the institutional pillars, the material conditions, and the human resources that he was convinced the country would require in the long run. The attributes the country needed, in his mind, included economic prowess, self-defence capabilities, achievement-orientated education and political stability.

OUTLOOK FOR SINGAPORE (1972)

With the birth in 1972 of his first grandson, Ken-Yi, Goh became a doting grandfather who spent memorable weekends with the boy. On 22 August that year, the Philippines government announced that Goh Keng Swee would be honoured with the prestigious Ramon Magsaysay Award for Government Service (*ST* 23 Aug 1972). The honour did not fall to him of being the first Singaporean to win a Magsaysay award, however. His old schoolmate Lim Kim San had received it in 1965 in the category Community Leadership.

In the general election held on 2 September 1972, opposition parties such as Barisan Sosialis and the Workers' Party mounted a serious challenge to the PAP. However, the incumbent party managed to win all 65 seats and 70% of the votes despite walkover constituencies consisting of only 10.5% of voters (PGE 72). Goh's hold on Kreta Ayer was uncontested for the second time (Tan 148). Flushed with this recent victory, he used the "Conference on Business Opportunities in S.E. Asia" organised by the *Financial Times* on 21 November to retaliate against the many doomsayers who had ever since Separation in 1965 been declaring Singapore's imminent demise. He reminded his London audience that already in the 1840s, there were pronouncements that "the zenith of Singapore's prosperity had been reached".

The purpose of his speech was certainly to attract British investments to Singapore. The content is worth some study nevertheless because it provides us with a further example of Goh's use of historical outlines for didactic purposes. In fact, this method was used so often that one must draw the conclusion that this was how he tended to understand Singapore's position in the greater framework of political economics, and consequently, his own role in history.

The rhetorical questions Goh put to the public were: Why such pessimism, and why have these prophecies never come to pass?

Where the first was concerned, one obvious answer was that the entrepot trade that was so important to Singapore seemed always to be at the mercy of outsider ambitions to bypass the middleman or establish competing trading centres. Such attempts had been made before, the first being in 1823, four years after Stamford Raffles came to Singapore.

Goh identified four reasons why Singapore, whether as a colony or as an independent republic, had managed nevertheless to survive and prosper. First, its central geographical location was enhanced by a natural harbour that did not suffer silting. Second, already from the beginning, a slim administration was put in place that favoured "the Victorian belief in free trade", low taxes, and the absence of harbour dues, which "allowed merchants and bankers full scope for the exercise of their talents". This resulted in the third reason, which was that efficiency in administration and business meant low costs. A discouraging cost differential would have to be paid by anyone adopting "mercantilist policies" to compete with Singapore. Finally, sustained economic growth was not a zero-sum game, and until the Great Depression at least, benefits were gained by most parties from the arrangement. The ability to adapt was what had kept things going. The government of the republic had had to adapt since 1959 to a whole series of challenges, such as unemployment, a growing population, political tribulations, and representative government, Goh reminded his audience, but the basic line had stayed unchanged.

> It might have been politically tempting to rid ourselves of institutions and practices that bore, or seemed to bear, the taint of colonial associations. Had we done so, we would have thrown away a priceless advantage for the sake of empty rhetoric.

Despite Singapore's shift from colonial status to nationhood, and from dependence on trade and shipping to an industrial economy, "government policy, now as before, must be directed to the support of this pursuit of business excellence".

In welcoming British manufacturers to Singapore, Goh was optimistic about the immediate future, but only assuming that "external factors [would] not deteriorate" and that the political climate in the neighbourhood would remain stable. Indeed, he had every reason to be confident. Singapore's GDP growth for 1965–1973 was an amazing 12.7% per annum on average. However, less than a year after he made this speech, his first assumption was invalidated. The OPEC Oil Crisis hit the world, quadrupling petroleum prices and precipitating a world recession. However, Singapore's average annual growth rate for 1973–1979 managed to stay at a very respectable 8.7%, and even after the second oil crisis of 1979, continued to retain an annual average growth of 8.5% for 1979–1981. The petroleum-service entrepot it had become placed it effectively as oil producer more than as oil consumer (Rigg 1988: 342: CS).

SOME UNSOLVED PROBLEMS OF ECONOMIC GROWTH (1975)

On 17 March 1973, Goh was in Manila to receive the Ramon Magsaysay Award for Government Service. At the same time, he was also conferred the Philippines' highest decoration for foreign dignitaries, the Sikatuna Award, for his efforts as Minister of Defence in making possible "the exchange of vital knowledge" between Singapore and the Philippines "in the field[s] of economics, education, social services and defence planning" (*ST* 17 March 1973).

If anyone still needs convincing that scholars of Asian nation building should study Goh's many speeches and writings, the lecture he gave to the University of Singapore Academic Staff Association on 30 November 1975 should win over the last doubters. This is one of the very few clearly academic papers that Goh wrote after he joined politics. It is heavily and properly referenced, but is also one that earned key mention 18 years later as one of his more enduring and influential works. Incidentally, this compliment was publicly paid to Goh when he received the highly prestigious Degree of Doctor of Letters (*honoris causa*) at Hong Kong University (HDU-HDG) on 4 March 1993.

Unlike most of his writings up to that point, Goh worked on the 1975 lecture with some external help. Understandably, this seemed to become more common in later years. In the present case, he acknowledged benefiting from discussions with fellow economist Augustine Tan, and from data collected by Chua Seng Kiat and Caroline Lee (Goh 1976: 1). The gist of this lecture, one that does seem to have resulted from a conversation with professional economists, was that the global economy was in serious trouble, and that the experts could not agree on the causes nor the measures required for solving them. As a result, their reputation had been suffering and no new consensus had appeared to replace the fall in status of Keynesian doctrines.

Before Keynes and before the Great Depression of the 1930s, economists generally believed that all who wished to work would be able to gain employment. Keynes showed this to be untrue, and even provided the remedies for that situation. Goh took

"modern growth" economists such as Roy Harrod and Elsey
Domar to task for their inability to explain current problems.
This, according to Goh, was because they assumed a continuing
state of full employment. Inflationary recession, where
unemployment and inflation rose together, was a new
phenomenon which challenged explanations advanced by A. W.
Philips for why the movement of the first should be matched by
movement in the opposite direction of the second.

Somewhat out of character, Goh dived into this theoretical
discussion, and introduced the Russian N.D. Kondratieff's
declaration that capitalism followed a 60-year cycle. Joseph
Schumpeter — "a difficult author" — had in 1939 added the
claim that major innovations coming at regular intervals were
what "disturbed the system", doing this mainly by reducing the
cost of production. Clusters of innovations spurred growth by
channelling investments into new and fast-expanding industries,
excited consumption anew, generated supporting industries and
encouraged a general expansion of markets through transport
and communication.

Using this perspective, three such cycles — named "Kondratieff"
by Schumpeter — could be identified. The first was the Industrial
Revolution itself, which ended around 1845 with a wave of
innovations. The third cycle started in 1898 with electricity,
industrial chemistry and the internal combustion engine being
the decisive innovations.

Though obviously impressed by this explanation, Goh was
left somewhat unsatisfied as to why inventions should generate
waves and why major innovations should be spaced over about
half a century or so. But using this pattern, one could venture
that a fourth cycle began after the Second World War. This was a
strong wave and in favouring rich countries greatly, made the
idea of full employment popular again.

Goh reasoned that if one followed Schumpeter's logic, then by 1975, the cycle would be peaking; profits would be at its minimal level and the next wave of new innovations would not have appeared yet. Should no new cluster of innovations appear soon, then rich countries would have to settle for a "natural rate of unemployment", and "a more deliberate pace of growth" would lead political agendas towards greater interest in social policies and quality-of-life issues.

Interestingly, if we were to revisit this pattern now, in 2010, we see that a new cluster of innovations did in fact appear. By 1990, Information and Communication Technologies and the Internet arrived to propel the global economy into a new "Kondratieff". New fields of investment harkened, new actors appeared, new supporting industries mushroomed, and new infrastructures came into being.

But back in 1975, what Goh was actually doing — again — was drawing attention to how concepts and policies thought up with the Western world as the standard did not always reflect conditions in Asia. Other dimensions had to be considered. Also, when he differentiated between rich and poor countries, he meant to distinguish the economic conditions separating urban from rural economies.

Goh commended the article "Economic Development with Unlimited Supplies of Labour" written by Arthur Lewis in 1954 for having "the advantage of being relevant to contemporary problems". Capital accumulation remained the key for "generating sustainable economic growth". By developing a capitalist industrial sector, excess labour from the rural population could be absorbed, and at low wages "so long as peasants [were] willing to offer their services at real wages slightly better than what they [could] earn in farms". The increase in profits for the industrialist would encourage savings, which in turn ensured future capital accumulation.

Unlike in rich countries, an increase in savings in poor countries was not realized through reduced consumption. Instead, it was credit creation that gave the stagnated economy the needed initial push. However, except for Korea, Taiwan and Brazil, this self-generating growth process had not taken place in poor countries.

Goh did not find the fault so much to be with the theories than with poor performance by governments. Wrong policies, combined with accelerated population growth rates, cornered these countries in two possible ways — the Malthusian Trap and the Ricardian Bind. At the same time, the manufacturing industries that were meant to power economic growth ran into trouble through bad planning and management, and shortages of foreign exchange for required imports led to capacity wastage and increased costs.

The Malthusian Trap involves two processes. First, population growth tends to exceed increases in food supply; second, rising standards of living may increase savings but they also reduce death rates at the same time, and if the increase in income is not large enough, then the population growth will outstrip it, forcing savings and income to fall.

The Ricardian Bind concerns food supply. In a closed economy, the rise in income and in urban population pushes food prices upwards due to land supply being fixed. This affects other sectors and the cost of industrial labour rises, reducing profits and stopping expansion. In an open economy, the same process works, but through the balance of payments. Food imports use up foreign exchange required by the industrial sector.

Here, Goh described how things went wrong through "three aspects of the growth process" deviating from the modelling. First, the urbanizing of the population in a rural country actually occurred at rates that were much slower than assumed. Reducing population growth was therefore a necessary measure for rural countries that were industrializing to move to a higher level of development. Second, the transfer of resources from countryside to city to stimulate growth actually worked in the opposite direction in the poorest and most crowded countries. This was partly due to the political power of landlords. But more importantly, poor families spent a large proportion of their income on food, and most of their income increments went directly to food consumption. In these extreme cases, a 5% GNP increase must be matched by a 4% increase in agricultural output over an extended period if the right effects were to be maintained.

Goh's third aspect on the rise of food prices was not properly discussed in his paper except through a mention of the Green Revolution based on the introduction of new strains of rice and wheat having to face its own problems as well. These latter included rich farmers with resources and education benefiting much more from the new innovations, accelerating the dispossession of poor farmers; and also great falls in food prices following sudden over-production. For a country to benefit from this revolution, political will was required that at the same time was able to respond to unexpected effects that worked against the original purposes.

What can perhaps be gleaned from Goh's paper about his own perspective on Asian development is this. Summarily, his view on development for Third World countries was that growth must kick off at such a rate that the economy shot away from the stagnating effects of traditional socio-economic conditions, habits and population patterns, and that a healthy growth rate must be maintained for an extended period. Political will and stability were prerequisites for such a project.

Chapter 4

DEFENDING AN ISLAND-STATE

Not everybody is well disposed towards the Republic; indeed, from time to time we have come across clear evidence of malice and hostility. And so, as the saying goes, the price of freedom is eternal vigilance.

— Goh Keng Swee
(Speech at Commissioning Ceremony of SAF officers
at the Istana, 26 Aug 1974)

Perhaps because of the sensitive nature of the subject, there is a relative shortage of revealing articles by Goh on national defence. However, the few texts chosen for analysis in this chapter are substantive enough to divulge some basic ideas that Goh entertained about defence. Indeed, they do more than that, showing as they do, that economics and defence were inseparable for him.

The first time Goh became Minister of Defence was on Independence Day, 9 August 1965 when Singapore suddenly became a country without a defence to call its own. He immediately began the first stage in the building of Singapore's defence capacity.

Interestingly, the possibility of a British pullout from Singapore was already being considered from the very beginning. On 2 September, Goh declared in Kuala Lumpur — with some show of tactical bravado, one might assume — that Singapore would simply put up "international tenders" if the British should choose to leave. Although he claimed that there were at least four countries willing to respond to such a tender, he did not name them. The suggestion he did make at the same time, that the British should take the initiative in the wake of Singapore's separation from Malaysia to negotiate a new defence treaty with Singapore, supports the idea that he was in fact putting public pressure on the British to do more where the defence of the island was concerned (*ST* 3 Sept 1965).*

News reports in September 1965 show that Singapore's defence at that time consisted of two badly equipped army camps, which Goh proposed to upgrade as soon as possible (*ST* 15 Sept 1965). By the end of the year, the Army Bill was passed by parliament for the establishment not only of a full-time armed force but also of a part-time People's Defence Force. Singaporeans of both sexes, and all who were medically fit would serve in this unit, but without their training seriously affecting their normal lives.

> The training they receive will not only prepare them for the part they will take beside our regular army, but also provide them with the necessary disciplines and skills to face the task of nation-building (*ST* 31 Dec 1965).

In Lee Kuan Yew's *From Third World to First*, the chapter titled "Building an Army from Scratch" deals at length with cases of racial stress and conflict between Malays and Chinese, and

---

* For a thorough study of the withdrawal of British forces from the Southeast Asian region, see Chin Kin Wah's *The Defence of Malaysia and Singapore* (1983).

between Malaysia and Singapore. The latter was more often than not a reflection of racial tension, and not a conflict in national interests. The same held true for the souring of relations between Indonesia and Singapore. Such anxieties configured much of the country's defence strategies. The use of Israeli advisors after India and Egypt had tactfully refused to help Singapore build its defence capabilities was a highly sensitive matter, as can be seen in how Singapore chose not to recognize Israel for diplomatic reasons, despite a request from the latter as a quid pro quo for helping the island create a credible defence force* (Lee 2000: 26–46). Indeed, from the very beginning, Singapore's external security and internal security were tightly interwoven. Many Malays in the Singapore Infantry Regiment, for example, had chosen to leave to join the Malaysian army in 1965.

CREATING AN OFFICER CORP (1966)

Some insight into Goh's understanding of the military can be gleaned from a couple of speeches he gave in 1966 at the Singapore Armed Forces Training Institute (SAFTI). On 7 May that year, he provided the first ever graduates of its Instructors' Course with a lesson on "fighting spirit". The age-old problem of generating sufficient fighting spirit was done among primitive tribes by participating in war dances which excited them into frenzy before they flung themselves at the enemy. What modern armies needed to learn, according to Goh, could be found in Sun Zi, the Chinese general who wrote his famed and influential treatise on warfare more than 2,400 years ago.

The old general taught that courageous commanders appeared in armies where "punishment and rewards [were]

---

* For a thorough study of Singapore's armed forces, see Tim Huxley's *Defending the Lion City: The Armed Forces of Singapore* (2000).

properly regulated". While extreme forms of punishment and reward would not suit a modern state, Goh told the officers, the basic idea was still relevant: Predictability in the military was what created great leaders. Furthermore, courage and cowardice were relative terms, and even the meek would rise to fight in the right circumstances, while a desperate situation might strike fear into the heart of the brave.

One could also militarize society, which post-Meiji Japan did, and create an army with fighting spirit in the process. But that was not for Singapore.

British fighting morale had subtler stimuli, summarized in Goh's mind as "the regimental mess, the aristocratic tradition, and the sense of historic mission". Americans, who had "neither the aristocratic tradition nor the sense of historic mission nor even experience in state-craft", were known to repeat a written code of honour among officers.

What the Australians did, Goh said, was as yet a mystery to him.

Ideological indoctrination was definitely another method that had been used with success for motivating warriors. This option, Goh explained, was not open to the government of Singapore either.

> Enforcement of an ideology means the repression of competing ideologies, the establishment of thought control, the suppression of dissent, liquidation of unbelievers and the introduction of all the paraphernalia of the police state.

Singapore had to come up with some other means of military — and civil — motivation in lieu of ideology, culture or outright coercion. Its society was too different from others. The point that Goh wished to make to the new officers that day was that he was not sure what these means should be.

We have to do our own thinking and find our own methods which will suit the style of our people and the social environment in which the army lives. I do not think that we can adopt in its entirety the system which was been found successful in one country or another. We may find a synthesis derived from different elements which I have briefly described, or we may strike out on a novel path of our own. I do not know.

HARD AND SOFT ARMIES (1966)

A month later, on 18 June, while speaking at the official opening of SAFTI, Goh continued to reason along the similar vein, as usual making full use of historical examples to frame his position. This time, he divided armies into "hard" and "soft", with ancient Sparta as a perfect case of the former. No doubt, a Spartan army was in close combat the equal of much larger armies, but the extreme way in which it was created left its generals with no sense of strategy. Worse than that, "being poorly educated by our standards or by the standards of the Greek civilization of the time, the generals showed all the weakness of men of low education: they were unable to control their avarice".

Examples of soft armies were more plentiful. These included those found in Medieval Europe and in China's *Chunqiu* (Spring and Autumn) era. But in both cases, "soft" would over time nevertheless become "hard". In China's case, the *Chunqiu* evolved into the period of the Warring States (*Zhanguo*), when war became a science analysed by prominent warriors like Sun Zi and Wu Qi.*

As Goh understood global military history, it was Frederick the Great of Prussia whose "methods of instruction and systems

---

* Goh's mention of Wu Qi here is interesting in that the name of this ancient Chinese general is seldom known outside limited circles of military scholars and sinologists.

of discipline" set a new standard for Europe's armies to follow into modern times. Just as impressively, the emperor did it all while remaining "a patron of the arts, a friend of philosophers and scholars like Voltaire and D'Alembert". Frederick had many imitators, and some, like Napoleon Bonaparte, were successful. Most were not.

> The harshness of his discipline was imitated without the understanding that this was a means and not an end in itself. So too with the precision drill which the Prussian Army practised.

Here, as elsewhere, Goh expressed a deep dislike for blind imitation, be it of Western permissive behaviour, trendy economic theories or pompous military uniforms and reviews. Singapore's army, Goh concluded, "will bear more resemblance to the armies of Frederick the Great and no resemblance whatsoever to those of his unsuccessful imitators".

SECOND READING OF THE NATIONAL SERVICE (AMENDMENT) BILL (1967)

Goh moved for the second reading in Parliament of the National Service (Amendments) Bill on 13 March 1967. This took two days, and the Bill was officially passed the following day. He presented the reasons for the special kind of defence that Singapore needed, the foremost of which was that the absence of a viable defence — as advocated by some — would mean that the island "must revert to a colony or satellite of whoever wishes to afford it protection". Furthermore, small states that failed to look after themselves invited civil war and disorder, tempting larger states to intervene and thus destabilizing the whole region. This danger was greatest when that small state was located in a strategic area, as was the case with South Vietnam or Singapore.

At the same time, Singapore's defence could be credible only if it worked within "a regional defence alliance". Such a framework allowed a small country to be "a more valuable partner and hence exert more influence". Another important reason for building a defence force was the contribution that it would make to the nation-building process.

> Nothing creates loyalty and national consciousness more speedily and more thoroughly than participation in defence and membership of the armed forces. [...] The nation building aspect of defence will be more significant if its participation is spread out over all strata of society. This is possible only with some kind of national service.

One of Goh's strongest arguments was that "many of our monied and intellectual elite" had failed to realize that "their status and position [could] only be justified and maintained if they [undertook] a responsibility in the defence of the nation consistent with their position". The country's "intelligentsia and wealthy citizens" needed to study Greek classics such as *The History of the Peloponnesian War* by Thucydides to learn how oligarchies were toppled when their sons were "spoilt by easy living and whose flabbiness [became] obvious to the citizens whom they [governed]". Goh amplified his position further with his disapproval of social immorality.

> [Ours] is a society which is deficient in many qualities, excelling only in the ability to get on in life whatever the regime. [...] Some of these indispensible qualities — social discipline and moral values — have unfortunately not been instilled in our education system to the extent that one would have wished. The result is a generation of young people who are largely amoral. They are easy victims of all kinds of ideas, passions and fads — be they the subversive doctrines of the Communists

underground or the seductions of Beatle music and beatnik philosophy.

Singapore's precarious position could not allow for its young to live in "a world of fantasy". Against such worries, the National Service scheme was worked out. In all four branches of the National Service — the full-time army, the People's Defence Force, the Vigilante Corps and the Special Constabulary — instruction in moral values would be given.

In winding up the debate, Goh was adamant that no allowance should be paid to the Vigilante Corps, aside from certain transport costs. Singapore's army would concentrate on both "brawns and brains" and all units would have the same type of uniforms. He also dismissed the inclusion of women in National Service. He argued that NS was a compulsory measure, with imprisonment being the punishment for refusal to participate, and Singapore had not come to a stage where it would tell its women to "do-this-or-go-to-jail" (ST 15 Mar 1967). Apparently, Lee Kuan Yew had wished for women to be included (Lee 2000: 35).

General Winston Choo, Singapore's first Chief of General Staff, who admitted that he was "greatly inspired" by Goh's courage and vision, credited him for being the "founder or father" of the Singapore Armed Forces. Realizing the "demographic and geographical constraints" of Singapore in 1965, Goh had set about acquainting himself with military strategy, and finally deciding that a National Service (NS) Army modelled after the Israeli example was most suitable for the island state (Chew 1996: 210). In an interview given in 1997, Goh summarized the beginnings of the Singapore Armed Forces thus:

> National service was the recommendation of a team of Israeli advisors. It was a small team, numbering 23 at the maximum.

The head of the first team to come to Singapore was Col. J. Ellazari, a brilliant man who mapped out the expansion of the army, beginning with a training school, the Singapore Armed Forces Training Institute. SAFTI was to produce the core of regular officers, and subsequently was to take in each year's NS intake of non-commissioned officers and officers. Many other training institutes were also set up, each preceding the setting up of a specialised battalion, such as artillery, engineers, and the like. We were confident that the Israeli programme was workable, although we were handicapped for many years by a shortage of experienced personnel. (*TowardSTomorrow* 1995: 25)

The Israelis had suggested a much larger defence force than Goh had at first imagined. The suggested size would have been large enough to support a military industry. That unexpected situation may have planted the idea in Goh for the creation of Chartered Industries of Singapore (CIS). In 1967, Goh began laying the groundwork for the CIS, which would introduce precision engineering into Singapore's nation-building equation. Characteristically enough, aside from small arms ammunition, CIS functions included the minting of circulation coins for the Board of Commissioners of Currency, Singapore (BCCS). Finance and Defence — civil and military matters — were integrated at a basic level and, one suspects, through the mind of a man fully immersed in these two areas of nation building.

OPENING OF THE CHARTERED INDUSTRIES OF SINGAPORE (1968)

In a speech given at the opening of the CIS on 27 April 1968, Goh — as was his wont — credited Sir Laurence Hartnett with being a key player in the creation of the CIS. Sir Laurence was the managing director of General Motor's Australian branch. Goh also mentioned R.H. Osbourne of the Royal Australian Mint for assistance rendered.

The Singapore Mint was part of the CIS, and shared their workshop with the ammunition production line. The CIS was licensed to produce the American M16 rifle and its ammunition. Over the next few years, a string of companies came into being for weapons production, and were soon organized under a company called Sheng-Li Holding Company ("Sheng-Li" — "Victory" was the name chosen by Goh himself). In 1989, its name was changed to Singapore Technologies and later ST Engineering Group (see Philip Yeoh's introduction in Kuah 2007: 15–19). Little was written about this in the early days, and a digital search of Singapore's major newspapers such as *The Straits Times* turns up no mention of "Sheng-Li Holding" from the early 1970s, suggesting the secrecy and speed that surrounded Goh's initiatives in bringing precision engineering into Singapore's industrialization.

Singapore's significance as an exporter of military hardware soon increased at a phenomenal rate, with total sales — largely of ammunition, small arms and mortars used by the SAF — reaching US$125 million in 1987, up from a mere US$1 million in 1983. All this was marketed through the country's own brokerage firm, Unicorn International. Over that same period, the Stockholm International Peace Research Institute (Sipri) ranked Singapore the 15th largest exporter of military hardware to Third World countries (Katz 1989). By 2009, ST Engineering had 20,000 employees worldwide, and had applied for 422 patents, 177 of which have so far been granted (*Today* 30–31 Jan 2010).

Thus, a row of crises in the late 1960s and early 1970s gave birth to the precision engineering arm of Singapore development — and also the financial market that Singapore would become. The shocking news that the British were pulling out of Singapore by the middle of the 1970s was announced on 18 July 1967. This must have upset Goh's plans badly. Given the improved security situation following the fall of Indonesian President Soekarno in March 1967 and the forming of the Association of Southeast Asian Nations in August that same year, the defence of Singapore did not need to be his major concern, at least for the moment. The economy was.

Goh needed to return to Finance as quickly as possible, and within a month after the British had made their plans known, he switched portfolios with Lim Kim San. On 17 August 1967, exactly two years after last leaving it, he moved back to the Finance Ministry (*ST* 17 Aug 1967). Despite the switch, however, Goh continued to be deeply involved in building Singapore's defence capabilities. Indeed, given the country's unique geopolitical conditions, her economic concerns and defence imperatives could not but be conjoined. This conflation was manifest in Goh's career; in the issues he involved himself most with, and in his thinking in general.

At the end of 1967, Whitehall dropped another bombshell, announcing that the deadline for British withdrawal of military forces from the region would be brought forward from 1975 to 1971. The economic challenge for Singapore was getting worse. Serious measures had to be taken immediately to prevent a recession. Lee and Goh flew off to London to bargain for more time. When they returned to Singapore from final negotiations with the Labour government of the United Kingdom on 18 Jan 1968, Goh dejectedly told the press that "the Labour Party has gone back on its word; the Labour government has gone back on its word".

As mentioned earlier, all that he and Lee Kuan Yew had managed to get out of their talks in London was a slight delay in the pullout, from March 1971 to December 1971.

It is going to place Singapore in a very difficult position, you
know, in the next 3 or 4 years. We have to work twice as hard
to remain just where we are. But I think we can pull through
this. Mind you there is just the odd hope that if the Conservatives
win the General Elections in 1971 they might not complete the
withdrawal to the end. Prime Minister [Lee Kuan Yew] and I had
discussion with Reginald Maudling, Ian MacLeod, and the former
Conservative Defence Minister, Duncan Sandys. There were just
aghast at this policy of scuttling by the Labour Government.
[...] Still, it is four years ahead. (Goh, press release 18 Jan 1968)

As it turned out, general elections were held in Britain on 18 June
1970, and the Conservatives under Edward Heath did fulfil Goh's
"odd hope" and pulled off an unexpected win over Harold Wilson.
However, no change to the withdrawal plan materialized even
under the new government, which must have been a great
disappointment to Goh. But by that time, Singapore's own
solutions to its defence concerns and its budgetary plans to
mitigate the depression were already underway.

Two days after returning to Singapore from London in
early 1968, Goh, not being one to waste time, was already in
Kuala Lumpur for talks with Malaysia's Prime Minister Tunku
Abdul Rahman Putra. Stressing that Singapore had "no need to
panic", Goh declared that Singapore and Malaysia would work
closely on defence matters after the British withdrawal. It
seemed obvious that the best fall-back plan for Singapore was
to align itself with the initiative proposed in June 1967 by the
Tunku to hold defence talks between Australia, Britain, New
Zealand, Malaysia and Singapore. Such talks were in fact soon
held, and by December 1971 — just when the British finally
left — the Five Power Defence Arrangement (FPDA) was signed
in Canberra between the five countries (*ST* 21 Jan 1968;
Australian Treaty Series).

Economic success with a growth rate of 12% on average from 1967 to 1970 brought full employment by the early 1970s (*ST* 3 Aug 1970). Despite the British withdrawal, this lessened internal security threats dramatically. The efficient domestic security intelligence organization in the form of the Internal Security Department (ISD), backed by the Internal Security Act, was also a contributing factor to a notable shift in defence policy towards external security. As a reflection of this, the Ministry of Interior and Defence was reorganized in August 1970 into a Ministry of Home Affairs and the Ministry of Defence (Huxley 2000: pp. 15–16). The former had disappeared after Singapore joined Malaysia in 1963.

And so, on 11 August 1970, sixteen months before the final withdrawal of British troops from Singapore, Goh left the Finance Ministry in the capable hands of Hon Sui Sen who gave up his position as chairman of the Development Bank of Singapore, and moved back to the diminished Defence portfolio that had been kept warm for him by Lim Kim San. Lim became Education Minister, taking the spot vacated by Ong Pang Boon, who took over the resurrected Ministry of Home Affairs (*ST* 11 Aug 1970).

As the British withdrew militarily from the region, Goh took the first steps towards establishing Singapore's own research and development facility for defence science and technology. He had in 1971 called together several young newly-returned engineers under cover of the Electronic Test Centre (ETC) to discuss "secret-edge technology".

This was Project Magpie.

The following year, three engineers — Tay Eng Soon, Benny Chan and Toh Kim Huat — started work "on the second floor of a converted detention centre on Onraet Road" (Chew & Tan 2002: 8). By 1976, the group had grown to 20, and in 1977 was given the name Defence Science Organisation (DSO).* By the turn of the century, DSO National Laboratories had been formed as a free-standing corporation with its own personnel scheme detached from the Ministry of Defence and the SAF.

The apparent rationale behind this impressively ambitious and visionary initiative reflected Goh's conviction in economics that climbing as fast and as high as possible up the value-add scale was what a tiny country of Singapore needed to do. For him, the string of crises it had had to face in its short life bore testimony to this. Even in defence, therefore, Goh wished to facilitate the leap upwards towards the technological cutting edge which he thought Singapore needed to make on all fronts in order to survive, and survive well.

ADAM SMITH ON DEFENCE (1976)

While seeing the need for Singapore to attain a technological edge in defence, Goh did not think it an adequate requirement. On 3 November 1976, he officiated at the commissioning ceremony for naval and medical officers at the Istana. Though short and obviously structured for the occasion, the speech he gave that day was illuminating in several ways.

Firstly, Goh used the broad vision of economics evident in Adam Smith's *The Wealth of Nations* published exactly 200 years earlier to poke fun at contemporary economists who "seem to develop a myopic vision as they become more and more learned about less and less". This dislike of narrow education was a recurrent topic in his speeches.

---

* For a thorough history of the Defence Science Organisation, see Melanie Chew & Bernard Tan (2002) *Creating the Technological Edge*. Singapore: DSO National Laboratories.

More interestingly, the speech, though relying heavily on Smith's rendition of human history, offers another example of the interfusion in Goh's mind of economics and defence. Through the realism embedded in this perception of social survival his reasoning led towards the conclusion that there was a price humanity paid for the separation of war from work. In primitive society, he reasoned, "war [was] a cost-free activity as it [was] merely an extension of peace-time activity, directed against human beings instead of animals". Among herdsmen, conflicts were often over rights to pastures, so that "warlike training, shooting, and horsemanship [were] normal peace-time activities". What was new at this later stage of development was that "such societies [had] much leisure to develop their martial skills, thereby making them good warriors". Whenever these tribal societies managed to unite, they were "invariably victorious". Even when farming communities appeared, adult males could be called to war during the off-season. Further progress led to war becoming a specialized business, "requiring a levy on the rest of the population to upkeep a standing army".

The point Goh wished to make with this simplified history of warfare economics was that "a people should want to defend themselves, that is to say that they should be patriotic and brave". Citing Adam Smith, Goh considered it the duty of a government "to prevent the growth of cowardice".

> Cowardice is the mutilation and deformation of the mind as bad as the mutilation of the body. [...] Prevention of cowardice deserves the most serious attention of the government in the same manner as prevention of leprosy or any other loathsome or offensive disease, because cowardice is contagious.

Goh concluded that Singapore's schools devoted too much time to examinations, and gave little encouragement to "manly games" such as gymnastics and sports. This neglect was happening "at our own peril", he warned. His concern about human weaknesses was recurrently apparent, especially when he touched on defence matters; and one would assume that he was to no mean extent painfully cognizant of this when constructing the defence infrastructure.

QUALITIES OF A STRONG MILITARY ORGANIZATION (1973)

At a promotion ceremony for the armed forces held at the Istana on 30 November 1973, Goh spoke about how different military culture had to be from civilian life. Successful armies, he told his officers that day, had "a high regard for physical courage and daring, for ability to endure hardship, for loyalty and patriotism" and where approach to work was concerned, for discipline and morale.

To inculcate these values, he reasoned, armies would — negatively — apply punishment or — positively — exercise leadership at all levels. Ideological indoctrination was also a common tool, as were rituals and drills. Goh listed some examples of how army commanders mistook "the show for the substance"; for example when the French army fell to the Germans in May 1940, or when the British lost to the Japanese in Malaya in February 1942.

Self-deception, he claimed, was a common fault for three reasons. First, we are given to wishful thinking, and believe what is comforting.

> Tell a battalion commander how fine his soldiers are and he will not only believe you, but judge you to be a singularly perceptive man. But tell him his unit is lousy and he will demand evidence and proof, which it never occurs to him to call for in the other instance.

Second, we prefer to be lazy than to work. When such an attitude prevails in an organization, reports upwards tend to be more positive than the situation warrants, so that "everyone can sit back and have a grand time, instead of picking faults, stirring trouble and being nasty to everybody".

Finally, incompetence in an organization, Goh suggested, encourages self-deception, and the only way to cure this condition is to remove the incumbents. However, when incompetence exists at the top, "removal takes place only as a result of defeat in war".

Self-deception was therefore a weakness that had disastrous circumstances, and he had witnessed many cases of "laxity and complacency" in the Singapore Armed Forces and the Ministry of Defence. Writing misleading assessments, covering up weaknesses and trying to be popular were often symptoms of these attitudes. The last seemed to concern Goh most.

> The desire to be popular and to be liked by people is a natural human feeling. It is also natural to want to avoid causing to others the pain and suffering that punishment involves. If you bring up the Army guided entirely by these decent human feelings, what we will get is what Tsun Tze [Sun Zi] called "a collection of spoilt children utterly useless in war".

The final point Goh made in his speech was how good generals were "voracious readers" who sought "thorough-going professionalism", and who were "proficient in methods of doctrine and alert to innovations and methodology". In fact, in 1978, Goh, who was Acting Prime Minister then, organized a six-month academic course on Marxism-Leninism for "selected senior commanders and staff officers" of the Armed Forces, at which he personally lectured twice in February and March that year on the political conflict between the PAP and the communists. As he put it, one of his aims was to follow Sun Zi's famous adage "know your enemy, know yourself and you can fight a hundred battles without danger" (ST 28 Jan 1977).

A public announcement on the arrest of fifty alleged communists in mid-1976 was made by the Singapore government just before a motion by the Dutch Labour Party to expel Singapore from Socialist International was to be discussed in London. The Dutch refused to withdraw their motion against alleged infringement of human rights by Singapore, which then left the organization. Judging from the newspaper report on this announcement, Goh's renewed interest in communism as "the enemy" stemmed partially from the fall of South Vietnam on 30 April 1975, and more immediately from the case of the lawyer Gopalan Krishnan Raman, who was arrested under the Internal Security Act in February 1977. G. Raman had been involved in the defence of the detainees, and admitted after two days of interrogation that he was a "full-fledged communist" involved "with a group of Euro-communists to exert pressure through the Socialist International on Singapore to release hard-core communist detainees" (ST 12 Nov 1976, 18 Dec 1976, 28 Jan 1977, 13 Feb 1977; Seow 1998: 113).

Another line of thought entertained by Goh where defence was concerned involved Singapore being a "rootless, migrant parvenu society". He mentioned in a speech made at a commissioning ceremony at the Istana on 26 August 1974 that Singapore's "roots are not deep enough". The "complacency, even euphoria" that he had warned against in the "collective psychology of the Singaporean" before the OPEC oil crisis had now turned into "defeatism".

[In a society without deep roots], minor success brings about overconfidence and the belief that good times last forever;

minor setbacks send people into a state of nervousness. In this situation, the Singaporean lends his ears to rumours of all kinds. Nothing is too absurd for him to listen to and pass on to others.

The rumours he referred to — popularized in a Hong Kong journal — were about him leading a Cabinet faction against Lee Kuan Yew in order to seek the latter's resignation and a re-merger with Malaysia. The "gullibility" of Singaporeans on this point, which he considered "bizarre" and a "patent absurdity", was what worried him.

> We must discard the migrant parvenu values I mentioned earlier. We must sharpen our awareness of our collective or national interests. In this way, we are not likely to be tossed about in any turbulence that may descend upon our part of the world in the years to come.

What seemed to leave him perplexed was that despite the fact that the only years when Singapore's GNP had dropped were when it was part of Malaysia, there were still those willing to believe that he would wish for a re-merger. His conclusion was that there was a clandestine organization operating in Singapore generating rumours about political change, and this danger was amplified by collective gullibility.

Chapter 5

CRISIS AS OPPORTUNITY

The misfortunes that befell Singapore in the first decade of her existence, from a self-governing state to a fully independent republic, are forgotten by observers who believe that ours has been a smooth and easy transition to self-sustaining growth. The truth is quite the reverse...First, the economic strategy was set in motion right from the beginning. It achieved some limited results. But more important than what we did, was the generally favourable background of the world economy.

— Goh Keng Swee
("A Socialist Economy that Works", 1976)

The withdrawal of British forces by 1971 necessitated long-ranging plans to secure for the island, firstly a viable defence force and secondly a string of institutional measures that would push its economy beyond mere defensiveness.

When final details of the withdrawal became known to Singapore's leaders, the Americans were reducing their forces in Vietnam, the confrontation with Indonesia had just ended, and problems caused by the separation from Malaysia were far from solved. How the country planned to minimize the negative effects of the withdrawal on the economy can be observed in two appearances Goh made on radio and television, on 30 March and 16 April 1968.

THE CRUCIAL YEARS (1968)

In the first talk in the series, appropriately titled "The Crucial Years", he forecasted a reduction in British spending of $900 million over the coming four years. In order to counteract this drop in expenditure, three areas where spending could be increased to a total of that same amount were identified by Goh. These were "Additional public sector building & construction", "Additional defence expenditure, mainly local cost", and "Additional induced private investment". The timing of these expenditures would be scaled according to the calculated annual rate of reduction in British military spending on the island ("Counter-recession strategy", 30 Mar 1968; *ST* 17 Apr 1968). An explanation for how money would be raised for this purpose was also provided, which included a reduction in the government's overseas assets, increased taxation and local loans, and official overseas aid and loan.

This counter-recession measure was however "a negative strategy", he ventured; and in his second talk, Goh announced plans to accelerate Singapore's progress beyond the big setback. He identified four fields where the country's economic growth rate could increase. These were the entrepot trade, tourism, shipping and the manufacturing industry. What he required of Singaporeans for his plans to succeed were "effort, self-discipline and perseverance".

> In particular, trade union leaders must accept the over-riding importance of the present climate of industrial peace and stability. They must also assist in implementing programmes

aimed at upgrading skills and increasing productivity. The way to wages is not by action to reduce profits but by increasing economic growth through improved skills and great output. We are all in the same boat — the worker, the employer and the Government — and we must pull together (*ST* 17 Apr 1968).

Where the entrepot trade was concerned, Goh realized that new transportation systems would open up new possibilities. New tankers had helped Singapore's entrepot trade in oil tremendously, and a fourth large refinery was being constructed. This development would affect other goods as well, such as fertilisers. Container ships were also bound to bring advantages, and in one case, an American tractor company had started using Singapore as its central depot for the supply of spare parts to the region.

Opportunities like this will grow in volume, as we improve our living and working conditions for managerial and technological staff and provide a stable and healthy climate for overseas enterprise.

Goh's uncanny instinct for what was to come and what was possible — and indeed his brilliance — is nowhere clearer than in his understanding of the tourism industry in the Pacific region. Dismissing "a lot of nonsense" found in "the minutiae of tourist promotion techniques", he outlined his perception of tourism as far as Singapore was concerned.

The main stream of our tourist trade has its origin in the West Coast of America. The first stage of this traffic stops in Hawaii, from whence it goes to Japan. From Japan it goes southwards to Taiwan, Hong Kong and Bangkok. A part of this traffic comes southwards to Singapore. We are at the tail end of this enormous Pacific tourist traffic. As such, we get only a small share of the trade.

Although Singapore also profited from being on the Europe-Australia route, traffic along it was not expected to grow much in the coming years. What would grow, reasoned Goh, was tourism coming out of Japan. The Japanese would be as rich as Europeans by 1975, and as wealthy as Americans by 1985. Taiwan was already receiving more Japanese than American tourists. For Singapore to gain greater advantage from this coming change in global wealth distribution, and not remain a terminal point for this new traffic of tourists, an attractive destination lying to the south of the island was needed.

This was potentially Bali, a former tourist paradise that had suffered greatly from the witch hunt on communists in 1965–1966, which left as many as 5% of the population dead.

Goh had held talks with Indonesian Finance Minister Dr Frans Seda about rejuvenating Bali into an international tourist resort. This, Goh proposed, fitted very well into "the spirit of the Asean agreement".

Should the Indonesians agree to such a development taking place, Japanese and American tourists would pass Singapore either on the way to Bali from Bangkok, or when returning from Bali after having gotten there via Manila. Singapore would be on the main stream of this growing two-way traffic.

The Indonesians did not need much persuading, given the bad state of its balance-of-payment at that time. The decision was taken already in 1969 to open the country to tourism. Bali had had the reputation of being a tourism paradise since the 1930s, and was therefore deemed most suitable as the focus for Indonesia's tourism development. Taking advice from a World Bank report published in April 1971, tourism was confined to the south side of the island but with excursion routes being created into the interior. Liberal landing rights for foreign airlines at Denpasar Airport saw arrivals rise nine-fold between 1968 and 1973.

However, this fell sharply after landing restrictions were put in place in 1973 by Jakarta (Picard 1995; Picard & Wood 1997: 49–51; 181–82).

Goh also argued that Singapore had not been taking full advantage of its shipping potential, and announced that his ministry was examining the matter "and we can expect important developments in this field in the years ahead for the seas hold out for us immense opportunities which we had hitherto neglected".

He cited figures to show that fixed capital investment in manufacturing had increased twenty-fold between 1961 and 1967, and employment in the Jurong area had jumped from 30 to 16,400 during the same period. In order to push development in manufacturing into the next stage, Goh planned to establish three key institutions.

First, a Development Bank would be founded "in which equity participation from the public, including the commercial banks of Singapore, [would] be invited". The Economic Development Board (EDB), which had been managing industrial development so far, would contribute expert staff and its profitable investment portfolio.

At the same time, through an Act of Parliament, Jurong Town Corporation would be created to manage all the industrial estates that the EDB had produced so far. This new body would have a board whose members were appointed from management, trade unions and the general public. Such a structure would "make Jurong not only an industrial complex, but also a thriving township".

Finally, one big worry for Goh was the limited availability of markets. To resolve this dilemma, most ambitiously, he wished to establish in a staggered fashion a government-linked company — "something like the great Japanese trading companies, which will study opportunities for our manufacturers in overseas markets and undertake their marketing operations there".

Goh's reasoning reflected sharply the nexus between his defence and economic concerns. The two were especially intertwined in his mind during these "crucial years".

> In the first stage, this trading company will confine itself to import and export trade with communist countries, especially trade in manufactures. Apart from being the first step to setting up the export trading company that we want, there are other reasons why we should do this. When our private businessmen trade with communist countries, they in fact become agents of communist Governments — true, business agents and not agents in the sinister sense. It is desirable that trade with communist countries should be done between Governments or between agents of Governments. This is what our trading company will do. It will trade with communist countries on behalf of the Singapore Government. In going about its business, it will as far as possible maintain established trade channels and will license present importers as the company's agents. The company will, of course, engage in new lines of business as trade with communist countries is likely to increase.

At a later stage, this company would gain the business expertise needed for it to fulfil its long-term and primary function — export promotion for Singapore goods.

And so, an impressive string of institutions came into being, all in a hurried and multi-frontal attempt for Singapore to meet the economic challenges it faced in 1968. On hindsight, it is impossible not to be struck by how the crisis precipitated by the British withdrawal generated solutions that define Singapore to this day.

Goh's belief in tourism as a major industry for Singapore proved well-founded. About 410,000 visited the island in 1969, a figure that would double by 1972. By 1978, more than 1.7 million tourists, many from Japan, Australia and Indonesia, were coming to Singapore (*ST* 2 Aug 1973; 29 Apr 1978). Indeed, Goh credited the impressive growth in the tourism industry to Singapore's ability to weather the world recession of 1973–1974. The country's Gross National Product actually grew during those two years by 6.3% and 4.1% respectively, with tourist expenditure in Singapore increasing three-fold between 1970 and 1975. What also endeared the tourist trade to Goh was the re-distribution of wealth between nations occurring without the need for advanced technology. The appetite that the rich had for "exotica" was something governments could take advantage of, he thought: First, the re-distribution is voluntary and is payment for services rendered; second, a satisfied tourist becomes an effective and unpaid ambassador for the country; third, the industry is labour-intensive and provides employment; and fourth, "the developing country retains its self-respect". Although the fourth point is more controversial than the rest especially in cases where the income gap between tourist and local is enormous, Goh's thinking here again discloses his concern and his constant search for means through which growth could occur without leading to demeaning dependence (*ST* 20 Aug 1978).

Goh had other ways of explaining Singapore's success as a tourism hub. He told staff of the Singapore Tourist Promotion Board at a dinner on 20 May 1979 that although Singapore could not offer what places like China, India or Bali could, tourists still came, and that was because it was "convenient". They could shop freely "in the clean and green environment of our city" from a comfortable air-conditioned base in a modern hotel.

Thirty years down the road, in 2008, over 10 million tourists would visit Singapore. The expected target by 2015 is an exorbitant

17 million, many coming from new markets such as China and India (PW).

Where Singapore's entrepot trade is concerned, growth would reach such an astonishing extent that in 2009, the PSA International (formerly Port of Singapore Authority, PSA) was handling "about one-fifth of the world's total container transhipment throughput", and was connected to 600 ports in 123 countries through a network of 200 shipping lines. This made the island republic the largest container transhipment hub in the world (PSA). PSA was established already in 1964 to replace the Singapore Harbour Board. It managed Jurong Port when this was formed in 1965 following the growth of the Jurong Industrial Estate, took over the British Naval Base Store Basin and converted it to the Sembawang Wharves in 1971 when the British left, and started the container terminal in Tanjong Pagar in 1972 and the Pasir Panjang wharves in 1974.

The shipping business was considered by the government to be vital to Singapore's future role as a port. The state-owned Neptune Orient Lines (NOL) was established in December 1968, with Hon Sui Sen as its chairman. Its first vessel, the Neptune Topaz, sailed for Hong Kong on 11 June to pick up goods for transport to Europe. The company would have 12 ships by the end of 1970 (*ST* 4 June 1969; 22 and 24 Aug 1969). Its Initial Public Offering in 1981 raised S$155 million (*ST* 1 April 1982). In 1997, NOL merged with the long-established APL, formerly known as American President Lines, a company specializing in "inter-modal capabilities — the seamless transfer of containerised shipments between ship, train, and truck" (NOL).

Hon thus moved from the EDB, where he had been chairman since that body was started in 1961, not only to manage NOL but also to head the Development Bank of Singapore (DBS), which was formed to take over the EDB's function of providing medium and long-term industrial financing. Things were happening in haste. DBS commenced operations on 16 July 1968 and by November that year was being listed on the stock market, offering 26 million shares to the public at a dollar each (Austin 2004: 43; *ST* 15 Nov 1968). Without doubt, Hon played a key role in the country's push at this crucial time. Goh would much later in life express regret that his old classmate's contributions to Singapore's nation building had not been properly acknowledged:

> [Hon] combined a high moral character and a powerful mind with a practical grasp of reality. This combination enabled him to sort out the complex issues which face all Ministers. It enabled him to separate the essential from the peripheral. In this way, he found the right solution and then could inspire those working with him to get the job done. Singapore is fortunate to have had a man of Mr Hon's calibre in charge of the economy (Cheong 1993: 8).

Strangely, much of what is stated here by Goh about Hon is what many who had worked with Goh tend to say about him as well. While praising Hon for the success of the EDB, Goh also commended Tang I-Fang, "Mr Hon's chief lieutenant in the EDB", for his role in developing the Board. Tang was originally employed by the United Nations Development Programme, and succeeded Hon as EDB chairman in December 1968 (*ST* 1 Aug 1991).

The EDB now handed over its many industrial estates to the Jurong Town Corporation (JTC), a body formed on 1 June 1968 to take charge of "the planning, development, leasing and management of all industrial sites in Singapore". JTC under Hon went on — in Goh's own words — to be responsible for "a Science Park, located next to the University of Singapore, the development of the Southern Islands for petroleum and petrochemical industries, and a special area for developing the aviation industry" (Cheong 10).

The Jurong project, sometimes called "Goh's Folly", was now being utilized to generate the institutions needed for Singapore to transcend the crisis precipitated by the British withdrawal. Apart from the DBS and the JTC, the EDB that was created to develop Jurong — the main suggestion made in the Winsemius Report of June 1961 — also spawned institutions such as the National Productivity Board and the Singapore Institute of Standards and Industrial Research (Cheong 20, 24, 89). These two were merged into the Singapore Productivity and Standards Board in 1996 (Wee 1997).

Among many physical creations soon to dot the Jurong landscape were the Jurong Hill Park that was completed in 1970, the Jurong Country Club formed in 1970, the Jurong Bird Park that opened on 3 Jan 1971, the Japanese Garden started in 1971 and finished in February 1973 and the Chinese Garden on which work began in 1971 and which opened to the public on 18 April 1975. Most, if not all of these were conceived or sponsored by Goh in one way or another (*ST* 4 Jan 1971, 18 April 1975; Cheong 87–95).

The EDB, now radically streamlined, would concentrate on promoting investments. It opened offices in Zurich, Paris, Osaka and Houston in the early 1970s, and established a Manpower and Training Unit in Singapore for industrial training. An overseas training programme was also started in 1971, which placed young Singaporeans in apprenticeships for example in Germany (EDB).

Exactly what institutional measure was undertaken by Goh at this time for the general marketing of Singapore products globally, the need for which he stressed so strongly in his broadcast, is not clear.

The intertwined threads that can be directly discerned from Goh's presentation on radio and television on 17 April 1968 were however only part of the story. Another web of institutions was being woven at the same time, which would anchor the fiscal sector of the country. A new Singapore dollar had already been issued on 12 June 1967 following the founding of the Currency Board of Singapore earlier that year. On that day, the old Currency Board ceased to exist, and negotiations between Singapore and Malaysia had fallen through. Malaysia's central bank took over the currency issuing function for Malaysia, while Singapore decided to retain the Currency Board System (CBS). According to Goh, Singapore singularly went against the trend common amongst ex-colonies to create a central bank with note-issuing powers, and retained the CBS's requirement of 100% asset backing for currency issue. The CBS was a colonial creation from 1906.

To fulfil functions similar to those of a central bank excepting currency issues, the Monetary Authority of Singapore (MAS) was established in 1970. Retaining the CBS disallowed the country's deficits from being financed through central bank credit creation (Tan 1992: 13–14). Incidentally, it was only in 1 October 2002 that the function of currency issuance was assumed by MAS when it merged with the Board of Commissioners of Currency.

Michael Wong Pakshong, a Chinese from South Africa who was posted to Singapore in 1961, and who later became head of the Monetary Authority of Singapore, reminisced about how "hard-headed" Lee Kuan Yew and Goh were, and how "very, very socialist" they were in their approach in the early 1960s.

But they were lucky in that they got independence a little later. By 1965, the problems of the so-called "welfare states", where people were looked after from the cradle to the grave, were

beginning to surface. I think they saw what was happening in
other parts of the world, in Britain, for example. And they
decided to follow another direction completely...They decided
against welfare...They decided to concentrate instead on
education, health, and housing (Chew 1996: 246).

Believing as he did that domestic savings were vital to "the scope
and effectiveness of a development plan", Goh moved in 1968 to
reform the Central Provident Fund (CPF) and to revitalize the
Post Office Savings Bank (POSB), both inherited from the British
(Goh 1965: 2–3). In mobilizing national savings through these
two institutions, Goh aimed to minimize inflation and provide
the government with funds for the development of infrastructure.

The CPF, founded in 1955 as a retirement scheme, underwent
major changes on 1 September 1968. For one thing, the
contribution rate was raised from 5% to 13% for both employer
and employee. More importantly, CPF savings were allowed to be
used for the purchase of low-cost housing built by the Housing
Development Board and Jurong Town Council (CPF Board 2005:
149). Employer CPF contributions had increased to 25% by 1985,
although the recession of –1.6% that hit Singapore that year
prompted the government to cut that quota down to 10% (Austin
2004: 79).

Where the POSB was concerned, after a publicity campaign
was launched and several new measures suggested by a specially
formed committee were adopted, it immediately noted an
increase in deposits by 23% in 1968 and 67% the following
year. To simplify its management, the bank was turned into a
statutory board on New Year's Day 1972 (Lim 1997: 29–30).
It was incidentally taken over by DBS in 1998 at a price of
S$1.6 billion.

Within a decade of the CPF and POSB reforms being carried
out, Singapore's investment rates had tripled to 33% of the GDP.

Its balance-of-payment surpluses jumped by 20 times between 1970 and 1997, and its foreign reserves by 40 times between 1970 and 1998 (Austin 2004: 50).

SINGAPORE'S MONETARY SYSTEM (1969)

Goh lectured on 20 September 1969 to the Economic Society of Singapore on the country's monetary system. Despite his Finance portfolio, this was apparently not a common subject for him to speak about publicly during the country's formative years. For that reason alone, the speech he gave on that occasion is worth dissecting.

One of independent Singapore's first problems was its currency situation. Malaysia had announced that the old Currency Agreement between Malaya, Singapore and Brunei would be terminated by the end of 1966. Singapore was thus left with two major problems to solve: should it continue having a common currency with the federation or create a new one of its own, and should it form a central bank or continue using a currency board, or something else.

Goh admitted in his speech that although he went along with the Cabinet decision to work towards a joint currency where each country would maintain its own serial numbers, he had wanted a separate currency from the very beginning. Although negotiations made impressive progress, the two parties finally failed to reach agreement over a legal technicality concerning ownership.

A major argument against an independent Singapore currency was that a joint one would have greater total reserves and would master greater public confidence and acceptability. Furthermore, close economic ties with Malaysia spoke for sustaining a common currency, and a break would distance the two from each other even more.

Where monetary authority was concerned, the Singapore Cabinet was more united in its reasoning and opted for a currency board. However, as a reflection of the intimate ties between the three countries, an Interchangeability Agreement was signed. That had been working well, according to Goh. This agreement is still in place today where Singapore and Brunei are concerned. Malaysia, on the other hand, decided to leave on 8 May 1973 (MAS — Heritage Collection).

A currency board for Singapore, Goh claimed, had to be only a short-term solution, and a central bank would have to be considered sometime in the future. The argument most often advanced by advocates for a central bank "in academic and other circles" was that it would offer control over monetary supply. In a downturn, it could create credit, and during an upturn, it could do the opposite and restrict credit.

The problem was, import leakages were enormous in Singapore. In 1968, as much as 60% of private consumption expenditure on goods was on imports. Keynesian intervention during extreme times could exacerbate the situation. In a downturn, reserves would already be diminished; and credit creation at such a time would accelerate the loss.

And so, instead of monetary interventions, Singapore decided to rely on fiscal measures. A budget deficit could be financed "by spending accumulated overseas assets or proceeds of foreign loans raised on the collateral of these assets". For this to be possible, accumulation of funds during good times was needed.

> So I am afraid the solution is prosaic and unglamorous. For us in Singapore, the road to greater wealth is through thrift, enterprise and hard work. The road to stability lies in prudence and foresight in prosperity, and patience and fortitude in adversity. In the swinging age of the new economics, all this

sounds old-fashioned and Victorian. No doubt it is, but I think
it is unrealistic to expect that doctrines worked out for developed
economies, where foreign trade forms a relatively small part of
the GNP, would apply in their entirety to the exceptional
situation that is ours.

Goh took time to explain how complicated Singapore's monetary
system was in 1969. The Ministry of Finance had to coordinate
the activities of ten separate authorities involved such as the
Currency Board of Singapore, the Exchange Control Department,
the Accountant-General's Department, the Clearing House, the
commissioner for Finance Companies, the Department Overseas
Investment, and others. Staff from these departments would
meet Goh on Monday mornings for discussion of reports handed
out before the weekend. At critical times, an extra staff meeting
was held on Fridays, and "during periods of acute tension", they
met on Thursdays.

"This system is doing very well," Goh claimed.

Be that as it may, Singapore still needed to have a central bank.
This was for reasons other than those normally ventured by bank
experts. For one thing, the system he described would gain from
being put under one roof. This would give it administrative tidiness
and a sense of purpose and direction, which was required for the
development of "a high level of professional expertise".

However, he wished for a central bank to evolve out of the
disparate units guided by his Ministry into "a central bank worthy
of its status as an independent monetary institution". For the
time being, the country had to wait for the international monetary
system situation to move into "a period of tranquillity" before a
central bank could be created.

Goh was in the event appointed chairman of the Monetary
Authority of Singapore (MAS) in August 1980.

WHY A CURRENCY BOARD? (1991)

In 1991, Goh wrote a paper titled "Why a Currency Board" in which he narrated the history of Singapore's financial system, two decades after the trying times of the late 1960s.

What was in fact unravelling at the end of the 1960s, Goh wrote, was the global financial system itself. Sustained Keynesian policies were ending in disaster. Britain was suffering severe balance-of-payment problems that led to its currency devaluation in November 1967; and American trade deficits were exerting inflationary pressure which undermined confidence in the dollar's convertibility into gold. In August 1971, currencies were allowed to float, and do so until today.

Goh understood Keynes as flawed on two counts. First, increased government expenditure financed by central bank policies involved the risk of inflation. Secondly, the theory did not consider foreign trade. A considerable part of the increased consumption would be used on imports, which if not checked in time would worsen trade deficits.

Singapore was too tiny an island country and too open a trading economy to contemplate budget deficits financed by central bank credit creation, or suffer a bad trade deficit. That would be "an invitation to disaster". "The old guard," he claimed, grew up under difficult conditions "and did not believe anybody owed Singapore a living."

> Hence, we were not impressed by claims — excessive as they turned out to be — that governments could bring about prosperity through spending. It did not surprise us that the Anglo-Saxon countries which adopted such policies got into trouble. We also noted that the Germans and the Japanese did not believe they could 'spend their way to prosperity', as the phrase went. Like Singaporeans, they set store by diligence, education and skills.

Nevertheless, Goh held great respect for Keynes, crediting him for creating what we today call "macroeconomics". As Goh saw it, modern states were able to manage their economies thanks mainly both to Keynes's approach and to Richard Stone (1913–1991). Stone was the 1984 recipient of the Nobel Memorial Prize in Economic Sciences, and is generally known as "the father of national income accounting". When Goh was working on his thesis in the mid-1950s on techniques of national income estimation, Stone's *Measurement of Consumers' Expenditure and Behaviour in the U.K. 1920–1939* had just been published, and Goh did refer to it in his own chapter on "The Estimation of the Value of Non-agricultural Product". In that book, Stone, who was one of Keynes' students, offered statistical methods for calculating government spending, investment and consumption, which acted as models for Britain's national bookkeeping system. These were later used by international organizations such as the United Nations (NPIA).

Singapore's chosen solution was to maintain a Currency Board System (CBS), which was legally obliged to issue currency only when backed by at least 100% of overseas assets. There were three reasons why Singapore needed to do this, according to Goh:

> First, to inform the financial world that our objective was to maintain a strong convertible Singapore Dollar. This remains the best protection against inflation. When nearly two-thirds of our citizens' expenditure is spent on imported goods, a strong Singapore Dollar helps to keep consumer prices down. The second purpose was to inform our citizens that if they wanted more and better services, they must pay for these through taxes and fees. There is no free lunch here. Third, we wanted to indicate to academics, both local and foreign, that what is fashionable in the West is not necessarily good for Singapore. A perceptive mind was needed to distinguish the

peripheral from the fundamental, transient fads from
permanent values.

Here, we observe a recurring mixture of concerns often noticeable
in Goh's thinking, and which together characteristically amount
to an effective and original policy not limited by ideological or
nationalist worries. The first identifies economic dynamics peculiar
to places like Singapore; the second seeks to influence the mindset
and behaviour of citizens, while the third asserts the independence
and uniqueness of the country, often in defiance of Western
academic perspectives.

In a unique move, Singapore decided that its finance minister
would also serve as chairman of the *de facto* central bank, the
Monetary Authority of Singapore. This flew in the face of World
Bank fears that such a solution would open the country to
budget deficits. Singapore's budgetary culture did not condone
deficits in any case, reasoned Goh. Incidentally, as an extra
measure against the use of state reserves for vote-buying, a
constitutional amendment was made in January 1991 for the
country's President to be elected, whose major responsibility
was to block any tendency on the part of the Finance Minister
to overspend.

In 1976, Goh gave a summary of his general view on economic
policy in his article *A Socialist Economy that Works*. Incidentally,
this article was Goh's contribution in *A Socialism that Works*, a
book edited by Devan Nair and published hastily in the wake of
the PAP's resignation from the Socialist International in May that
year (*ST* 12 Nov 1976). By then, the two problems that Goh
considered most in need of a fast solution had been solved. These
were unemployment and inferior housing. Both stemmed from a
fast growing population; and one cannot but induce that his
conclusion was rooted in the social surveys he carried out in
exemplary manner back in the 1940s and 1950s.

Taking an overall view of Singapore's economic policy, we can see how radically it differed from the *laissez-faire* policies of the colonial era. These had led Singapore to a dead end, with little economic growth, massive unemployment, wretched housing, and inadequate education. We *had* to try a more activist and interventionist approach. Democratic socialist economic policies ranged from direct participation in industry to the supply of infrastructure facilities by statutory authorities, and to laying down clear guidelines to the private sector as to what they could or should do. The successful implementation of these policies depended on their acceptance by the people, generally, and on the active cooperation of organised labour in particular. All these conditions were fulfilled.

On that occasion, he also gave ample credit to the crucial role that Singapore's organized labour played when it "took the path of enlightened long-term self-interest". Winsemius held the same view and once listed unionist leader Devan Nair as the third most important contributor to the economic development of Singapore, after Lee Kuan Yew and Goh (CORD Winsemius).

INTERNATIONAL FINANCIAL SYSTEM (1978)

What Goh thought wrong with the international monetary system in the 1960s was presented in a speech delivered to the International Chamber of Commerce at Singapore's Shangri-la Hotel on 23 June 1978. The Bretton Woods system was breaking down in the late 1960s due to American budget deficits which had naturally led to huge accumulations of US dollars outside America — the so-called Euro-dollars. As long as there was enough gold in Fort Knox, Goh said, there was stability. But when American gold reserves fell sharply in the 1960s, turmoil ensued, leading finally to the Dutch Guilder and the Deutschmark being allowed to float upwards. Subsequent attempts at fixing currency exchange parities failed, and floating currencies became the norm, growing out of "a situation that was increasingly unmanageable and when the experts had run out of options".

This new state of affairs promised certain advantages. First, speculators now ran great risks of incurring huge losses, and second, floating currencies would "iron out more easily [...] problems created by trade and payment surpluses and deficits". Market forces would depress the currencies of countries with trade deficits and strengthen the currencies of countries with trade surpluses. There was general agreement on this, and yet, balance of payments equilibrium failed to appear despite the freely adjusting mechanism.

This, according to Goh, had several related reasons. For one thing, industrial nations did not form a homogenous whole, and were in fact made up of two economic sub-systems. The Anglo-Saxon countries and several hangers-on subscribed to Keynesian doctrines, and understood economic policy as having the basic function of creating full employment. Through the "management of aggregate demand", the government generated demand for unemployed resources through fiscal stimulation, or reflation. As long as unemployment was significant, such government spending would not lead to inflation. It soon became the prime mission of the government to generate prosperity. Along with it came certain core weaknesses.

> The political factor intruded upon the scene. The timing of stimulus had to take into account the next general, presidential or congressional elections. This was bad enough in itself, but the impact on public opinion was even more damaging in the long term. The electorate began to expect their governments to give them secure jobs, better wages and higher standards of

living without having to put in greater effort. One result of continuing reflation over the years is rapidly rising government expenditure, exceeding 40% of GNP in some instances. Eventually it became politically unacceptable to phase out inefficient and uncompetitive industries so that resources released could be directed to more profitable uses. Indeed, the notion of profit became suspect and big business — banks, oil companies, multinational corporations — came under increasingly close scrutiny for alleged misdemeanours of all kinds.

The second sub-system included countries like Germany and Japan, which had had to rebuild their flattened economies after the war. Where they were concerned, budget deficits financed by central banks did not lead to prosperity. Their economic formula was to create better products more cheaply.

In the Keynesian system, inflation set in once politics had become more important than economics. The currency would then devalue itself and allow for exports to increase. But since underlying weaknesses — listed by Goh as aggressive unions, subsidized uneconomic industries, excessive taxation, and decline in work ethic — remained, the problem of inflation soon returned.

What seemed to happen in the second sub-system when the currency got more expensive and exports were threatened was that companies tried to reduce cost and increasing productivity, or even merged. Such moves could be successful. A recent 30% increase in the value of the yen, for example, was followed by a rise in Japanese export prices of only 13.5%.

Central banks in surplus countries would fight inflation by either absorbing the inflow of dollars or revaluing their currencies, or both, knocking out the self-adjusting mechanism that floating rates amounted to.

MAS AMENDMENT BILL (1984)

On 24 August 1984, Goh spoke in parliament at the second reading of the Monetary Authority of Singapore (Amendment) Bill. Five days earlier, Lee Kuan Yew had announced in his National Day Rally speech that Goh was retiring and "[could] not be moved" from that decision. The MAS itself had recently undergone reforms after Goh jumped in as chairman in late 1980 on Cabinet worries that the body was not investing Singapore's reserves effectively. Western consultants were brought in and investment strategies radically changed. The Government of Singapore Investment Corporation (GIC) was established by Goh in May 1981, with Lee Kuan Yew as chairman, Goh as deputy, and Yong Pung How as managing director. The GIC handled the government's financial reserves in the beginning, but soon came to manage the reserves of the Board of Commissioners of Currency, Singapore, as well as the long-term assets of the MAS. These developments took Singapore's position as a financial centre to a new level, and by 1996 had turned the island into the fourth-largest foreign-exchange trading centre in the world. Incidentally, Singapore's financial system weathered crises in 1987 and 1997–1998 well, and even consolidated its position as a financial centre in their aftermath (Goh 2007: 161–67; Lee 2000: 89–102).

According to Professor Lee Sheng-Yi, this was achieved through a series of measures. No withholding tax was levied on earnings from foreign-owned deposits; numerous monetary, banking and financial institutions were established and liberal immigration regulations for skilled personnel and experts were adopted with the aim of attracting international banks. Other measures included liberalization of interest rates; abolition of exchange control; the development of the Asian Dollar Market and the Asian Bond Market and related instruments; and, other sophisticated enhancements of the financial system (Lee 1983: 4–5).

The Asian Dollar Market had been established in 1968 as an extension of the Euro-Dollar market founded in 1957. As explained in a pamphlet issued by the First National City Bank in 1973 to attract investors, Asian Dollars were "off-shore funds" sold as Asian Currency Units (ACU) issued by banks licensed by the MAS. The success of the Market was dramatic. ACU deposits at the end of 1968 amounted to USD33.6 million. By the end of 1972, it had surpassed USD3 billion (*The Asian Dollar Market* 1973).

Goh used his final parliamentary speech to explain Singapore's unique conditions where financial management was concerned. Central banks, he said, dealt with three matters: the regulation of money supply, the regulation of banks, and, since 1971, looking after the external value of the national currency "by active intervention or benign neglect or, in some unhappy instances, by desperate improvisation". The first function was necessary because, on the one hand, "people [were] fed up with inflation" and, on the other, "people also [did] not want to pay the price of fighting inflation in the only sensible way, that [was], for the Government to balance the budget and for the country to live within its means".

Western central banks had to watch their money supply because their governments were chronically given to overspending. Their countries' currency volume was tracked through M1, M2 or M3, which were money supply measures that stretched from a narrow to a wide definition of money. But since Singapore's public sector was in a state of chronic surplus as a matter of policy, the MAS — unique among all central banks — did not have to bother with the three M's. What it had to watch instead were foreign exchange rates, the new function that central banks were laden with after 1971.

Goh regretted the collapse that year of the Bretton Woods system because the resultant fluctuating foreign exchange rates made things uncomfortable for small countries like Singapore. The solution is best given in Goh's own precise words:

> We create what is called a basket of currencies based on the value of trade with major trading partners. We — that is, the Ministry of Finance and the Ministry of Trade and Industry, in consultation with the MAS — decide the future worth of this basket, or in other words, the value of the Singapore dollar in terms of the US dollar, the Japanese yen, the Deutsch mark, pound sterling, etc. Upper and lower limits are then set and the MAS given authority to manage the float within these limits. This is done by buying or selling foreign currencies against the Singapore dollar or by swap operations. The intervention currency usually is the US dollar, as is the practice with nearly all central banks.

The surplus flow of funds into the MAS would go back into banks through the purchase of foreign currencies, keeping the Singapore dollar from appreciating excessively. An overall surplus was vital. For example, although Singapore had a bad merchandise trade deficit, this was more than outweighed by the surplus in services.

As Goh put it, this system worked very well, "guided by Adam Smith's gentle and invisible hand". There were of course some visible state measures which allowed for this hand to act so gently.

> So long as we continue to work diligently and skilfully, so long as we spend carefully, and so long as we don't lend Singapore dollars to foreigners, it will continue to work beautifully.

The third function of central banks — controlling foreign exchange rate fluctuations — was a "complex and delicate matter", especially in light of banking failures in the West in the 1970s and early 1980s. The Basle Committee and its Basle Concordat came into being in 1975 to guide the supervisory function of central banks, and in 1980, Singapore joined something called "The Offshore Supervisors Group", with a membership of fourteen countries. These bodies had agreed to encourage banks to stay away from financial centres that did not have "proper and adequate systems of supervision". Be that as it may, there were as yet no "comprehensive, binding and clearly defined principles" to follow. As Goh noted;

> It could well be that central banks can never be reduced to working within rigorously defined rules and we must learn to live with uncertainty. The subject is of concern to Singapore and the well-informed Singaporean should keep abreast of events.

Chapter 6

THE HUMAN ELEMENT

The early stages of economic growth are necessarily a cruel and harsh process, and it needs a robust, philosophical outlook to go through with it.

— Goh Keng Swee
(Radio broadcast on 30 January 1967)

There is no doubt that most of Goh's intellectual energies were targeted at the fields of economics, finance and defence. However, throughout his life, he held strong views that he voiced publicly about what can only be called "The Human Element" and how this impinged on the best laid plans of mice and men, including Goh.

How humans are prone to act under tightly identified situations is part and parcel of basic economic theory. National macroeconomics, however, provides ideas and tools of coercion and manipulation that put the human element in another light; human propensities have to be controlled for the greater good, and not merely acknowledged and utilized. Given Goh's early economic training in the 1930s when Keynesian intervention was parrying the worst criticisms that socialism could throw at capitalism, along with his interest in the workings of a war economy in the early 1940s, one can safely assume that Goh's approach to economics — as is evident in his 1940 work, *The Economic Front from a Malayan Point of View* — is national economic in essence.

His early career as a civil servant and his surveys on poverty and housing contributed to his perception that state intervention was inevitable in creating economic growth and sustaining it without causing an excessive income gap through excessive reliance on private entrepreneurship. Where the political aspect of housing policies was concerned, Goh's old roommate Lim Kim San, the man Singaporeans remember as the builder of the ubiquitous HDB blocks that are today more a physical depiction of the country than the Esplanade Theatre can ever be, recalled the following many years later.

> Dr Goh had already seen the situation on the ground. He did the Social Survey when he was in the civil service in 1952. He wanted me to look at it personally, to see how urgent the housing problem was. The overcrowding was a breeding ground for gangsterism and crime. It was difficult to catch criminals who would just run in and out of these buildings. Politically, it was a dangerous situation. The Communists were exploiting it to win support. Housing was critical. (Chew 1996: 163)

Where defence was concerned, human weaknesses such as self-deception, complacency, laziness and cowardice, or the propensity of commanders to put show before substance, could easily lead to disaster. There was little room for such faults where the country's armed forces were concerned. Partly for this reason, he sought to raise the technological know-how of the army and the country, just as his handling of Singapore's economy had led to enormous and effective institutions being generated to lead growth and avoid disaster.

The unease he felt where the human element was concerned steered him towards the last ministry that he was to head before his retirement. This was Education. But before his contributions in that field are discussed, a study of some of his opinions about the individual, society, bureaucratic culture and political contingencies of the times should provide some understanding of his philosophy outside of purely economic and military matters. To be sure, it is difficult to detach Goh's ideas on psychological and sociological matters from economic or defence contexts, for his mind never seemed to leave the larger project of nation building for long. One could say that he was generally holistic — though with a partiality for economics — and practical in his approach; or that his mind was for most of his life fully fascinated and consumed by the mission of constructing a political entity that would survive, and survive well.

Being strongly aware that market forces were endlessly active, he realized that the constructing of a state had to be done on the wing; there was essentially no other way. What he had to say about socio-cultural matters — and he did write a lot about them — is therefore of great interest to us. It is hard to miss or dismiss the fact that Goh in much of his writings expressed a low opinion of social theorists, or at least social theorizing. At the same time, his understanding of economic development was tempered by his complaint that "the human aspect" was seldom given enough attention. Accordingly, he was more often than not highly critical of developmental economists.

In an address at a seminar on international labour held in 1965, he compared the disappointing performance of developing countries in the 1960s — which had optimistically been titled a

Decade of Development in such countries by the United Nations — to the impressive achievements of the Germans and Japanese after the Second World War. What concerned him was identifying "the social values which [motivated] the people of modern societies". These included "respect of law and order as the basis of social discipline"; "awareness of rights and obligations"; "attitudes towards work, willingness to endure the disciplines of the wage system, eagerness for advancement in education, and, at a higher level, insatiable intellectual curiosity and abounding business enterprise" (Goh 1965; April).

These "intangibles", he proclaimed, were more basic to economic growth than obviously economic factors like "capital investment, the infrastructure of social overheads and the like".

> I believe that most developing countries have been misled by economists as to the importance of economic factors. I will be the last, being by training an economist myself, to deny the importance of economic factors, but the process of development and modernization does not begin and end with economic factors. It is necessary that we should pay due regard to them, but it is not sufficient merely to do so.

MAN AND ECONOMIC DEVELOPMENT (1961)

Already in 1961, Goh wrote in *Commerce*, a journal published by Nanyang University's Commerce Society, that economists tended to put too much emphasis on details, and so lose sight of "basic human and sociological principles". Ricardian ideas about man's rational economic behaviour, he ventured, held true "only in a limited sense".

> Where large changes have to take place, then it by no means follows that the assumptions under marginal analysis [i.e. analysis of small change] hold true.

For a start, it was not always true that humans sought to improve their basic material living conditions, noted Goh. He then showed an economist's bias against societies or sub-cultures that did not exhibit material ambitions by concluding that unless such "lethargy" was first removed by "the sociologist and the politician", there was nothing much an economist could do. On top of that, the postulation made by economists on complete mobility of workers to change careers and migrate freely was badly misguided. Such mobility simply did not exist. What was thus needed for national development went beyond economic computations. The point of understanding human motivation in this context was for it to be engineered in a definite direction.

> The problem resolves itself into the policies which a government should adopt to achieve the changes in society and in individual human beings that will permit the objective facts of economic development to assert themselves.

In short, economic development for non-advanced countries required a social revolution of a certain type. First, an educated citizenry was needed. With literacy came an awareness of "the benefits of economic development" as well as a social discipline that would guide citizens away from "frivolous pursuits" towards "a fuller and more cultured life". Education had to be functional as well because individuals were endowed differently and in any case, "no society [could] consist entirely of the intelligentsia".

The second important factor for growth was "the opportunity which a society [afforded] to those with talent, ability and skills to rise to the position for which they [were] best fitted". For this to happen, an able leadership was needed, which was free from corruption.

> In advanced countries, it is not so much open nepotism which is to be feared but the insidious "old boy" type whereby no

illegalities are committed, but in which the pinnacles of power, influence and wealth are the reserve of those born into the right families.

For Goh, what the social engineering side of nation building should result in, potently if indirectly, was entrepreneurship.

Entrepreneurs are something which the state cannot directly create. Entrepreneurial talent emerges if the conditions in society are appropriate. All the state can and should do is to remove the restrictions on the development of such talent.

Such a need was most strongly felt in developing countries. Society would stagnate, if entrepreneurs were not allowed to "pursue their goals unhindered". This stagnation was what Goh perceived to be happening in advanced countries, where entrepreneurs were being discouraged, either through naivety or socialist dogma.

When applied to Singapore, Goh's analysis depicted a fortunate situation. The island nation's population consisted mainly of immigrants or recent immigrants who had "cast aside [...] rigidities, taboos and prejudices of the past and [who were] willing to permit a degree of social freedom and mobility that [was] quite remarkable by Asian standards".

For Goh, even if one provides for some politically expedient optimism on his part, conditions in 1961 were commendable where political leadership, administrative machinery, the lack of corruption, social services, educational opportunities and entrepreneurship were concerned.

MANAGEMENT IN THE DEVELOPING SOCIETY (1963)

Social organization was something Goh considered thoroughly, and in that context he often distinguished between modern values and traditional values. Modern values to him were tellingly those conducive to political stability and economic progress, while traditional values were seen as a hindrance to those goals.

What Goh brought to the discussion was a harsh surgical precision in terminology and an accompanying wish for action. At a symposium held at the University of Singapore on 15 March 1963 on "The Role of Management in Industrialization", for example, he drew attention to the common "curious illusion" that differences between the Soviet Union and Western democratic states were "fundamental and enduring". The two were more similar than they would admit, he claimed.

How Goh thought them similar is of course revealing of his understanding of contemporary human history and global politics. First, both sides were children of the Renaissance and the Enlightenment who believed in man's ability to exceed limitations imposed by his natural environment.

> Both the modern Communist states and the Western democratic states accept this belief almost without reservation, and accordingly, the keenest intellects that they can muster are concentrating their talents and energies towards extending the frontiers of human knowledge.

Material improvement was also a common pursuit in both systems. In the West, although voices of protests were heard from "poets, painters, novelists, even in Victorian times" against the industrial society, their impact had not extended beyond their "narrow artistic and intellectual circles". The common man, however, guiltlessly sought "better homes, motor cars, scooters, household gadgets, foreign travelling and the like".

Where production was concerned, the two were similar in their "respect for meritorious performance in the creation of wealth", and having to deal with issues of management and labour, technical innovations and incentives for work.

These beliefs led to "recognition of the value of the managerial class", and were in stark contrast to certain pre-modern values that inhibited economic growth, such as pre-ordainment and fatalism. Vested interests continued to maintain superstition among the masses and to resist "any attempt to awaken them". Spiritual values held priority over material progress. This was however a minor hindrance, being more a secondary condition born from "despair over the prospects of success in the conquest of age-old poverty" than a deep-seated attitude.

What provided more serious resistance to the creation of modern societies in Asia was the fact that status and position continued to be determined "largely by birth and heredity". Asian countries often failed because governments would not adopt economic growth as their first priority. The deeper effect of this was "its inhibitory effect on enterprise and the growth of an energetic and self-assured managerial class".

For a start, political instability in these countries meant that resources were directed towards "non-economic objectives" such as building a strong military, which drew money and skills away from capital formation. Such a situation discouraged foreign and local investments, and what was worse, led to political posturing.

> Such political postures are likely to take the form of exaggerated nationalism with its concomitant anti-foreign and anti-capitalist content. When the economic situation goes from bad to worse, the political gestures become increasingly extreme. At some stage in the debacle, there is a resort to the incantation of magic words as a remedy for all troubles.

Nevertheless, Goh remained optimistic about Asian countries, partly because they did not have to overcome the pioneering difficulties faced by European societies, but more importantly because the global trend was towards profound change, which would undermine traditional structures and ways of thought.

Just as Goh exhibited great flexibility in defence and economic matters — and much of his brilliance definitely came from this aversion to ideological short cuts — his pragmatism also condoned a gungho attitude where societal phenomena were concerned. His confidence in his ability to engineer, which had stood him in good stead in the fields of economic and defence, was also evident in his approach to society in general.

The late 1960s was a globally turbulent period. China was sunk in an earth-shaking cultural revolution whose consequences could only be guessed at; while the West was experiencing a cultural revolution of its own fuelled by opposition to the Vietnam War and by the coming of age of post-war baby-boomers. There was fear that Singapore, petite and toddling, would suffer cultural changes that could jeopardize its survival.

On 7 April 1967, Goh gave a speech at a variety show organized by the PAP's Bukit Merah branch. The points he drove home that evening were elucidatory of his statist view on cultural development. No doubt, his audience consisted of many party loyalists, but his advice on how plays should be produced clearly held cultural phenomena subordinate to state concerns.

> Firstly, the themes of the plays should be in keeping with the realistic life in Singapore and its multi-racial, multi-cultural and multi-religious spirit. Secondly, they must discard the crazy, sensual, ridiculous, boisterous and over materialistic style of the West. In the same way, the feudalistic, superstitious, ignorant and pessimistic ideas of the East are also undesirable. Thirdly, they must emphasise the spirit of patriotism, love for the people

and for sciences, and cultivate diligence, courage, sense of responsibility and a positive philosophy of life. Fourthly, they must be free from crudeness in production, opportunism, monotony, vulgarity, copying and backwardness. Fifthly, they should provide noble, healthy and proper cultural entertainment for the people.

Later that year, on 5 December, he gave a reply in parliament on the possible opening of a casino in Singapore to boost tourism. He was opposed to such a thing happening unless two conditions were fulfilled. He had to be satisfied firstly that it would bring "substantial benefits to Singapore" and secondly that "firm safeguards against Singaporean citizens using it" were put into place first (*ST* 6 Dec 1967). The human element, especially in fellow Singaporeans, was evidently a source of worry to him.

THE HIPPIE CULTURE (1970)

On 25 October 1970, Goh spoke at the fifth anniversary dinner and dance of the Democratic Socialist Club. His subject was "the dissident movement" that had been spreading across the world. As was his wont, he started by providing "essential features of youthful dissidence in Western countries". Two "well-defined" groups of dissidents interested him most. The first were children of wealthy families who had become disillusioned with "evident inequalities, injustices and cruelties", and whose attitudes in contradistinction to their parents' supposed views formed "the generation gap". The second consisted of those who believed they were discriminated against as a group "or because they [did] not have the intellect or character to make the grade". From these emerged the many manifestations of the movement, penetrated further by "the lunatic fringe", apparently meaning loosely defined anarchists.

Aside from violent demonstrations, other deplorable acts included "the taking of drugs, the craze for psychedelic music, the practice of sexual promiscuity, [and] bizarre styles in dress".

> These are the inevitable consequences of people who have decided not to strive and achieve in a society whose values they reject as pernicious. Once they reject established values, once they consider conventional ethical codes as a hypocritical cover for unjust practices, then the door is wide open for uninhibited hedonistic practices of all kinds. This is the basis of the hippie culture.

Whether these cultural developments would destroy "the complex industrial economy which [was] sustaining the high living standards of the West" was still an open question, according to Goh. What he was interested in was Singapore's defence against the spread of this "dissident movement".

He argued that independent Singapore had been providing educational and other opportunities to sons and daughters of poor but able migrants; and so, the generation gap was measured through the rise in affluence and not in "acceptance or rejection of ethical codes". Singapore's "harsh competitive society with good rewards for the successful [was] hardly an environment which [favoured] hippie activity, drug-taking and opting out of society". The "external trappings" of hippie culture found in Singapore were "timid self-conscious imitations of the West".

> As is usual when the Singaporean apes the West, he goes for the froth and the frills and not for the substance. In this instance, it is well that this is so and that the result has been that the hippie threat to Singapore is largely an illusion.

His reading of the Western youth culture of the 1960s was certainly harsh. However, what seemed so far to be a mere nationalistic speech meant to praise Singapore at the cost of the West turned at this point into a criticism of Singapore's educational culture. The fixation with examination results had led to "a stultification of intellectual development".

> And so we have in Singapore intellectual conformity in place of intellectual inquisitiveness. And the sum total of it all adds up to a depressing climate of intellectual sterility. [...] If we are honest with ourselves, I think we can detect in contemporary Singapore a strange and striking similarity of intellectual climate and social values with Victorian England, together with much of the hypocrisies and cruelties of that age.

There is common agreement among Singapore's older civil servants today that Goh was bad at delivering speeches. This was a weakness that Goh would have agreed with. However, judging from the high quality of his transcribed speeches, that failing was indeed a great pity, and his ideas certainly warranted much more attention and debate than they got. The talk he gave on the night of the 25 November 1970 was characteristic of the man — comprehensive, honest, substantive, without punches pulled, and rational.

The next twist he turned on his audience that night was to argue that this intellectual sterility and intellectual timidity in the universities should not be blamed on the government. The problem went deeper, and its causes were more sociological and historical in nature than political. Gerald De Cruz, Goh said, had recently pleaded for "a heroic intellectual" to emerge in Singapore. Such a person would not do any good, Goh countered, for he would not be listened to.

Thinkers of that calibre came out of "a leisured class, people of independent means who [did] not have to work for a living". Singapore's goals had to be modest on that front, he reasoned and gave his own solution.

What we should try to do is to build up a respectable research
effort in various disciplines of learning. This means strengthening
the position of postgraduate studies in the university. It also
means establishing full-time professional research institutes.

The logic here relates to the reason for the founding of The
Pyramid Club in 1963: since Singapore lacked "an Establishment",
one had to be created. Goh discussed this apparent need with Lee
Kuan Yew in early 1963, and after studying examples such as The
Athenaeum in London, they decided to form such a club whose
members were drawn from "the highest echelons of private and
public life" (Chew 2005: 34–35). This will be touched on in more
detail later, as will be Goh's creation of a "full-time professional
research institute" for Southeast Asian studies.

Among those who reacted to Goh's claim of "intellectual
sterility" was the sociologist Professor Syed Hussein Alatas, head
of the Malay Studies Department at the University of Singapore.
Alatas insisted that Singapore society as a whole was to blame for
this state of affairs, and for not showing sufficient interest and
recognition to intellectual activity. Calling for more debates in
newspapers and television, he added that Asian governments
tended to pay more attention to foreign scholars than to their
own, "with the result that they [were] not aware of the
contributions of their own scholars".

Goh had also ventured that the scope of the intellectual had
to be necessarily modest and limited. The professor also disagreed
with him on this point, stating:

The infrastructure for an intellectual creativity of a world
standard is present here — what is lacking is a sufficient number
of individuals who will be encouraged by society to undertake
intellectual accomplishments (ST 27 Oct 1970).

Goh was especially worried that Western influences on Singapore's young and within the armed forces would continue — and grow — for some time to come. On 10 December 1972, while he was Acting Prime Minister as well as Defence Minister, Goh spoke at a fund-raising dinner in his constituency of Kreta Ayer, and famously warned that the practice amongst young Singaporeans of copying Western fashions would turn the country into a nation of "Wogs". "Wogs" — short for Westernized Oriental Gentlemen — was a term of contempt originally used by British civil servants for English-educated Indians when India was the Empire's crown jewel (*ST* 11 Dec 1972).

> The brainless young, who follow Western fashions and wear long hair are part of the Wog culture of Singapore. Wog women wear mini-skirts and nylon stockings and think they look smashing. [...] A Wog society has no survival value in Southeast Asia.

However, what he seemed to think was the problem was not so much Western culture as what he saw to be evidence of a lack of "a set of sound basic values" needed for the development of "a wholesome well-integrated personality".

> An understanding of one's own cultural heritage and a knowledge of the history one's own people would help to give a man some cultural ballast. He will then not easily become a Wog. This is why it is important to be educated in at least two languages.

He said he shared the fear that Lee Kuan Yew had recently expressed that an education done exclusively in English would produce "a Caribbean type of person with no roots in the past". Interestingly, Maurice Baker, head of the department of English Language and Literature at the University of Singapore and Goh's old friend from their London days, discussed the speech in the same day's newspaper. While agreeing with Goh on most points, Baker added that even if education was in one language as in the past, "a reasonably intelligent child," given basic moral values from home, would still be able to "resist drugs and avoid vice".

> I myself do not share Dr Goh's disapproval of nylon stockings, though I must confess myself sometimes disturbed by mini-skirts and disgusted by untidy and excessively long-haired boys. (*ST* 11 Dec 1972)

Two months later, when opening the Japanese Garden in Jurong, Goh continued his barrage against contemporary Western youth culture. This time he denounced its musical taste.

> Let us not consider the subject of music as a trifling matter, of no import in the affairs of the state. The ancients knew better. Both Plato and Confucius correctly recognised the crucial role which music as an instrument of state policy could play in producing the desirable type of citizen. Neglect in Singapore on this subject has given rise to serious problems. I refer to the widespread popularity of the barbarous form of music produced by the steel guitar linked to an ear shattering system of sound amplification. Voice accompaniment takes the form of inane tasteless wailing. It is barbarous music of this kind that is mainly responsible for attracting the mindless young of Singapore to the cult of permissiveness of the western world.

He called for action from the Home Ministry against this "barbarous music", and for an initiative to right "the minor scandal" of Singapore not having a symphony orchestra. His irritation over "the cult of permissiveness" led him to the extent of lamenting that many of Singapore's *nouveau riche* were not "rounded or cultivated men", and who allowed their fortunes to be squandered by the children that they had not brought up properly. Quoting Tunku Abdul Rahman, Goh thought their ruin could be traced to a preference for "fast women and slow horses" (Goh, 16 Feb 1973).

Incidentally, Singapore did finally get its own state-sponsored symphony orchestra. This happened officially on 1 January 1979, apparently after some persistent arm-twisting of Cabinet colleagues by Goh. It performed for the first time on 24 January 1979 (Tan 2007: 181). Choo Hoey, the Singapore Symphony Orchestra's first musical director, recalled how he was called home from Europe to meet Goh, "a nice man, a very nice man". According to him, Goh had wanted a 100-man orchestra but was persuaded to go with a chamber orchestra of 40 musicians (Chew 1996: 294).

BUSINESS MORALITY IN LESS DEVELOPED COUNTRIES (1979)

One might have expected that after joining politics in 1959, Goh would have had less and less time to put across his ideas publicly. This did not seem to have been the case. Instead, through the decades and into the mid-1990s, the range of his writings was as impressive as the policies and institutions he helped initiate. A lot of his thoughts did find expression in short interviews, political speeches or keynote presentations at conferences, but some of his latter works were impressively lengthy and substantive.

He gave lectures on occasion, to the Singapore civil service and at respected institutions around the world. Some were widely noted, while others were too technical to arouse public interest. As late as in July 1996, when he was 78 years old, Goh co-authored a weighty academic paper with Linda Low, titled "Beyond

'Miracles' and Total Factor Productivity", which was published in the ISEAS journal, *ASEAN Economic Bulletin*.

Two of his more significant international lectures were "Business Morality in Less Developed Countries" (1979) and "Public Administration and Economic Development in LDCs" (1983). The latter — to be discussed later — was the fourth in the Harry G. Johnson Memorial series held at the Trade Policy Research Centre in London. The former was delivered as a Barbara Weinstock lecture on January 1979 at the University of California in Berkeley. Goh was at this time in the process of moving from the Ministry of Defence where he had been for so long to take over the Education portfolio. He had already been heading a task force since August 1978 to assess the country's education system. Officially, he became Minister of Education on 13 February 1979.

Dubious business practices in less developed countries (LDCs) is an issue to be studied in a chapter on economic development rather than one on the human element; after all, Goh seemed to see business practices as the resultant of political and economic conditions. But since it is the corrupt behaviour of businessmen and bureaucrats that he was analysing, it is hoped that locating the talk he gave in California in a discussion on the human element will provide insights into his understanding of the nexus between ethics and economics in Third World nation building.

Judging from the footnotes, Goh made extensive use of articles found in *Political Corruption*, a 1970 classic on the subject, edited by Arnold J. Heidenheimer. Goh dissected corrupt business practices in LDCs by focusing on the condition of being "less developed" more than on specific cases of corrupt practices and the means of curbing them. Excusing himself for using sweeping generalizations, he claimed that "the deplorable state of business morality which [existed] in so many of these countries [was] one of the results of their attempts to solve [their] problems by modernising their economies and their societies".

Goh's point of departure was that most people in LDCs were involved in subsistence farming.

> Farmers in third world countries are poor because their output is low. Output is low because technology is backward and the size of farms is small. Backward technology is both the cause and the effect of poverty. Most poor farmers are illiterate and so find it difficult to acquire capital and to use modern technology which requires the use of capital. It is a depressing state of affairs, escape from which is not easy.

Land redistribution or resettlement schemes often failed because these needed enormous and competent state support. The prominence of illiteracy and traditional customs did not help. On the positive side, "the seeds of progress and modernisation" were planted in most places by imperialist powers, in the form of "official agencies and business enterprises".

> Wage employment is the general rule. And the exchange economy exists with currency, banks and other financial institutions. Production is for the market, although invariably for the export market.

It was in this modern sector where contact between LDCs and industrial countries now took place that corrupt practices were to be found since its gradual expansion offered "eventual escape from harsh poverty". Goh contended that "in many of the third world countries this process [had] been subverted by unethical business practices and corrupt administration, and that unless the situation [was] changed, less developed countries [would] not be able to emerge from poverty, no matter how much aid they [received] from rich nations".

Since the end of the Second World War, the common wisdom was for poor countries "to stage a re-play of the actual historical process" that had made advanced countries successful. This basically meant import-substitution as nation-building strategy.

There were a few things wrong with this way of thought. First, little consideration was given to population growth eating up economic growth. Focusing on urbanization and industrialization done at the cost of the agricultural economy, Goh did some quick calculations using Japan's case and argued that Third World countries would have to grow at much faster rates than Japan had so impressively accomplished between the Meiji Restoration and 1940. Second, the need for investment planning by the state was obvious, and foreign exchange had to be properly controlled. Wastage of funds and resources and the building of excess or insufficient capacity had to be avoided.

The need for legislative and administrative control of raw materials, capital, distribution, and finally prices, would soon multiply. Controls put in place — rationing, licensing, monitoring, and so on — quickly fostered a culture among businessmen of sidestepping or smoothening the official process. On one side, the businessmen were eager to speed things up, and on the other, the bureaucracy tended to gain from slowing things down.

Paying bribes might seem a way of speeding things up, but what often happened was that the other side would respond by increasing the number of signatures required. In petty corruption, the spoils were shared "by spreading decision-making over large number of officials". This in itself might not seem serious because the end result was that business transactions gained legitimacy. What was much worse was that monopolies or oligopolies would soon appear since the local market tended to be limited, and in many cases, a permit was tantamount to a winning lottery ticket.

When the stakes are high, the system works in the opposite direction — concentration of decision-making. The bigger the prizes and the higher the level of decision-making in the Government, the fewer are the decision makers and the higher are their positions. For the really big prizes, it is the Big Boss who decides.

The effect of such leadership on society was "widespread cynicism and apathy and finally acceptance of corruption as normal conduct in public administration". In some countries, the situation could reach such a "kleptocratic" stage that teachers would have to pay the headmaster to remain on his payroll, police would levy illegal tolls, and murderers would have the police helping them to erase evidence and hang innocent parties.

In the second part of his talk, Goh targeted "revisionist" economists for arguing that corruption was actually beneficial. He singled out Nathaniel H. Leff as "the most prominent revisionist". Leff had argued in articles such as "Economic development through bureaucratic corruption" first published in November 1964 in *American Behavioural Scientist* that the understanding of corruption was generally oversimplified and its ills exaggerated.

Revisionism, according to Goh, argued firstly that businessmen were better informed than bureaucrats and planners about what customers wanted and their bribery of Third World officials limited the wastage that would be done by misguided policies and inefficient implementation: "According to this school, the reason for corrupt business practices is 'market imperfections' caused by wrong-headed Government policies".

Furthermore, the revisionist would argue, the businessman who managed to out-bribe the field showed superior entrepreneurship. Bribes were also most beneficial at high bureaucratic levels, where the huge sums involved could be channelled as capital into manufacturing industries. Petty corruption would not have that potential. To stop these sums of money from being secreted overseas, bribery and corruption should be made "acceptable to public opinion". The absurd but logical conclusion of such reasoning, according to Goh, was "the more bribes the better".

Goh refuted "these bizarre assertions" in four ways. First, revisionists mistook visible industrial hardware as evidence of beneficial economic growth and failed to consider "production costs, competitive ability, or dependence on high tariff protection for survival". Second, bribery would not correct "market imperfections" caused by state control because the obtaining of a major licence held no guarantee that the monopoly was broken. In fact, the bribery might merely cement the presumed monopoly in the hands of one entrepreneur instead of the state.

Third, these economists made grave erroneous assumptions about industrial establishment in less developed countries in thinking that such initiatives were the result of entrepreneurship and innovation and constituted "the seizure of business opportunities not foreseen by inept economic planners of the Government". What LDCs did in general, Goh elucidated, was to scan lists for imported products that could be locally made instead. Whether bribes were paid or not in attaining a licence to start a factory in line with central planning, one could not term it as a seizing of opportunity or an innovation. Such businessmen, Goh exhorted, did not deserve the title of "entrepreneur" at all.

Fourth, bureaucrats functioned in hierarchies where decision-making powers depended on rank. And at the end of the line were the politicians. Revisionists tended to treat bureaucrats as "faceless functionaries" while the reality was that there were "levels of discretion in Government decision-making" that they failed to consider.

In the end, a culture of corruption would not be conducive to economic growth and would offer little incentive for corporate expansion or for keeping price levels competitive.

Good business ethics and sustained economic growth seemed to gel smoothly in Goh's mind.

> When businessmen earn money the hard way, i.e. the honest way, they do not engage in meaningless extravagance. Profits are not spent in conspicuous consumption but are ploughed back into the business. Where, however, business profits are the results of favours granted through bribery, the effects are different. The businessman himself may or may not re-invest profits earned. This depends on whether he can secure more favours to start new monopolies. In that event, he would be imprudent not to stash a good portion of his profits in an unnumbered Swiss Bank Account. Patrons behave differently. Since they have acquired vast fortunes by virtue of the positions they hold and not because of work put in, the temptation to spend freely becomes irresistible. Almost invariably, there is competition among patrons to impress one another and the general populace. This is why we so often witness gross extravagance among the wealthy in third world countries.

Goh ended by reverting to the incongruence with which he started his talk, between peasant values and the modernization that emanated from urban centres. He relied on George Rosen's study on *Peasant Society in a Changing Economy* (1975), which argued that less developed countries could only be understood through a study of social factors and not merely economic variables.

> Peasant societies have different social structures, different perceptions of right and wrong, good and bad, and different expectations of life as compared to people in modern industrial

countries. Thus, when the forces of modernisation work in
their societies through the growth of cities, the establishment
of business corporations, and the expansion of government,
the impact on these societies can take curious and unexpected
forms.

What interested Goh most about Rosen's study was the patron-
client relation that was central to peasant politics, culture, security
and ethics. A modern government based on the hierarchic
structure of traditional peasant life would "run along the lines of
the peasant family or village" (Rosen 1975: 233). Goh quoted
extensively from Rosen's argument on this point, since he could
"do no better".

> In relations with the private sector, all too often the governments
> have regarded the private industrialist as a client. Controls are
> seen as a way of enforcing this clientage, and of thereby
> exchanging a private contribution to the governing group for a
> required permit. When controls have been used in this fashion,
> they have contributed to the building up of inefficient firms,
> which in turn require special protection and assistance. [...]
> This incestuous relationship creates an oligarchy of political
> leaders and industrialists who jointly control the political and
> industrial system. (Rosen 217, 234)

In contradistinction to the caricatured revisionist view that more
bribery was better, Goh's remedy for corruption in less developed
countries, given how licensing and patron-client culture fostered
dubious practices, was "to free the economy of licences wherever
possible, especially those which [provided] incentives for large
scale business corruption", largely meaning import and foreign
exchange controls. Where the economy was too weak for such a
measure, licences should be publicly auctioned.

At the same time, Goh doubted that such remedies would
be applied anywhere, due to "powerfully vested interests

established in corrupt practices". Revolution was not to be recommended either, judging from the fate of those who had suffered that process.

Nevertheless, there was hope. This was embodied in the success stories of Taiwan and Korea. Both had highly competitive export industries as well as high agricultural productivity at the same time. In fact, manufactured goods in South Korea went from constituting 14% of total exports in 1960 to 82% in 1975. Somewhat prematurely, Goh supposed that the type of corruption described earlier no longer existed in these countries.

The success of these countries, as Goh saw it, was due to a successful switch from import substitution to export-oriented industries. The competitiveness of the international market helped to eradicate the inefficient companies that were based on the patron-client system. A new breed of entrepreneurs thus emerged "not through patronage but through natural selection in the hard school of competition".

Interestingly, Goh did not include Singapore in this comparison despite the switch to export industries that he had masterminded in the 1960s. While modesty before an international audience might have been a reason for this, what is more probable was that Singapore could not be properly considered an agricultural economy at independence, especially when compared to the other two polities.

Be that as it may, two others factors that worked in Taiwan's and South Korea's favour were equally applicable to Singapore. The first was that a small domestic market acted as a compelling force for the economy "to join the international rat race, in the course of which the nation must abandon the immoral habits of the past". Second, lacking resources, they could not continue "living the easy way by exports of raw materials as a means of solving their problems with balance of payments".

Goh ended his already extensive talk with two matters that continued to puzzle him. Did Taiwan and South Korea manage the shift in economic systems because of the rise of a class of industrialists and financiers who demanded new rules, as had been the case in Victorian England? Or was it their leaders — namely Chiang Ching-kuo and Park Chung Hee respectively — who "realized that their countries could not make the progress they aspired to unless higher moral standards of conduct in the government and in business were enforced"? Goh left the question to the revisionists that he had adopted as opponents in the debate to answer.

Lastly, he used the example of Latin American countries caught in the middle income trap, with their politics swinging between populist governments and military regimes, to discuss Max Weber's postulation that the Protestant Ethic was a necessary ingredient in "the difficult and painful transition from an agrarian to an industrial society". Such a journey, he ventured, could not be achieved "purely through correct economic measures".

> What is required, in addition, is a strong commitment at some stage to high standards of moral conduct on the part of both government and business leaders. Only then will it be possible for a backward society to go through the prolonged trauma which we call modernization.

As a sign of the Singapore government's growing interest in social values, be these styled "Confucianism" or "Asian Values", Goh affirmed that what was needed for such a transition was "positive attachment to government and spiritual involvement in society, both of officials and people".

Goh's understanding of this issue in 1979 echoed views he had aired on an Australian Broadcasting Commission radio talk show in early 1967. The separation from Malaysia seemed still fresh in his mind when he spoke on "The Abolition of Poverty". He noted then that Malay culture considered "the spectacle of the Chinaman working like a demon possessed, and ruthlessly brushing aside any one or any obstacle that stands in his way...not one that [aroused] Malay admiration". He asked: "And yet without this passion for wealth generating a fanatic determination to accumulate, is it possible for the Malays to achieve the economic success of the Chinese?" Using the Malaysian case, he generalized his point to cover Asian societies in general.

> The trouble is that, given the traditional order and the prevailing ethos, none of their leaders dares even to contemplate the stern measures that need to be taken to propel their societies forward. To me this, rather than the technical problems of economic planning, is the real dilemma facing Asian countries today. [...] The integrated, comprehensive, all-embracing approach to these vital problems of the modernization process has yet to be made. Asia has produced a Mao Zedong; it has yet to produce its Max Weber. (Goh 1967a)

Goh's conviction on this point was strong and consistent, and his reasoning concerning the painful transition from traditional values to modern materialism remained unchanged throughout his life.

THE DANGER OF ANOMIE (1980)

In gripping synchrony with his involvement in education policy-making, Goh's concern grew about the negative moral and psychological problems that Singapore's speed of advancement and its need to adapt to global dynamics had generated. His dislike of the 1960s dissident movement in the West, for example, was palpable enough.

On 2 August 1980, he chose to speak on "The Danger of Anomie" at the inaugural meeting of the Tamil Language and Cultural Society. He adopted the sociologist Robert MacIver's definition that "anomie signifies the state of mind of one who has been pulled up by his moral roots, who has no longer any standards but only disconnected urges, who has no longer any sense of continuity, of folk, of obligation".

The tail end of MacIver's definition, which Goh did not use for the occasion, is even more damning of this modern human condition.

> The anomic man has become spiritually sterile, responsive only to himself, responsible to no one. He derides the values of other men. His only faith is the philosophy of denial. He lives on the thin line of sensation between no future and no past. (MacIver 1950: 84–85)

Goh's short speech to the Tamil society that day was of a gloomier nature than was normal for him. What was causing worry — and this concerned the Chinese in Singapore as well as the Tamils — were two things: "the wholesale adoption of a foreign language and the chase after money".

The global trend towards the use of English was putting pressure on Singapore families. The dropping of various mother tongues to accommodate this development was quite unique, and there was real cause for worry that "anomie" would set in. A policy of bilingualism was therefore being implemented in Singapore, along with "Speak Mandarin" campaigns. If the majority group were to suffer from anomie, then all groups would be even more threatened.

At the same time, the relentless pursuit of wealth was leading to the abandonment of "social norms of conduct such as honesty and moderation", and "if there [was] something to what the sociologists say about anomie [being] disruptive of social order and political stability", then there was indeed cause for concern, he said.

Singaporeans were losing their traditional values. Moral education may help to a point, Goh noted, but what was obvious was that "we must not abandon our cultural past". Some incongruence in Goh's thinking is evident here. While he had often argued that "traditional values" stood in the way of successful modernization and industrialization, he was now responding positively to recent calls by the public to introduce moral education in schools based on "what [was] vaguely called 'traditional values' ".

Chapter 7

EDUCATION AND KNOWLEDGE

The road to modernity in higher education may need a reinforcement of [...] traditional values, not a break with the past.

— Goh Keng Swee
(University of Hong Kong, March 1993)

In August 1978, Goh was tasked by Prime Minister Lee Kuan Yew "to look into the problems of the Ministry of Education with a team of your own choice". No terms of reference were given because "the field was vast, the problems innumerable, the objective simple". This objective, Lee later wrote in his official response to the final report, was "to educate the child to bring out his greatest potential, so that he [would] grow up into a good man and a useful citizen" (*Report on the Ministry of Education* 1979: iii).

The team concluded its report on 10 February 1979, the same day that Singapore had its largest ever by-election. The latter event was triggered by the demise of a PAP Member of Parliament. The timed resignation of six party veterans as part of the party's drive to renew its ranks meant that seven constituencies held polls that day, two of which were walkovers for the PAP (SE). Significantly, on 13 February that year, Goh became Minister of Education, and would remain so until his retirement. Heading this new ministry was thus a heavy responsibility that came at the end of his political career. He had however always held strong views on education, and his early opinions can here act as a point of departure for our appraisal of his later contributions.

Interestingly, Goh participated in a student debate held at the University of Malaya in October 1958 where he led the opposition against a motion that read: "Where the state largely finances a university it should have the right to determine and direct university policy". *The Straits Times* reported him arguing against the "absurd and indefensible" motion, saying that the university's primary duty was "the pursuit of knowledge and not turning out leaders for political parties or staff for the civil service". His side, which included student Ernest Wong and lecturer Dr Wang Gungwu, won the debate (*ST* 30 Oct 1958).

EDUCATION REFORM (1967)

Goh was Guest of Honour at the 81st Founder's Day reunion dinner at his alma mater, the Anglo-Chinese School, held on 1 March 1967. The speech he gave that evening, titled "Education Reform", was written in uncharacteristically simple language. This could have been in consideration of the mixed audience of about a thousand comprising "Old Boys (not to mention Old Girls), teachers, parents, friends, students and well-wishers" (ACS 1966/67: 27).

And so, twelve years before he was asked by Lee Kuan Yew to lead a high-powered team to work out education reforms, he publicly presented views on the subject. The times were different no doubt, but in studying the earlier case, we can at least gain a glimpse of what he personally — and not as head of a committee — considered essential in the education of the young.

Singapore, he said that evening had now come to the end of "the first phase", which was simply to provide a place in class for every child of school-going age. His approach to the next phase, he said, was to consider what the "model citizen of the future" should be like in order to discern what changes to the school system were necessary.

To start with, there had been "far too much emphasis on academic performance". Railing against "this obsession with getting outstanding results in the Cambridge examinations", he argued that too much time was spent on studying and not enough on "the physical and moral side of life". If examinations were for distinguishing the bright and clever boys and girls from the less bright and clever, and such a divide was certainly needed "for purposes of university entrance and maybe eventually for selection of candidates in the Civil Service and other occupations", then "three or four subjects" would do just as well as a larger number to discriminate between "excellent, good, fair and mediocre".

> In fact, that is what we should do and what people in advanced countries are doing. The preoccupation in Singapore with examination results is unnatural and unhealthy and we should bring it to an end as early as possible.

Good performance in exams only proved one thing, he believed, and that was "the possession of good examination techniques", and did not say much else about the person's integrity and character, which were "just as important as intelligence and more important than the mastering of examination technique".

Apart from participation in physical activities, Goh identified three other "aspects of education" which had been neglected in Singapore. These were namely creative imagination, character and moral values. Imaginative thinking, he said, was cultivated through intellectual games like chess or through physical activities such as outward bound training courses.

> It is inhibited by parrot-like teaching of textbooks and I hope that abominations of this kind will cease in all schools. [...] It is only when a person thinks creatively that he is capable of initiative, that he can form his own judgements on matters and that he can be entrusted with great responsibility.

Character, Goh ventured, was something quite separate from intelligence. A person could have one without the other. The British public school system put stress on character-building, and that was something Singapore should follow, he said. But then, character and intelligence were not sufficient in the creation of the desired citizen. After all, "pirates, brigands and gangsters [had] imagination and character in ample proportions". What they lacked was moral stature.

> Without a widely accepted code of moral values, Singapore will remain what it is now — a community which is basically self-centred and selfish. Such a community may be all right if it is governed by others, but it will not survive long as an independent democratic national state if the more successful citizens continue to place their self-interest before the interest of the community. [...] At present we have a community which tends to be complacent and arrogant when successful. At the first signs of coming troubles, our people are liable to panic.

HOW THE INTELLIGENTSIA CAN MAKE THEIR CONTRIBUTION TO SOCIETY (1967)

Goh agreed to officiate at the annual dinner and ball of the Australian Alumni held at the Chinese Chamber of Commerce on 11 March 1967, and was asked to give a speech on how the members of the alumni could contribute to society. Goh said that he had recently noted that the intelligentsia in Singapore were becoming more aware of "the responsibilities which they [had] to assume". The start of the People's Defence Force had encouraged staff and students from the University of Singapore to come forward, and the fact that doctors sometimes disqualified "lecturers and professors whose shoulders [were] stooped by age and whose vision [had] been dimmed by the reading of books" only showed that medicine was not a science: "It is an art, and doctors are no better than economists or historians in diagnosing what has gone wrong".

In what seemed a discharge of sustained irritation, Goh attacked "a curious view" held by some and that had been communicated to foreign diplomats and journalists that the Singapore government disapproved of dissenting opinions, "even to the extent of dispatching Special Branch agents to search for the heretics and persecute them in one way or another, for instance, by disqualifying them for jobs, refusing them passports and so on".

> These timid people flatter themselves if they believe that they are worthy of being targets of Special Branch operations. The Communists and their open-front operators, in whose activities the Special Branch has professional interests, have at least the quality of courage, which is what these people manifestly lack. And without guts, they cannot be a danger to anyone, least of all to the PAP Government, however much they may delude themselves into believing they are. I suspect that the raising of the Special Branch bogey is really a psychological defence mechanism, to rationalise away their feeling of inadequacy.

The PAP government, he said, actually welcomed controversy. The absence of open debate — apart from "Barisan mid-summer madness" — in Singapore, except on trivial matters, was serious, and had to stop. The unfounded fear of the government, he ventured, was one reason. If that were the only reason, then the intelligentsia in Singapore would count as "the most cowardly and spineless intelligentsia in the world". If they really believed that they were ruled by tyranny, then it should be their duty to rebel, "even to the point of taking up arms against the Government".

Such words could not have been conducive to a comfortable and relaxed mealtime for Goh's dinner companions. He did, however, think that there was a second and more acceptable reason for this "deplorable absence of articulation", which was that "the English-educated intelligentsia [were] uncertain of their position in society, and in fact, [did] not understand in all its complexities, the society in which they [lived]".

This echoes Goh's deep conviction, expressed at various times throughout his life, that analyses of Singapore's politics and economics relied excessively on "abstract principles *in vacuo*", or concepts born of alien assumptions.

> But if you go to any other country, you will find that the Australian academic will discuss Australian education, the American academic will discuss American education, the French, French education. It is only among the Singapore egg-heads that you will find this extraordinary propensity to discuss abstract principles unrelated to the surrounding reality. I think it is this factor which is the main reason for the small amount of dissenting views and, indeed, any other kind of opinion on Singapore's contemporary affairs.

What the intelligentsia needed to do, suggested Goh, was to enact close contacts with people who constituted society's grass-roots, be they living "in the slums of Chinatown, in the new housing estates of Queenstown, Redhill, Aljunied and elsewhere, in the scattered farms and hamlets of rural Singapore". They could join "grass-root organs of the Republic, such as the Citizens Consultative Committee found in each constituency, or management committees of community centres". As a rule, these committees were run voluntarily, by "small businessmen, hawkers, an occasional teacher or clerk, workers, farmers and so on", unrewarded and unrecognized. The absence of the intelligentsia was total.

Not pulling any punches, Goh assumed snobbishness to be a reason why the intelligentsia distanced themselves not only from the common man but from the reality of society itself and from the ability to understand its workings. In a rare show of socialist sentiments and a recurrent expression of his low regard of the educated class, Goh promised that the intellectual would find "the common man" quite a discovery.

> He is a sturdy individual, honest, dependable, hard-working, generous to a fault. You will take great pride in leading people such as these. You would have re-established your contact with your society. In this way, all of you will discover your proper role in our society and some of you may find in it your fulfilment.

His apparent aversion to the intelligentsia may seem odd, given that he was one of the most, if not the most, educated minister in the PAP. But the basis for this sentiment seemed to be the intelligentsia's tendency to find refuge behind a wall of privileges and abstractions. This timidity was what irritated him. He wished for their participation, Singapore being uniquely "a government of egg-heads [...] and not a government of generals, landlords, money-lenders, professional politicians or plain down-right thugs". But what got to him was how slowly they were going about it.

His final observation that evening was scathing, honest, and brilliantly insightful; perhaps more revealing of him and his concerns than of those he reprimanded.

> There is a regrettable habit here to equate political views and action and even nation building activities with passionate declamation of lofty ideals and high principles or the striking of heroic postures and attitudes. Frankly, I find all this repellent. I think it is a lot of pretentious humbug. I am more interested in what people do, not what they say. The important thing is to tackle concrete problems as they exist, not to lay down woolly abstract principles. There are no crusades to mount, only a lot of work and a myriad of problems at all levels of society. You may be an idealistic kind of person or you may be a selfish one. That is between god and yourself. But you have a function to perform, the function of leadership, and if as a class you abdicate this responsibility you only have yourself to blame if collectively you come to a sorry end.

Goh himself was considered by Lee Kuan Yew to be his own "resident intellectual *par excellence*", who "with his clear mind and sharp pen [...] was my *alter ego*, always the sceptic, always turning a proposition on its head to reveal its flaws and help me reshape it". His "intellectualism" was obviously fixated on practice, where the context that specific concepts were coined to function within, and the presuppositions that made them valid, were always clear to him. From this grew his intolerance of what he saw as lazy and opportunistic intellectualism, where "heroic postures and attitudes" tried to pass for profundity and ethical positions (Lee 2000: 510).

A reminder is in order at this point that between 1942 and 1958, Goh was almost uninterruptedly a top civil servant engaged in ground-breaking social research, and his academic credentials were gained during breaks from this, his main adult occupation before he openly joined politics to participate in the 1959 elections. This observation helps explain his strong conviction that social science — as with economics — had to be practical in essence. Already in *The Economic Front from a Malayan Point of View*, the monograph he published in 1940 soon after leaving Raffles College, his tendency to adapt approaches to context was evident. During the Japanese Occupation, he was recruited to work at the tax office, and after the war, he joined the Social Welfare Department and managed Singapore's first social survey. Before that had been finalized in 1948, he had moved on to study in England, where he stayed for three years. Soon after his return to Singapore, he led pilot studies on the health situation on the island, and when that initiative was ended prematurely, he directed the momentous survey that led to the influential report published in 1956 on *Urban Income and Housing*. By then, he had been immersed in his doctoral research at the London School of Economics for over a year. When he was awarded his Doctor of Philosophy degree at the end of 1956, the PAP had been in existence for two years, and Goh's increasing involvement in politics was irreversible.

Thus, there was no time in Goh's adult life when academic work had taken place without him being simultaneously involved — and deeply — in social or political questions. His appreciation of the role that the social sciences could play in Singapore's nation building was therefore strongly infused with a spirit of social activism, and although much of his pre-PAP writings were admirably academic, the passionate intention to identify practical solutions was always proximate.

His disappointment with what he saw as a cop-out by Singapore's post-Independence intellectuals in deference to class-based snobbishness and intellectual timidity must therefore have been deeply felt.

PROPOSAL FOR A RESEARCH INSTITUTE FOR INDONESIA AFFAIRS (1966)

The man all acknowledge as the architect of Singapore's economy and defence was thus one who was unendingly engrossed in analysing the educational structure of the country and its role in nation building. When he took over as Minister of Interior and Defence in 1965 in the midst of the confrontation with Indonesia, he could not but have been deeply cognizant of the fact that Singapore's security — and the future of international ties within the region — relied on correct knowledge about the political economy of surrounding countries.

Indonesia was in a very unstable state at that time. The Partai Komunis Indonesia (PKI) celebrated its 45th anniversary grandly in Jakarta on 23 May that year, putting a scare into President Soekarno with its talk of a "council of generals" allied to it. The President was rumoured to be having serious health problems as well, and inflation was running at an astounding 60%. The 30 September Movement that year unleashed a six-month witch hunt for communists and their sympathizers, with deaths finally totalling anything between 500,000 to 3 million people. By March 1966, the President's power had been properly curtailed by Suharto, who would officially take over power exactly a year later. The confrontation between Malaysia and Indonesia was still ongoing, and would wind down to a close only in August 1966. (Hardoyo 2007: 13–14: Yusuf 2007: 18).

On 1 October 1966, on returning from attending the United Nations General Assembly and visiting European and American universities, Goh told reporters at the airport that he would propose to Cabinet the establishment of a post-graduate study and research institute for the study of Southeast Asian affairs. This body would be distinct from the two universities (*ST* 2 Oct 1966).

His proposal was ready within two weeks. In a memorandum dated 14 October 1966, he laid out his thoughts about the research institute in his typical thorough fashion. He had been studying top research institutes in the West during his recent trip and had discussed various issues with academicians such as the Indonesianist Professor George McTurnan Kahin at Cornell University. Goh now wished to start a research institute on Indonesian affairs, sensing that "our ignorance of Indonesia and her people [was] at once vast, comprehensive and frightening".

> We know more about Melbourne than Medan, more about the English Channel than the Sunda Straits. We know that General Nasution and Adam Malik are Bataks, but we do not know what a Batak is, and how many there are of them, where it lies, and how is it that they produce two of the top leaders in Indonesia. How is it that General Suharto consults a Sooth-Sayer? What kind of army is it that throws into prominence a person who believes in the occult?

As long as Singapore retained its ignorance about important neighbours such as Indonesia which colonialism's expediencies had forced on its subjects, its policies were going to be "reactive", and not proactive. Small countries like Singapore "[did] not shape world events or history but [were] shaped by history and world events", he proclaimed, and what she needed was "a delicacy of perception" of affairs in neighbouring countries.

The best way to develop this 'delicacy of perception' was "to bring together high quality intellects trained in a variety of disciplines and get them to address their minds to these problems as a full-time occupation over a long period". Official reports and assessments from the Foreign Service and Intelligence sources did not suffice: "One does not acquire the perspective of history either from producing or reading these".

There were other less obvious and equally important advantages that would come from having close contacts with scholars from other countries studying the same thing, be they stationed in Indonesia or USA, he said. In the late 1960s, the USA was also investing a lot of resources into Indonesia research. Knowing what others thought they knew and how that influenced policy would be of advantage to Singapore.

One further benefit that such an institute would bring was to provide a place where promising personnel from Foreign Service and Intelligence personnel could do a spell of research work. It could also be a source of recruitment in the longer term.

In his study of research institutions in the West, Goh had concentrated on three: the Royal Institute of International Affairs (Chatham House), the Council of Foreign Relations, New York, and the Rand Corporation, apart from graduate schools in the USA. None of them was what Goh thought should be his institute's focus, which was "research into matters not of immediate value in policy making but which [were] necessary to the development of well-rounded expertise".

Something that fascinated Goh more was the comprehensiveness of the Area Studies Programme that he witnessed in American universities. Indeed, he was impressed by the "tremendous volume of organized study on Asia" that was going on in the States. This university-based model would be easiest to implement in Singapore, he thought, except for the fact that the government and the University of Singapore suffered a "regrettable lack of rapport". This he blamed fully on the university, where the culture, due to "the expatriate faculty members of the University, especially those recruited from India, Pakistan and Ceylon and serving in the Philosophy Department", propagated "an extraordinary doctrine of loyalty to the international community of mankind", and not to nation-building concerns.

Goh worried that the power the institute's director would have may allow personal interests to override core areas of research. Furthermore, the University of Singapore, being based on the British system, lacked experience in inter-disciplinary co-operation, and the jealous guarding of domains would prove an "insuperable" handicap. Nanyang University was in the midst of reorganization, and could not take on the extra burden. A third alternative was to create the institute as a government body. He advised against this however, because there were too few capable officials available for any to be spared for this new field of work. Besides, if mediocre scholars from neighbouring countries were to be refused positions at such an institute, the government could be placed in a sensitive situation. Some of these countries, Goh stated, were "exceedingly sensitive to imagined slights to their national honour".

The solution, then, was to start an autonomous research institute. This would work closely with the ministries and the universities under a board of trustees representing key ministries, academic departments, the business and professional world, and important foundations. This board would guide the director without interfering in administration or research, which would be the latter's responsibility.

Goh also thought it wise to have someone with an academic background as director in the beginning, since such a person would be more capable of establishing good relations with Singapore's universities. Professor Wang Gungwu — a Malaysian historian — was the person he thought most suited to be the first director, "and every inducement should be offered to secure his services". But should Wang not be available, then some American involved in the Area Studies Programme could be recruited for "two to three years". Someone from the Rand Corporation, for example, could then take over.

However, Mao Zedong's Cultural Revolution was then in full swing, and Wang's academic curiosity was strongly drawn towards China and not towards Indonesia or Southeast Asia. He therefore declined Goh's offer. Incidentally, this interest in China led Wang in September 1968 to accept an offer from the Australian National University to head its Department of Eastern History (Benton & Hong 2004: 5).

In a letter to George Kahin dated 19 October 1966, Goh wrote that he was sending him a copy of his research institute proposal under separate cover, and was quite confident that he could convince Professor Wang to be the first director. Some Cornell publications had already been sent to Goh, which in effect were the first acquisitions for the institute's library (George Kahin papers).

In later correspondences, Goh thanked Ruth T. McVey, who was also at Cornell, for help rendered to him especially through her book, *The Rise of Indonesian Communism* (1965), in his preparation for a talk to be given at the Australian Institute of Political Science on 28 January 1967. His wide-ranging lecture was titled "The Nature and Appeals of Communism in Non-Communist Asian Countries". In this context, what Goh had to say about communism in Indonesia at that time is of great interest to us.

What made PKI, the Indonesian communist party, different from other Leninist parties, Goh said, was its decision in the early 1950s to abandon the principle of being a conspiratorial vanguard party in order to re-enter the nationalist mainstream by becoming a mass organization. Despite many apparent successes, the party was strangely vulnerable.

> Security against their arch enemy, the Indonesian Army, depended not on a Leninist secret organization of cadres nor on a Maoist rural sanctuary, but on the goodwill of President Soekarno.

Perhaps it was this condition, Goh ventured, that encouraged the PKI to mount what became known as the 30 September Movement following rumours that President Soekarno was gravely ill. The structure and the strategy of the PKI therefore differed greatly from the Malaysian Communist Party, which remained Leninist in structure throughout its existence. The realization of this key difference on Goh's part may have been a factor that convinced him that Singapore was dangerously ignorant of details concerning its southern neighbour, and the country was therefore in need of an institute that would specifically study Indonesia.

In any case, the institute that Goh envisaged in 1966 was more academic in nature than it was anything else. It would cover subjects such as Economics, Political Science, History, Geography, Social Anthropology, Demography, Linguistics and Art. Research staff would consist largely of Singaporeans or those willing to take up Singaporean citizenship, and the search for talent would cover even outstanding pre-university students who would be sent to top American universities against an agreement to be bonded on their return. Researchers would also be encouraged to teach at undergraduate or postgraduate levels, but should in normal cases not accept supervision duties.

Goh's sense for vital details was evident throughout his presentation of how the institute would come into being, and how its structure would be like within a decade. What was immediately needed, he reckoned, was recruiting the right director, building the premises, finding a librarian, and funding the purchase of materials for the library. The librarian should be versed in English, Dutch and also Bahasa Indonesia and Chinese.

The institute should be sited on the university campus as close to its own library as possible, and its initial stage of development should be completed by 1976 when the first selection of staff done in 1967 were back from their studies. Although ministries may submit research projects to the institute, the director should nevertheless have "a right to refuse to undertake such work". Relations between the government and the institute were best kept informal, Goh decided, and researchers could benefit ministries with their expertise by acting as consultants from time to time. Also, studies of other Asian countries should not start prematurely "to the detriment of Indonesian studies". He also cautioned that "any attempt to sacrifice quality" in order to complete staffing arrangements in time should be avoided.

Throughout the memorandum, Goh's mind was indubitably oriented towards security issues; however, his perspective stayed long-ranging and comprehensive. The estimated cost by 1976 was in his calculation definitely worth spending, being only "equivalent to the annual cost of maintaining a battery of heavy mortars". Never wandering far from practical considerations in envisaging an autonomous institute, Goh suggested that its staff not be paid better than university staff so as not to "engender resentment and jealousy and thus inhibit co-operation with the University". What the institute, being new, had to offer was "quick promotion prospects". He even asked that reflection be given to the problem of staff being lost to the university, the government and even foreign institutions, and concluded by suggesting that "it may be in the interest of the Institute to have its less able staff (possibly recruited in the initial period) transferred to the University or Government".

The Institute of Southeast Asian Act was passed by Parliament on 7 June 1968, after a third reading. By then, Goh had returned to the Finance Ministry. The Association of Southeast Asian Nations had also come into being, providing a new infrastructure for intra-regional security and cooperation which was not there when Goh first envisaged the institute. Although security was its immediate concern, the Bangkok Declaration signed on 8 August

1967 to found ASEAN did interestingly include among its goals the wish "to promote Southeast Asian studies" (Aseansec).

When the Act was first read in parliament on 31 October 1967, Singapore's Minister of Education, Ong Pang Boon, stated that the institute would "carry out systematic research into affairs of South-East Asian countries, their history, geography, ethnography, economics, political science, culture, etc." (Parliamentary Debates). In between the Bill readings, Singapore had gone through its first general elections, with the PAP winning all the seats on 14 April 1968, thanks to a boycott by Barisan Sosialis and other opposition parties.

In the event, the institute's first director was Prof Harry J. Benda, the Professor of History at Yale University and concurrently Acting Director of the Southeast Asia Studies Programme in Yale University. Benda began his year-long stint in July 1968 and was succeeded by Prof. J. D. Legge from Monash University and then by Prof Josef Silverstein from Rutgers University (1970–1972). The Malaysian geographer Prof. K.S. Sandhu took over in 1972, and stayed until his death in December 1992. The librarian identified to run the ISEAS library, which she did from 1969 to 1987, was Patricia Lim Pui Huen, also a Malaysian (Lim 1998).

The Act passed on 22 May 1968 showed some notable changes made to the ideas listed in Goh's 1966 memorandum. First, the idea of a research institute on Indonesian affairs was now broadened into an institute for Southeast Asian studies, with the research focus being widened accordingly. Interestingly, when Goh first broached the subject with journalists on 1 October 1966, it was Southeast Asian studies, and not Indonesian affairs which he talked about. Second, the establishment of a printing press at the institute was now included.

Interestingly, Legge wrote a letter to Benda on 22 October 1969 to inform him that Goh had been very reassuring where financing for the institute's expansion was concerned. Apparently, the board of trustees had expressed the wish for Legge's successor to be "a permanent man", meaning a local scholar. Goh, who according to Legge's report to Benda was not pleased by this, had exclaimed "with that delightful throaty chuckle":

> Where did they get a silly idea like that? There's no reason why we shouldn't have expatriates for a while yet. There's no Singaporean whom we could appoint. I must let the Board know that they mustn't make silly policy decisions on questions of this kind.

One pressing issue was Indonesian suspicions that the institute was a front for espionage activities, which were strengthened by the fact that Benda and Legge were both experts on Indonesia. Partly to assuage Jakarta's fears, the third director did not have Indonesia as his field of expertise. Silverstein was a Burma expert.

TOWN AND GOWN (1972)

Singapore held general elections on 2 September 1972, and although broadly challenged, the PAP managed to win all contested seats. Exactly a week later, flushed with victory and perhaps still in campaigning mode, Goh spoke at the annual dinner of the University of Singapore's Academic Association.

For the occasion, he said, he had been reading up on the history of Europe's university systems. While the business of running a government was studied in universities under "political science", he felt that much could be learned from studying the ancients, especially by Third World countries. Here again, he expressed misgivings about the usefulness of modern disciplines for developing countries. Such countries, he quipped, did not really need to go beyond Adam Smith for guidance, while a more advanced one, like Singapore, could perhaps adopt David Ricardo. "Anything later than Ricardo is of doubtful value," he proclaimed.

Italy's Bologna emerged as Europe's first university after the Dark Ages following the fall of Rome, Goh continued. Ties between paying students and professional teachers were rather informal at first, and it was only when these law students formed bodies to protect their interests vis-à-vis landlords and professors that what was recognizable as a "university" took shape. A full-time executive was appointed from among the students to deal with administrative matters and as negotiator. Goh titled him anachronistically as "Vice-Chancellor" (VC), a title that appeared only after the Middle Ages. Being a representative of the students, this person wielded substantial power over professors, requiring them to produce detailed lesson schedules that they were bound to keep to for fear of forfeiting a deposit, or being fined. Even their lectures were strictly regulated.

Pushing their advantage, student bodies would sometimes play one city off against another, and sought to improve their conditions by threatening to move. Such student mobility was what led to universities being formed in several other Italian cities.

Competition among cities soon led them to provide stable and improved conditions for their professors in order to attract students. The tide had turned for the professors to such an extent that cities soon used oaths and laws to keep professors from migrating. Professors were now dependent on salaries paid by the city administration and not on student fees.

This nexus between political power and professorial prowess — between "Town and Gown" — took a different course in England. There at Oxford on 10 February 1354, an argument between scholars and a vintner over the quality of the wine served led to an armed battle between the townspeople and the scholar population. No one was killed that evening, but an attack by country folk the following day left many scholars dead. The Vice-Chancellor then asked for royal help. The king complied, and the defeated townsmen and country folk paid a hefty collective fine, and had to do public penance on the anniversary of the episode. This practice was terminated only in 1825.

The Vice-Chancellor of Oxford and his successors pushed their advantage, and much of the jurisdiction over the town, including the taxation of the privileged, was handed over to the university. The town was also divided into districts, and the morals of their inhabitants were scrutinized by a board made up of academicians.

To illustrate further his story about universities, the church, state authorities, power and violence, Goh included the English Peasants' Revolt of 1381. This was a highly significant and bloody rebellion led by Watt Tyler to protest against a poll tax levied to finance the king's wars. It involved scholars at Oxford, but by 1411 was tamed and remained tightly controlled by the church for over a century.

The situation in Paris, where students tended to be very young, was different again. The University of Paris had mastered "the art of playing one part of the establishment against another — city against church, church against crown, dukes against kings and the Pope against all comers". It became extremely powerful and independent to the point of sending envoys to foreign lands. All that ended when Louis XII invaded the university at the head of an army.

Goh asked his audience what the reason could be for the academic community's early history of "violence and lawlessness". Universities in the Middle Ages constituted "a truly international community that used the common language of Latin, and were usually protected by Popes against stately power":

> [They] enjoyed what we now call extra-territorial rights. These
> had their origins in the medieval practice of regarding the
> academic community as members of the church. As men of
> God, they were not subject to civil law but came under the
> jurisdiction of the bishop. The Vice-Chancellor, as the bishop's
> representative, exercised these rights except for major crimes,
> such as murder.

Judging from his references, Goh had apparently based this history
of European universities on H. Rashdall's three volumes edited by
B. Emden and M. Powicke, titled *The Universities of Europe in the
Middle Ages* and published in 1936 by Clarendon Press (Oxford);
and on Nathan Schachner's 1962 publication, *The Mediaeval
Universities* (New York: A. S. Barnes). After giving his history
lesson, Goh wished to touch on two issues regarding the University
of Singapore, namely, its position as "a member of the international
community of academics, and its role as a highly important
teaching institution in Singapore".

> Some years ago, some expatriate teachers, Asian expatriates
> mostly, set out the doctrine at the university that its members,
> both staff and students, really belonged to the international
> community of scholars, and as such owed no loyalty to
> Singapore. This seems to me a manifestly absurd proposition.

Goh denied that academics today actually formed an international
community as they did in the Middle Ages. Strangely, his
argumentation that evening was as strongly Eurocentric as the
"international community" of academics in the Middle Ages he
described in his talk. He was obviously thinking of universities
understood as Western creations, and was therefore not thinking
about institutions of higher learning in general. The history of
such institutions found in other civilizations would certainly
have varied greatly from the European case.

It is when Goh discussed the "internal role" of the university that the reason for his history lesson becomes clearer. He frequently referred to what he saw as erroneous views on Singapore matters being spread by expatriates and foreign experts and being adopted by locals, only to the latter's detriment.

Touching on a sore point, Goh denied that the University of Singapore could be considered part of the establishment. Although individual Cabinet members and prominent figures may also be involved with the university, that did not mean that it was part of the establishment, "in the way that the Oxbridge Universities [were] in Britain", he pointedly added.

The misconception, he ventured, had several reasons. Firstly, expatriate teachers "who have brought with them the anti-establishment attitudes fashionable in their own countries", had spread that notion in Singapore; secondly, some local academics felt that the government was "doing the wrong things". These academics were "misguided", and Goh felt that "their understanding of the social situation and the political process [was] seriously defective".

For example, just before the recent elections, Goh told the dinner guests, some study of Housing Development Board areas concluded that the level of dissatisfaction among the population was high. Foreign journalists echoed this view, and the opposition acted accordingly and contested in those areas, only to be "well and truly slaughtered" by the governing PAP.

> And then there was constant harping on individual liberties. In one party political broadcast during the general elections, an opposition leader even referred to the "garrison state mentality", a phrase used by a geographer from a minor British university who wrote the most fatuous book on Singapore that I have read for a long time. [...] The ghost writer of that occasion as well as others who convinced the Workers Party that individual freedom

> was a momentous issue greatly agitating the minds of the
> electorate — these academics have rendered the PAP yeomen
> service. I hope they remain totally unconvinced by what I say
> for at least another five years, when, with luck, they may
> ensnare yet another opposition party into a false position.

If there was a thread that ran through Goh's thinking over the
years, it was that he thought many so-called experts in reality
lacked concrete knowledge about Singapore, and relied instead
on abstractions and generic ethical positions to generate
arguments. Often, local intellectuals would adopt attitudes from
foreigners whose theoretical insights were incongruent to
Singapore's situation.

Goh also defended the government's decision to put a cabinet
minister as the chief executive of the University of Singapore,
arguing that it was the only practical solution given the various
problems faced by the nascent nation. Toh Chin Chye, the Minister
of Science and Technology and chairman of the PAP since its
formation in 1954, was then the Vice-Chancellor, and had been
so since 1968. Toh's stint was controversial and he was criticized
for being authoritarian. He stayed at that post until 1975.

Goh's reason for highlighting the difficult relationship
between universities and the state to the academic crowd that
evening was to argue in conclusion that "we should not be
unduly worried we have not hit off as well as we could".

EDUCATION IN SINGAPORE AND THE 'TEACHER IMAGE' (1973)

On 17 October 1973, Goh inaugurated the Institute of Education.
He chose that day to speak on the loss of self-confidence among
teachers in Singapore. Interestingly, his point of departure was
some comments made by Phua Swee Liang at a 1971 seminar

held by teachers, called "The Teacher and the Dynamics of Nation Building".

Phua, who would become Mrs Goh Keng Swee in 1991, had obviously left a strong impression on Goh. Phua had stated two years earlier that "the teaching profession [suffered] from a low economic and social status", and what was worse was that "teachers themselves [felt] they [had] lost their identity as individual teachers".

Historically, Singapore's main role as a trading centre meant that education was given very low priority by the colonial masters. After independence, although a lot of resources were put into providing schools, economic growth through manufacturing for export remained the major direction for government policies. The lower risks faced by the teaching profession in comparison with the competitive world of business meant higher incomes in the latter.

But the fall in self-esteem among teachers was more complicated than that, reasoned Goh. What the government had been doing over the last decade was to concentrate strongly on creating attractive opportunities for investors and to increase the chances for these investments to make profits. A strong awareness about business opportunities came into being.

> As a result, people begin to admire wealth, and make the effort
> to accumulate it. In an extreme form, it leads to the worship
> of money, or 'moneytheism' as my colleague Mr. Rajaratnam,
> puts it.

While agreeing with Rajaratnam, who was then the Minister of Foreign Affairs, Goh thought that "no one in his right mind would want to stop our economic growth in order to do away with moneytheism". However deeply he regretted the behaviour of those who had suddenly become rich, he did not at the same time see any way through which this "foolish ostentation" could be corrected; except by "raising cultural standards". That would take time.

Since the prevailing practice was to judge a man by his bank balance, teachers could not possibly enjoy a high social status, though he disagreed that the situation was as bad as Phua had claimed.

Since the government was caught in the business of building the nation, the problems and troubles of teachers did not get the attention they deserved, and again quoting Phua, "the views of teachers [were] never sought before any educational decision [was] made".

Higher pay for teachers was of course an appealing solution. Goh argued, however, that there were limits to this, and what was important in any case were "relative pay rates". These were however determined by forces of supply and demand, "and these unfortunately [operated] against teachers everywhere". While agreeing that a host of suggestions such as a stronger union, better public image of teachers, etc, would help, he thought the basic solution was for each teacher "to believe that you belong to a profession of which you are proud".

> If you want to hold yourself in esteem when you believe that many people do not, you *must* believe that you are proficient in your work. And the best way to cultivate this belief in your proficiency is to be proficient.

Proficiency, he generalized, came from "mastery over techniques" and "a right attitude of mind". The former required a liking for the work being done, and a conviction that it was important work.

While there is wisdom in these words, one has to wonder if the crowd of young and worried prospective teachers listening to

Goh that day appreciated his advice to develop the right attitude instead of being given higher salaries. Goh's final advice to them was that, although their salary scales were not "dazzling", they were not "meagre" either, and what they should do was live within their means.

REPORT ON EDUCATION, AND PARLIAMENTARY SPEECH (1978)

Goh ended his long stint as Defence Minister on 13 February 1978. Just when the so-called Goh Report on Singapore's education system was being finalized, he took over the Education portfolio.

Prime Minister Lee Kuan Yew added his comments to the report four weeks later. These comments are helpful in providing us today with a quick understanding of what the key issues were. Lee reminisced about how difficult it was in the early years for the government to gain authority over the schools. "The communists", he said, "exploited the Chinese voters' natural pride in language and culture." It was only at the end of the 1960s that the PAP secured authority over the educational system. He cautioned the committee that they had to be flexible in implementing changes, and that parents had to be allowed to choose the standards they wished their children to attain in a bilingual system. He vouched for proficiency in English to improve, and that Mandarin had to gradually prevail over the Chinese dialects. Bilingualism would take time to achieve, and in the meantime, society could become more "translingual". By this was meant that one could "speak to each other in different languages [and] understand each other without translation".

The report had failed to discuss two things. These were the moral and character building aspects of education, and the issue of having teachers capable of being good moral examples.

The best of the East and the West must be blended to advantage in the Singaporean. Confucianist ethics, Malay traditions, and the Hindu ethos must be combined with sceptical Western methods of scientific inquiry, the open discursive methods in the search for truth. We have to discard obscurantist and superstitious beliefs and practices of the East, as we [...] reject the passing fads of the West. Particularly important are intra-family relationships. We must reinforce these traditional family ties found in all Asian societies. But we must excise the nepotism which usually grows out of this extended family net of mutual help. (Report 1978: v)

Lee's comments illustrate quite succinctly the policy direction being envisioned for the Ministry. Needless to say, both these comments and the Report itself were widely discussed in the mass media.

Instead of merely summarizing the rather technical *Report on the Ministry of Education 1978* at this point, a study of what Goh said in parliament on 27 March 1979 about the motion promises to give an easier outline on what he thought about the issue. He claimed that his committee had identified "real causes of trouble" in Singapore's education system. These were, *ad verbatim*:

1. The languages of instruction in our bilingual system are not spoken at home for the great majority of schoolchildren;
2. The rapid switch from the Chinese stream to the English stream made necessary the mass production of teachers for the English stream schools, to the detriment of the quality of teaching;
3. One system of education, lasting 12 years, has been tailored to suit the brightest 12%.

Basically, the motion was meant to revise the educational structure to "allow each pupil to study at a pace suited to [his] learning capacity", and which would make him as bilingual as possible. The ultimate goal concerned Singapore's economic future, as well as the relative importance of English vis-à-vis Chinese and other languages used in the country. English was bound to increase in relevance in the years ahead, whether in the service sector, the manufacturing industry or in high technology. Furthermore, one of Singapore's major advantages in competition with economies like Taiwan and South Korea was the population's proficiency in English. Providing multinational companies with appropriately skilled personnel at as many levels as possible would retain that advantage for the country. At the "non-manual level" in work places, English would continue to be the language of choice. What the situation would be at the blue-collared level was uncertain. Automatic promotion — a system practised in the beginning — had meant that more and more students understood less and less. This was replaced in the late 1970s with retention, which was a traumatic experience for those involved, and was therefore counterproductive.

The old scheme of keeping a pace suitable to "the brightest 12%" of students had led to "high wastage" both in primary and secondary schools. The "logical consequences" of this insight was that children should be taught at "different rates according to their capacity to absorb learning". Given that Singapore's situation was unique, one should not expect "too much too soon". "A very good education system" would take time to build; there were "no magic cures, [...] no quick fixes and no short cuts".

The report recommends different streams of education to suit the slow, average, above average and outstanding learners.

Goh would have been aware that his solution did not really dismiss the possibility of traumatic experiences for students classed lower than their mates. The country that the Education Study team finally chose as the model for closer study was Switzerland. But while the Berne system that they found most interesting "[made] no pretensions to being egalitarian" and as many as 50% of students did not move beyond primary school, it was expected that Singapore's streaming would see less than 20% going into the monolingual stream. Streaming was to be based on performance in school and on intelligence tests aimed at identifying so-called late developers.

Goh noted the shortcomings of such methods of assessment, and asked for "flexibility in implementation" particularly to accommodate the varied wishes of parents. The difficulties that would arise were impossible to foresee, he admitted, and aside from giving parents the right to reject an "adverse assessment" of their children, the policy required "a more efficient and sensitive management system in the Ministry of Education" than had existed. This meant that the opinion of school principals and teachers about how the new system worked had to be continually sought.

Here, we should jump ahead in time to study a light-hearted but informative speech that Goh made at the inauguration of Schools Council on 22 February 1981. Exactly two years after becoming a Minister of Education brought in for troubleshooting purposes, he spoke openly about strategy.

The talk illustrates the general task that he saw himself facing. School Councils were being formed, he explained, to rectify the appalling lack of communication between schools and the ministry. These were due to what he kindly termed grave defects in "management practices" within the ministry. A minister, he revealed, had to be a generalist, and not a specialist. Furthermore, he had to be sensitive to public opinion, and be responsible for his ministry and answer to the Prime Minister, the Cabinet and parliament. To do his job well, he had therefore to depend on "a strong organisation staffed with competent professionals and administrators" to which he could delegate tasks. What stayed his main responsibility was "identifying the crucial problems and seeing to it that they [were] solved".

The solving of problems, Goh thought, was not a difficult matter. Once the problem had been identified, the information that was needed became quite obvious. Once sufficiently reliable information had been acquired, the options and the costs could be worked out, based on financial and other trade-offs. The final solution, in truth, was a collective effort.

But after that came the stage of implementation. In the case of education, the schools were where policies became reality in some form. On taking over the ministry, Goh had found that although the staff had integrity and were devoted, "the management was dreadful". He boiled down the problem of defective "management culture" to two factors: the cult of obedience and the cult of secrecy. The first signified the related habits of "giving unquestioning obedience to superiors and demanding the same of subordinates", and any departure from this was "tantamount to disloyalty". In fact, Goh had closed down the Education Development Division because such behaviour was found to be strongly entrenched there, and he had preferred to start things afresh by creating the Curriculum Development and Information Services (CDIS) to replace it. He had also reformed the Schools Division where school inspectors were housed.

[The cult of obedience] stifles initiative among subordinates, encourages servility, gives rise to the formation of cliques and promotes favouritism. Most damaging of all, it is impossible to attract talent to an organisation which engages in such practices or is believed to do so.

This, Goh admitted, was the reputation the ministry had among teachers. Strangely, the army was less authoritarian than the Education Ministry was. The army, in his experience, had an evidently healthier work culture than in schools, where he found the "bowing and scraping" and "the desire to impress" too much to bear. He had actually stopped visiting them.

In fact, Goh had formed a study team in September 1979 to look into the case of the Education Development Division, the resultant report of which enumerated many weaknesses that it graciously noted "were not in any way due to the negligence of professional officers in the Division but rather to *a disorder in the system of working*" (italics added). As Goh himself noted, the report was done by a team of "Systems Engineers, Administrative and Professional Officers" and was therefore limited to "procedures and organisation". He considered it a complement to another report he had commissioned from overseas experts who dealt with curriculum development. Limited in its own way, that report contained no suggestion for reform. Noting that detecting errors was an easier task than recommending remedies, Goh wisely arrived at the conclusion that the problems would not be solved unless they were made known to "the general body of teachers and school principals" (*ED Review* 1979).

The cult of secrecy Goh found harder to understand. In Finance and Defence, the need for secrecy in certain areas was obvious. In Education, where the common goal of all concerned was the best possible education for schoolchildren, open discussion, and not secrecy, should be encouraged.

By creating the Schools Council, therefore, Goh hoped to reverse the lack of confidence, trust and communication that the field of education suffered from in Singapore. This council would have 33 members: thirteen would be from the ministry and 20 principals from schools and junior colleges. Each principal was allowed to bring along one other school member to each meeting, which would be held on the first Saturday of every month. Attendance would be voluntary, and the rate of attendance would indicate the usefulness of the scheme.

(Incidentally, the Schools Council initiative would prove unsuccessful.)

The Goh Report admitted that although the team could identify weaknesses in the system, they could not provide details for solutions. This was a job that would take many years to complete, and would need "the expertise of Ministry professionals directed under an efficient management system".

Two months after his team was formed in 1978 to study the ministry, Goh had ordered a complementary study of "the existing moral education programme in schools". The appointed committee was to "recommend ways to develop a programme that [would] suit the specific educational needs of Singapore" (*Report on Moral Education* 1979: ii). Led by then Communication Minister Ong Teng Cheong, it handed in its report seven months later. The basic conclusion, aside from identifying weaknesses in the existing programme, seemed general in nature, claiming that "the best moral education on paper" would not succeed if "the home and society" propagated conflicting values, and if moral education was confined to school premises. The team maintained that "a loyal, patriotic and useful citizen [could] only be trained through the combined efforts of family, school and society". This ambitious — and necessarily centralist — approach to the inculcation of social morality was functional, and sought not only to produce "good, useful and loyal citizens", but to do so in an inclusive manner involving all the social contexts affecting students.

Specifically, the proposed moral education programme was to cover Personal Behaviour, Social Responsibility and Loyalty to the Country, and was to be taught in the mother tongue. In a final suggestion, the team asked that mission schools be allowed "greater flexibility in implementing their religious instruction programmes" (*ibid*: 12).

After reading the report, Goh remarked that "there must be an intellectual basis which [would] bind the various moral qualities we [deemed] desirable into a consistent system of thought". While the schoolchildren would not be able to grasp "the intellectual content" behind the programme, those who prepared the curriculum and wrote the textbooks had to understand the value assumptions involved. Outside help was needed if the ministry was to turn the committee's recommendations into policy.

When allowing to have the report published, Goh disagreed with the committee on a couple of points. He feared, for example, that its suggestion for students to "avoid dangerous games and acts" would discourage "manly games such as football and rugby" and would undermine the building of "a rugged and robust society". More importantly, Goh thought that a couple of points were in need of greater discussion. First, he thought the "Hua-chiao" — the Overseas Chinese — mentioned filial piety a lot "but [did] not understand its deeper sociological implications and its role in under-pinning the Confucian political system". Second, while tolerance was a virtue in inter-cultural communication, "tolerance of wrong conduct" was not.

> There is too much of this in Singapore. People are reluctant to report to the police misdeeds which they come across. Professionals, such as lawyers and doctors, keep to themselves unethical conduct of their colleagues which come to their knowledge, instead of reporting it to their professional bodies for disciplinary action.

The uniqueness of the Singapore situation often noted by Goh, along with the importance attached to education by parents and the state's proclivity for fast, comprehensive and effective policy in all areas including education, were — and are — major reasons why Singapore's expansive education system was — and is — notorious for continual shifts and innovations. Needless to say, over the years, some of these measures were in effect reversals of earlier initiatives.

For the period when Goh was at Education, the Ministry's 2007 anniversary publication listed the following changes, among others (*Many Pathways, One Mission*): in 1979, the New Education System was introduced with examinations at the end of Primary 3 streaming pupils into Normal, Extended and Monolingual streams, the Special Assistance Plan was implemented in nine secondary schools, Moral Education and the Humanities Programme were introduced, and a merger of different boards created the Vocational and Industrial Training Board (VITB); in 1980, the National University of Singapore was formed through the merger of the University of Singapore and Nanyang University; streaming into Special, Express and Normal courses at secondary level was introduced; the CDIS was formed, along with the Schools Council; in 1981, ethnic Chinese pupils had to register in Pinyin, and Nanyang Technological Institute was established; in 1982, the Music Elective Programme was introduced; in 1983, the Basic Education Skills Training programme was introduced, and; in 1984, a very eventful year, English became the medium of instruction in all schools, the Primary School Proficiency Examination for Primary 3 Monolingual Stream was introduced, primary school leavers were automatically admitted into VITB, the Art Elective Programme and the Gifted Education Programme were initiated, Religious Knowledge became compulsory in

Secondary 3, and the College of Physical Education (merged in 1991 with the Institute of Education founded in 1973 to form the National Institute of Education) was established.

Early in 1982, Lee Kuan Yew had announced that Confucianism would be part of Moral Studies. Later that year, after consultations with Tu Weiming of Harvard and Yu Ying-Shih of Yale, Goh invited a group of scholars to Singapore to help construct the curriculum for Confucian studies (Dirlik 1995: 238–39). The government's worry that Singapore's young people were proving too susceptible to negative Western influence helps explain why the reform of the education system placed so much weight on moral values. The way morals had been taught up to that point was considered highly dissatisfactory, and so, by 1984, Religious Knowledge was introduced to provide the missing but vital philosophical coherence.

However, the subject — in practice sub-divided into Hindu Studies, Confucian Ethics, Bible Studies or Buddhist Studies, etc. — was withdrawn five years later. The programme accentuated differences in religious practices and beliefs instead of providing common ground for moral behaviour, leading to cases of aggressive proselytization. The religious revivalism apparent in the 1980s was also blamed on the government's adopted method of teaching moral values; it drew students away from the ritualism of traditional religious practice to the rationalized versions that they were being taught in schools (Tan 2008: 324).

PUBLIC ADMINISTRATION AND ECONOMIC DEVELOPMENT IN LDCS (1983)

The deterioration of morals in light of the push to modernize society was thus a steady concern for Goh. Not one given to piecemeal measures, he sought a comprehensive solution in the study of classical Confucianism. For this purpose, the Institute of East Asian Philosophies (IEAP) was established in July 1983. He was the chairman of its board of governors until it morphed in 1992 into the Institute of East Asian Political Economy (IEAPE) to reflect a shift in interest from classical to contemporary studies. Goh was the executive chairman and chairman of the new board of directors as well, until 1996. IEAPE was closed down in 1997 to be incorporated into the National University of Singapore as the East Asian Institute (EAI). Its first director was Professor Wang Gungwu, who had just retired as Vice-Chancellor of the University of Hong Kong (Tan 2007: 166).

Goh was invited to give the fourth in the Harry G. Johnson Memorial Lectures series in London. He accepted and gave a talk on 23 July 1983 on developmental difficulties facing less developed countries (LDCs), where he argued for a solution through education policy.* The lecture made use of some comments by Johnson on poor countries as a point of departure.

Goh wished to compare less developed countries with advanced nations, and felt that he had two immediate difficulties doing that. First was the phenomenon where "Western intellectuals and even administrators and businessmen [thought] of LDC institutions more or less in terms of their own". He recognized that habit to be a major source of error in academia and in foreign affairs. Universities in poor countries, for example, were not centres of excellence for learning and teaching and research

---

* In what was a more common habit in later years, Goh relied on the help of others especially when preparing lectures. In this case, he was aided by Quah Kung-Yu, Dr Phua Swee Liang, Dr Teh Kok-Peng and Dr Song Teck-Wong.

Harry G. Johnson (1923–1977) was a prolific Canadian economist who was globally active as a teacher. His work was largely in international trade and monetary theory and he also wrote on growth in less developed countries.

as was assumed in advanced countries. Second, in these less developed countries, "academic freedom and the liberty to speak one's mind in public [were] luxuries which political leaders [had] sometimes to forgo".

Summarily, there were six "blessings" that distinguished advanced countries from less developed countries: the Western respect for law was based on citizens being "members of an orderly society in which individual liberty and property rights [were] ensured in the administration of justice"; universal franchise made leaders sensitive to public opinion; a long tradition of public service allowed for smooth power transitions; a highly competent civil service was maintained; a high level of education existed, and; corruption was absent in high places. Less developed countries tended to lack several, if not all, these conditions.

Goh decided to limit his talk to the issues of corruption, education and the civil service since he believed these to have the most immediate impact on development in poor countries. Furthermore, these were subjects that were generally avoided in the academic literature and other areas as "matters not discussed in polite society" or as "distasteful". As he had argued in *Business Morality in LDCs*" in 1979, Goh said that import-substitution strategies actually encouraged corruption, for various reasons. The end results were that less developed countries were caught in a bind that was quite difficult to escape from — corruption and tax evasion by the rich increased along with income inequalities. Although the last was not necessarily an obstacle to growth, political discontent would be the most likely outcome, when conditions for new international loans led to sudden austerity drives that affected the poor.

The connection between education and economic growth in less developed countries was a harder one to grasp, and experts seemed to be in substantial disagreement on that point. Goh had been reading up on the subject for his lecture, but as usual, he was most insightful when noting conditions relevant especially to these poor countries.

> In many LDCs, pay in the civil service is higher than pay for equivalent work in the private sector because civil-service pay, in the higher echelons at any rate, is related to what expatriate civil servants were paid before the countries achieved independence. One result of these abnormally high rates of pay for graduates has been an excess supply of graduates leading to the widespread problem of unemployed graduates in many developing countries.

This idea is delightfully reminiscent of the protest against high wages that Goh, Kenny Byrne and L.C. Goh launched back in January 1957. All three were with the colonial civil service, and wished to declare publicly when they were about to be promoted to permanent secretaries that their pay scales were too generous. They thus wished for cuts to be made when locals filled those high positions. Goh said then that that demand was part of an inevitable trend moving towards a more egalitarian society (*ST* 5 January 1957).

What was often ignored in studies about education and development — as with the case of corruption — was how distressing the situation was in less developed countries. Goh said that studies showed that an average student in such a country fell into the bottom 10% of students in an advanced country. Why such poor standards?

Goh's hunch was the "brain drain", especially from the more promising countries. Admitting that this idea was disputed, he argued with support from an article by Don Patinkin (1968) that the difference between a first-rate university and a mediocre one lay in "a relatively small number of outstanding people who set the criteria and lend the tone". The loss of a few top personalities could therefore change an institution's level of excellence considerably.

The crucial role played by a crucial few applied in the civil service as much as in the political leadership, Goh reasoned. Here, we are confronted again with his conviction that nation building succeeded or failed depending on the ability of key elite groups. This informed his creation of the Pyramid Club, and his tactic of identifying and employing whomever he thought to be the best man from anywhere in the world to head new institutions.

Again, he argued that "traditional culture" did not encourage "the pursuit of intellectual excellence". It was up to schools and universities to nurture such a culture, pushed on one side by government investments and on the other by rewards offered by success on the open market. Indeed, a spiral mechanism was involved here.

> The loss of talent through the brain drain or, indeed, the failure to develop talent through a proper educational system, results in the deterioration in the quality of government not only in terms of performance standards but also in terms of standards of ethical conduct.

Goh ended his lecture with substantial references to Meiji Japan, one of his favourite examples of a successful case of nation building. Here, he identified lessons that less developed countries today could learn from the Japanese case. Economic modernization and the modernization of political and social institutions, he reiterated, were inseparable processes. The creation of modern institutions had to take place first for industrialization to succeed; and a crash programme was bound to fail for the lack of adequate management and work skills. As in other countries, the release of energy that followed the end of feudalism in Japan had to be properly channelled, and the difficult choices that had to be made during such troubled times were made by "a cohesive leadership of talented and dedicated men over a long period".

Western models, Goh said, had to be meticulously studied before they were industriously applied and astutely adjusted to local needs. Education was rightly seen as an investment in human beings, but that worked only if quality was maintained. It was also proven by the Japanese that success was possible without "tariffs, aid or privileged access to export markets" if the nation's natural advantages were properly utilized.

Beyond all this, Japan had at least two further advantages. First, the population was homogenous, unlike those in many less developed countries today; and second, no brain drain was really possible during that time, when they needed all the talent that they possessed. As Goh saw it, the reason developing countries today were failing was "not inadequate aid or trade, but their failure to establish competent organs of public administration and their failure to develop durable and enlightened social and political institutions".

Chapter 8

THE CASE OF CHINA

If our experience can be used as a general guide to policy in other developing countries, the lesson is that the free enterprise system, correctly nurtured and adroitly handled, can serve as a powerful and versatile instrument of economic growth. One of the tragic illusions that many countries of the Third World entertain is the notion that politicians and civil servants can successfully perform entrepreneurial functions. It is curious that, in the face of overwhelming evidence to the contrary, the belief persists. And so in the name of socialism, equality and justice, millions are denied the escape from age-old poverty which rapid economic growth can provide.

— Goh Keng Swee
(Preface to *The Economics of Modernization*, May 1972)

Goh's retirement from politics was announced on 19 August 1984, four months before general elections, and seven weeks short of his sixty-sixth birthday. A year later, he was decorated with the Order of Temasek (First Class), the country's highest award. He remained deputy chairman of the Monetary Authority of Singapore until 1992 and of the Government of Singapore Investment Corporation until 1994. He was also chairman of the Singapore Totalisator Board from 1988 to 1995.

China's strongman Deng Xiaoping had visited Singapore in 1978, and according to his host Lee Kuan Yew, he went home convinced that the island state was worth studying in light of the reforms that were about to be unleashed in China (Lee 2000: 668). Goh was made Economic Advisor to the State Council of the People's Republic of China on the Development of the Special Economic Zones and Advisor on Tourism in1985. His role in the latter position was to give advice, more on how tourism could earn foreign exchange for China, than on developing tourist sites (Phua 2008). His conviction that foreign exchange was central to the economy was already evident in his first book, *The Economic Front*, and was behind much of his thinking when Singapore's financial system was constructed. Also evident early in his life was his concern with China's needs, as mentioned in his short essay "My Ambitions" written when he was barely a teenager.

He also brushed up on his Mandarin in later years.

Goh separated in 1986 from Alice Woon, his wife of over forty years, and moved to a rented apartment on Orchard Road. He married Phua Swee Liang in 1991 (Tan 2007: 169). The pair travelled regularly; and he spent a lot of time reading about military history and equipment and watching wildlife documentaries (*Today* 17 May 2010). According to Phua, Goh would try to avoid news about Singapore, mainly because he was no longer in a position of power and would presumably feel powerless following Singapore events. This was despite his attachment to the Monetary Authority of Singapore and the Government of Singapore Investment Corporation until the early 1990s.

Goh was further honoured in March 1993 by the University of Hong Kong with the degree of Doctor of Letters, *honoris causa*. In the speech given at the university on that occasion, Goh quoted from Cardinal John Henry Newman, the influential

19th century English writer, that university education aimed "at raising the intellectual tone of society, at cultivating the public mind, at purifying the national taste...at giving enlargement and sobriety to the idea of the age, at facilitating the exercise of political powers, and refining the intercourse of private life". These views, Goh addressed the Vice-Chancellor, conformed remarkably well "with the beliefs of the traditional Chinese scholar on the role of the educated man", and he hoped that the university could persuade the Beijing government to provide its intellectuals with proper pay: "The road to modernity in higher education may need a reinforcement of their traditional roles, not a break with the past".

Newman's views on education were best elucidated in his volume *The Idea of the University* written in 1845. The quote used by Goh is not found there though. Given Goh's concerns about Singapore's lack of high culture, one can imagine that the cardinal's words about "cultivating the mind" and "purifying the national taste" appealed greatly to him.

In order to avoid any repetition of ideas presented earlier, this concluding chapter will concentrate as far as possible on Goh's views about China and her role in global politics and economics. He did indeed concentrate on China after his retirement, partly because that was the direction his thoughts about nation building were moving in, and partly because the People's Republic had come under the control of the pragmatic Deng Xiaoping, who like Goh tended to place economic growth before ideological purity.

PARASITE STATES (1968)

China seemed always to have interested Goh. In 11 November 1968, when Singapore was caught in a multiple crisis and he was moving between the portfolios of Finance and Defence, Goh delivered a speech at the Public Services International Second Asian Regional Conference where he discussed China's history.

Modern times, he said, were marked by three new qualities. First, government intervention had become extremely great and continued to grow; second, the income gap between nations was enormous and expanding; and third, established codes of conduct were being increasingly challenged. Nevertheless, this state of uncertainty needed to be properly contextualized to afford "some relief from the perplexities which confront us", and he believed this could be done through a comparison with ancient China's civil service.

The imperial system was something that evolved over hundreds of years, and Confucian ideas began to be implemented only a half millennium after the Sage's death. Several features characterized it: entry depended on complicated three-tiered written examinations; it relied strongly on ethical principles developed by the Confucian schools, corresponding to what we would classify as "the humanities"; and thirdly, the civil service was an extension of the absolute monarchy.

Chances for entrance into the civil service were minute indeed, and only an estimated one percent of all hopeful candidates could pass. Accordingly to certain scholars, this strange system achieved, first, a cheap method of self-indoctrination where orthodoxy was absorbed voluntarily by the candidates, and in the process, a form of meritocracy that allowed humble folk to gain social status maintained; and second, a way of keeping the best brains occupied, but that kept the emperor dependent of feudal princes.

Goh suggested a third function practised by the civil service, namely keeping imperial excesses within tolerable limits.

Nevertheless, ancient China did experience dynastic cycles of about 350 years, during which a royal house would go from frugality and principled governance to corruption and decay. Given this civil service straitjacket, it was difficult for China to develop what we now know as science and technology.

In Europe, the limiting of monarchical excesses had a more *ad hoc* nature, ranging from power-sharing with barons and bishops to parliaments and free cities. But since there was little of the sudden jumps in productivity that we are now used to, imperial extravagances meant little being left over for the people to enjoy. Governments tended to become parasitic. This state of affairs changed with the Industrial Revolution.

Here, Goh credited Karl Marx for being "a thinker of great originality and power", who realized that the standard of living would now increase tremendously, and poverty could become a thing of the past. For Marx, the enemy were the owners of capital who wished to keep surplus value for themselves. History might have proven Marx wrong, but Goh argued that the man did in his time have "strong justification for his belief".

In response to the tumult of the Industrial Revolution, the state's role increased to cover most aspects of social life. In Europe, parasitic states came to an end, and two new classes — the industrialist and the industrial worker — demanded and obtained "a form of representative government in which rights of the individual, the rule of law, and sanctity of contracts were enforced". "Arbitrary government" came to an end. But alongside this process, warfare became more tragic as well.

In the developing world, even where "the paraphernalia of a modern state" had been adopted, often by leaders "inspired by the vision of rapid and continuous progress", the "parasitical tendencies" of past societies remained strong. Even universal franchise had proved ineffective when the electorate were largely peasants.

In summary, what signified a failing programme of modernization, Goh concluded, was "the lowering standards of public service, both among the professionals and among the political leadership". In olden days, excesses could invoke excuses like divine right. Today's parasitical tendencies relied instead on graft.

> It is this decline in the standards of administration and in the standards of public service that is at the root of economic stagnation. Opportunities for parasitic activities are much more numerous and profitable in emergent countries of today than they were in traditional societies. The modern sector which has been established in most new countries produces a surplus value which the parasites of government prey upon.

Too much emphasis had been put on "the technical aspects of economic development", Goh stated. A backward society could in principle be transformed through education and "the application of science and technology to all forms of production". But we were dealing with societies that were "confused, bewildered and demoralized"; so what was needed for success was an "enlightened government of integrity".

Where less developed countries were concerned, the insecurity of modern times, in Goh's view, was like that experienced in the age of Confucius and in the Greek classical age. But despite us having greater opportunities, the intellectual vigour of those bygone times was lacking in our age.

CHINA'S ECONOMIC POLICIES IN A HISTORICAL PERSPECTIVE (1987)

On 22 October 1987, two years after Goh became an advisor to the Deng regime in China, he spoke at an international conference called "China's Foreign Trade and Investment Policies: Expectations and Opportunities". His argument was that China had entered the final phase in "transforming an ancient civilization into a modern industrial state", and in order to understand its implications, we had to consider thoroughly China's modern history.

A communication gap did exist between China and the West-oriented world, widened further by the keener sense of history that the Chinese had as compared to others. Goh started his history lesson in a conventional manner, taking 1793 as the point of departure, when Lord Macartney visited the aging Qianlong Emperor to vainly ask for trading rights. The Qing Dynasty was at its peak then, and China's doors could not be pried open until a half century later through the Opium Wars. Unlike the Japanese, whose gates were also forced open in the mid-1800s, the Manchu Dynasty did not seek knowledge about its new enemies. Here, Goh quoted again from Sun Zi: "Know yourself, know the other side and you can fight a hundred battles without danger".

External pressure opened up the China market and accelerated the decline of the central authority, leading to chaos and great suffering in the empire for over a century. Civil wars fractured All under Heaven. The Communist Party therefore took over a land that was in desperate need of economic growth in 1949, and gratefully adopted the Soviet Union's system of central planning. Internal conflicts typified the coming three decades. By 1978, after the death of many of the old guards, the party reached a consensus on the need for a thorough reform of economic policies.

According to Goh, the highly centralized planning system brought greatest advantage in the early years. Though heavily criticized, the State Planning Commission managed to produce an impressive network of industries, and almost all products were made within the country. However, production was never enough, and the designs followed were often outdated. The focus on quantity meant that quality and design suffered, and given the centralized system, any initiative could potentially lead to conflicts with central sourcing and bureaucratic practices.

What Deng Xiaoping's attempts to "learn truth from facts" led to was that economic logic as well as the institutional structure concerned with production had to be given major consideration. The first was a simple matter of computing production costs, outputs and demand. Institutional arrangements were a bigger challenge since the large state-owned enterprises were responsible for the total welfare of their employees, and changes within them affected most aspects of the life of huge sections of the population. This situation exerted as much conservative drag as did the party's stiff enterprise management.

Another aspect of the centralized economy was that prices had been kept stable for three decades, and anything other than a slow pace of liberalization on price control would risk high inflation. At the same time, a slow pace of change would lead to a multi-tiered price system where profits would depend more on access to controlled supplies than anything else. Such a price system would nurture corruption.

The Chinese government carried out concerted reforms on the large enterprises. These sought partly to motivate production by permitting some profit retention and allowing more autonomy concerning what to produce and what prices to keep, and partly to reduce the symbiosis between professionals and party committees.

Attracting foreign investments featured prominently in China's scheme of things, alongside "the re-equipping of her factories, communications industries and infrastructure with imported plants and equipment", and the reorganization of research institutes.

What the country was striving for was the creation of a "planned commodity market". Goh thought that "a solid beginning [had] been made but a long journey [lay] ahead". There was no turning back.

> What we are seeing in China today is the final phase of the historical process of transforming an ancient civilization into a modern industrial state. Just as Meiji Japan did 120 years ago, China has decided to come to terms with the modern world of science and technology, of business management and information systems. In the process of modernization, she offers some unique opportunities to foreign investors who understand her policy objectives and who take a long-term view of their investment.

Goh's understanding of Dengist reforms seen against the backdrop of China's difficult relationship with the Western world over the last 200 years was that they would lead to the kind of success that marked Japan's experience in the 19th century. He also kept to the conviction that the survival of non-Western cultures depended on their ability to imbibe the special work ethics, managerial methods, epistemic attitudes and production infrastructure that defined modern economics.

This speech from October 1987 was Goh's take on the first decade of Deng Xiaoping's reform programme, and dealt with dilemmas that stemmed from how the centralist mode of production developed painfully over the thirty years prior to 1978 was being reformed. He did not go into detail about the phases into which some analysts divide Deng's reform process.

Richard Evans for example postulated that after securing power in 1978, Deng first sought to restore institutional patterns formed in the mid-1950s which in effect meant the propagating of the rule of law and the removal of all sorts of political and discriminatory labels. The party and its security apparatus withdrew from their hitherto deep intrusion into society, and instead allowed private life to regain some space. Between 1982 and 1986, Deng worked at rejuvenating state institutions, including the Communist Party, and managed to encourage elderly officials and party members to retire. From 1986, he sought to develop "socialist democracy" through a decentralization of decision-making and management and to recruit better educated and professional younger people into the party. This third phase was a slow one that met with internal resistance. Small-scale student demonstrations had been taking place, mainly against corruption and inflation that in 1985 had risen to 9%.

A key player during these years was Hu Yaobang, the apparent heir to Deng Xiaoping. Hu became the party's third chairman in 1982 and when that post was abolished the following year, became secretary-general. Hu pushed for accelerated reforms in 1986. Encouraged by this, student demonstrations grew in frequency in Shanghai and Beijing, leading to internal disciplining that affected more ardent reformists within the party, including Hu. Hu disappeared from public view. News of his death on 15 April 1989 from a heart attack led immediately to student rallies commemorating him but which soon became the lightning rod for general discontent. His funeral ceremony on 22 April saw 100,000 students congregate on Tiananmen Square. That gathering soon developed into an indefinite strike that swelled in numbers and became more militant. The power struggle that this movement precipitated within the party ended with the tragic entry of the People's Liberation Army into Beijing and the killing and wounding of thousands of civilians (Evans 1993: 251–52; 256–60; 275–300).

The reform movement was in deep trouble.

ECONOMIC GROWTH AND THE INTELLIGENTSIA (1990)

On 8 January 1990, Goh gave the opening address at a conference organized by the Institute of East Asian Philosophies, called "Confucian Humanism and Modernisation: The Institutional Imperatives" (1990). His talk was titled "Economic Growth and the Intelligentsia — A Comparison of Experience in the Mainland and the Periphery", in which he asked the question, "If the economic success of the four small dragons is due to the Confucian tradition, why has the homeland of Confucius not achieved similar success?"

The speech was a long one, comparing the four small dragons to China, and then contrasting the ancient Confucian system of government to the contemporary Communist system.

China's economic future following the Tiananmen Tragedy did not look good, and observers were generally pessimistic about the potential for change under the Communist regime. Goh would not speculate on why some obvious reforms had not been implemented, and which trade-offs and ideological constraints had been decisive: "...the privilege of writing in ignorance of the facts I shall leave to journalists and suchlike bold spirits".

Goh observed one common aspect in the developmental strategy of the four small dragons, namely their export-orientation policy of growth. Huge volumes of low-technological products consequently flooded Western markets, quickly leading to protective measures against them. This in turn forced these small dragons to climb the "technology ladder" and find relevance at higher levels.

What should be noted, Goh said, was firstly that they relied on free enterprise and could take advantage of revolutionary advances in "transportation, telecommunications and information systems"; secondly, fierce competition on the export market tested their ability to adapt and to read customer demands correctly; leading thirdly to the emergence of outstanding entrepreneurs. But unlike the other three, Singapore had to import such entrepreneurs.

Goh admitted that too much praise had been given to government involvement in these cases. Governments merely maintained "a conducive economic environment"; the determining factor was entrepreneurship.

> We should note that competition in the international market produces a Darwinian process that eliminates the unfit among the dragons' entrepreneurs. Darwinian selection separates those with energy, judgement, organisation ability, vision and daring (and a dash of luck) from those deficient in these qualities. Patronage by the powerful counts for little.

As a consequence, incomes became very unequal, but "the adverse political consequences usually associated with it" did not appear. Agriculture workers were absorbed into the tight labour market, and the income of "brainworkers" rose, with entrepreneurs caught in the competitive process of recruiting the best staff from the universities. South Koreans and Taiwanese had the added advantage of easier access to American universities, where they could learn about the American market close up.

The importance of the point about brainworkers laid in the fact that the "major source of discontent in Third World countries", namely unemployment or lower pay among university graduates, did not grow into a big problem. In such an environment, resentment against the successful remained weak: "Ostentatious spending to establish status noticed in stagnating Third World countries is absent in the four dragons".

Undeniably, the Confucian ethic did contribute to their success, Goh said; but at the same time, market competition had eliminated certain traditional attitudes, such as the disdain for merchants or the wish by talented youths to become officials. Proven ability had become more important than nepotistic connections.

In China's case, the growth rate under Deng averaged 7.5% between 1980 and 1983, and increased to 11.7% in 1984–1988. These were impressive figures by any measure, and easily matched those of the four small dragons. Yet, it all ended with a blood bath on 4 June 1989. Why? How was this to be explained?

Goh's point of departure for a deeper analysis of China's inability to match the small dragons was a document published by the Communist Party, titled "Decision of the Central Committee of the Communist Party of China on the Reform of the Economic Structure". This came out in October 1984 in the middle of the second phase of Deng's reform programme.

What the party now sought to do, Goh indicated, was to enlarge further the space for enterprise autonomy and reduce the dependence of enterprises on government departments. Furthermore, ownership had to be separated from management. Pricing reforms had also to be carried out to reflect the relation between supply and demand. The document urged planning authorities to rely increasingly on "macroeconomic levers" such as "money supply, interest rates, taxation and state expenditure".

It was imperative according to the document that "a mighty contingent of managerial personnel for the socialist economy" be created and that "the social standing of intellectuals" be raised along with their "working and living conditions". In 1987, as many as twelve management schools were started throughout the country, with foreign assistance.

According to Goh, weaknesses that developed in this transition from the centralized economy included the multiple pricing mechanisms where "the cultivation of good relations with suppliers and planners could affect profits more decisively than efficient management". A culture of cronyism and corruption was generated and sustained by the transitional system itself.

Breaking the "iron rice bowl" proved more difficult than expected, having to deal with strong habits in the formal distribution of salaries, bonuses and extra items. Thus, "slovenly work attitudes, low productivity and hostility towards quality control" continued to define Chinese workers. The practice of assigning workers to their positions affected the intelligentsia badly, keeping wages and mobility low. And so, while workers tended to favour the system, the intelligentsia did not.

There were more immediate causes for what Goh called "the breakdown" of the 1984 reforms. Certainly, in January 1990, the reform movement seemed stalled. The causes were related to the provincial governments. For one thing, these tended to create their own monopolies and start protected enterprises for the sake of acquiring resources, lowering unemployment and raising tax inflow.

Since the reform of China's banking system was not pursued in earnest, and the central bank continued to function as the state's "chief cashier" even while enterprise reforms were moving ahead rapidly, provincial manipulation of the system to secure loans for pet projects became common. Local branches of the Central Bank were manned by local people, allowing for personal connections to eclipse banking professionalism.

Currency circulation increased fourfold between 1983 and September 1988, when urban inflation almost reached 29%. Goh pointed out that the rural population and industrial workers managed to keep ahead of the inflation, and the ones who suffered most were those with fixed incomes, and government employees whose departments were not involved in economic activities. For the staff of "schools, universities, media agencies, hospital, transportation services as well as the administrative departments" as well as university students, rising prices were a serious problem.

The Tiananmen Tragedy was unlike protest movements in other communist countries in that organized labour did not play a role. Not only was the protest movement in Beijing led by the intelligentsia, the issues were ones that concerned the intelligentsia most. What added fuel to the discontent was the fact that the newly rich were not wealthy through merit, "as in the dragons", but through being relatives of people in high places. Workers, Goh suspected, were not as easily affected by this condition since they generally did not aspire to managerial positions. The intellectuals, in accordance with Confucian tradition, considered such positions to be their natural right.

Here Goh wondered what Confucius would think about the present plight of the intelligentsia. The Confucian State was governed economically by a tiny group of intellectuals, and as one went down the hierarchy and away from the Centre, lower officials trained by the same examination system populated government offices. Communist members numbered 40 million,

compared to the 1.2 million literati found during the later
Qing period.

Confucius would have found these communists lacking in
two other aspects. First, "they [did] not possess a doctrine of
government, such as the literati had in Imperial China, which
[could] serve as a reference point as to what decisions should be
made and how authority should be exercised". Second, the ancient
examination had an authority that stemmed from its long history
and from the social institutions of the time. Those who failed to
make the grade might have envied those who did, but they
would not harbor resentment. The modern system encouraged
both these sentiments. While the first leaders based their
legitimacy on their proven military prowess in uniting the country,
the successors could not.

Nevertheless, the modern Chinese state, according to Goh,
practised at least two doctrines of the past. The first was the
centralized nature of power. The ancient system however was "an
unintrusive government", while the communist government
could not possibly be described as "unintrusive". What the state
seemed not able to do was stop provincial governments from
interpreting central dictates to their own advantage. In a statement
fully reminiscent of Sun Zi, Goh stated:

> In reserving all ultimate power to itself, the State finds itself
> caught in the predicament not unlike that of a general who,
> wanting his army to be strong everywhere, distributes his forces
> equally along the front, only to find that he is weak everywhere.

The second similarity was in the absence of a legal system. This,
Goh claimed, must count as a "serious deficiency". The Chinese
state today was therefore engaged in introducing modern laws
into the equation, for without them, control over the provinces
could not be properly attained. Goh concluded:

> We also sense that at the root of China's troubles, lies a
> fundamental incompatibility between policy objectives on the
> one hand and the operational capabilities of implementing
> institutions on the other, while the mindset of opinion makers
> hinders rather than promotes action to reform those institutions.

The Sunday Times published this lecture as a three-part series in
November 1990, almost a year after it was first given. This strongly
suggests that Goh was contented with his own analysis of China's
situation and its dilemmas. The views that he presented in it can
be cogently complemented with points made by him in several
related contexts over the coming five years. Some of these are
studied below.

LI PENG ON CHINA'S STATE ENTERPRISES (1991)

Two years after the lecture discussed above was given, Goh
wrote a paper on 21 December 1991 in which he drew some
conclusions based on statements and comments made by China's
Premier Li Peng, a conservative who rose to prominence after
the Tiananmen Tragedy.

Following the 1989 crackdown, ideologues in charge were
convinced that large and medium-sized state enterprises (LMSEs)
would be the backbone of the socialist economy and had to be
protected. The preferential treatment given these enterprises
very quickly led to serious budgetary difficulties and great
losses. Li seemed preoccupied nevertheless with them and
recommended 11 measures aimed at invigorating them. What
Li wished to do, Goh said, bore close study since it would decide
the coming course of events, at least as long as Li remained
in power. In summary, Li's strategy sought to improve the
production system through the use of advanced technology, as
well as the management system. The common wisdom among

free market economists was that the state could not be entrusted with making the right decisions on resource allocation; but Goh was willing to admit that it could be done, using Japan as case study. However, the conditions under which that could happen did not exist in Communist China. While they may be able to properly connect enterprise demand for resources to resource availability, it was highly unlikely that they could make correct judgments on the future development of technology. While Japanese multinationals could maintain good information flow internationally and within the home economy and financial institutions, China could not.

Goh was even more pessimistic about post-Tiananmen China's ability to improve its management system. The measures undertaken in the early 1980s may have boosted production, but bad habits had reemerged. This regression had at least three causes. First, the "iron rice bowl" structure meant that efficiency could not be improved and the welfare system could not be dismantled; second, the egalitarian ethos undermined mechanisms put into place to stimulate productivity; and third, the two-tier price system encouraged corruption and inefficiency.

The great fear among the conservatives was that thorough reforms would cause social disruption, and their tendency was to protect what had been gained instead of taking greater risks. As things looked to Goh in 1991, therefore, proper reforms would have to be completed by a future generation of leaders. Such a completion would need at least four conditions being fulfilled. First, price reforms would have to be finalized and the subsequent inflation accepted and managed; second, the large and medium-sized enterprises which were welfare states in themselves would have to be dismantled; third, a labour market would have to be established in place of the iron rice-bowl system; and finally, a free capital market would have to be set up on the back of banking reforms that included the creation of an independent central bank and of commercial profit-driven banks.

Beyond these, a professional civil service would have to be created, as well as a Federal Constitution that clearly defined the authority and responsibilities of the different levels of government. Furthermore, a modern judiciary system would also have to be established.

All these were in conflict with "cherished tenets of socialism", said Goh, and would not come easy.

INTO THE 21ˢᵀ CENTURY (1994)

The ideological conflict within the Chinese Communist Party was indeed the key hindrance to Deng's plans to turn China into a consumption-based economy. This was clearly recognized by Deng, who at the ripe old age of 87 took a fateful trip down to the Shenzhen Special Economic Zone on 19 January 1992. There, far away from the Maoist hardliners who had gained prominence after the Tiananmen Tragedy and who placed ideological purity before economic growth, Deng declared that "making revolution [meant] liberating the productive forces", and called for pragmatic acceptance of any economic strategy that showed promise: a cat's colour did not matter as long as it could catch mice.

Deng warned that leftism in the party was more dangerous than rightist leanings. That claim led to news of his trip being ignored by the mainstream media for a whole month. Only after the speeches he made on what has become known as his "*nanxun*" — his "southern inspection tour", referring to an imperial tradition — had been collected and published by allies were they publicly endorsed by top leaders (Schell 1999). In the event, this intervention by Deng to stop China's drift towards the left proved highly successful. And so, when Goh spoke on China and the future of Asia in early 1994, the general perception of China's reform movement was much more optimistic than had been the case for several years. However, the kick start that Deng's intervention gave the economy was partially responsible for the inflationary period that soon followed, with prices increasing by 21.7% in 1993 (Brahm 2002: 17).

On 7 March 1994, Goh talked about the 21st century to teachers at the History Teachers' Conference in Singapore. Again, he used pre-modern history to frame his ideas about the immediate future for China and Asia.

He perceived a "logical and coherent order" to how the diverse and complex 20th century had been developing. Calling it the "Age of Violence", Goh noted that in the century's enormous wars, more combatants were involved than in all preceding centuries put together. Furthermore, citizens had been killed in incredible numbers and cities carpet-bombed.

Most wars fought before the Industrial Revolution were over territory; which was in keeping with the fact that wealth was generally gained through "ownership and cultivation of land". But with science and technology becoming the new and effective means of wealth creation, land grabs and control of raw material lost geographical limits. Although European states became wealthier, rivalries between them remained strong. Some countries grew faster than others, weapons became more lethal, and the whole of society was mobilized in times of war. All these conflicts led to the Cold War, with American industrial prowess becoming irrepressible by the end of the Second World War.

After Mikhail Gorbachev became the Soviet Union's president in 1985, radical reforms were carried out, partly through *glasnost* (openness) which granted some independence to the mass media, and partly through economic reforms. Consumer goods produced in the country had been abysmally bad in quality and did not correspond to the actual needs of the population.

Fatefully, economic reforms were implemented hesitantly while political reforms moved rapidly. This "released forces that the Soviet leadership could not control". The Union thus fell apart in December 1991.

After his summary of political development in the West, Goh turned his attention to Asia, especially to the four dragons and to China. Their growth had been rapid, with China's averaging 9% in 1978–1993. "The Pacific Rim countries" had been effectively coined and the World Bank had published a report called "The East Asian Miracle". Typically, that report made use of a range of economic variables for comparison. Goh however identified one single condition as "the real reason for the dragons' ascent". This point of view, he reminded his audience, was not really accepted by the "so-called neo-classical school of academic economists".

That school postulated that savings and investments were directly associated with economic growth. This missed the point, Goh stated, for what was important were the reasons for high savings and investment.

Improvements in scientific knowledge as well as the spread of benefits to the population at large had been relatively slow processes in the West. But where Taiwan was concerned, the victory of the Chinese Communist Party in 1949 meant that the island became a virtual protectorate of the United States. Over forty years, more than 100,000 Taiwanese students studied in the USA, enjoying access to the most advanced knowledge of the day. Many remained there, making up as much as 20% of the semiconductor engineers in Silicon Valley by 1989.

When the Taiwanese government decided to move from labour-intensive industries to technology-intensive ones in the late 1970s, special inducements were offered to entice talents to return to the island. As many as 19,000 scientists and engineers had taken the bait by 1988. At the same time, huge investments were put by the government into the tertiary educational system, expanding it significantly. Low salaries and top-end knowledge about industrial production thus came together, creating a highly successful export-oriented economy. This was most obviously seen in Taiwan's foreign exchange reserves, which became the largest in the world. Continued development saw Taiwanese investments in neighbouring countries growing phenomenally.

> One point should be noted in production for export. Taiwan's enterprises have to obtain their inputs of raw materials, components, capital and labour in a free competitive market and they also sell in a free competitive world market. Neo-classical economists believe — and in this I agree with them — that production conducted in such an environment encourages the best use of economic resources unlike production under a centrally-planned economy such as once operating in the former Soviet Union.

Here, Goh compared Deng Xiaoping with Mikhail Gorbachev. The former, he claimed, understood "the essential priorities involved in reforming a Communist state that had existed for several decades". Deng realized that the party was the glue that held society together, and its sudden removal might cause the system to crumble. Gorbachev's reform of the political system did exactly what Deng would not allow to happen in China. Deng proved to be right and the Chinese Communist Party remained dominant throughout the reform process until today.

Goh claimed that the Chinese also realized the importance of education, "unlike our neo-classical economists". Communist

China's economic development had relied heavily on the Soviet Union throughout the 1950s, and continued developing state-owned enterprises even after the break-up between the two communist giants.

In the reform period starting in the late 1970s, Deng opted for a gradual process while Gorbachev, who came to power in the mid-1980s, followed the advice of "foreign academic economists" and adopted the "Big Bang" approach of complete change, which failed badly. Nevertheless, China still had some serious problems to face, said Goh.

In the 21st century, Goh argued that Europe would have to restructure the welfare state no matter how strong the political resistance to that. America's problem was its tendency to overspend. Its ability to attract talent from around the world however would give it what might prove a decisive edge over competitors. The Russians, having "a capacity to bear hardship far exceeding other European people", would need to "abandon Karl Marx, follow Adam Smith and introduce the market system to guide production". The failure of the Big Bang approach should convince them to follow the step-by-step method preferred by the Chinese.

Goh was basically optimistic that the Russians and the Chinese would succeed in transforming their economies. But should they fail, the results for the rest of the world would be "calamitous".

Where Southeast Asia was concerned, Goh advised Malaysia, Indonesia and Thailand — the three economies rushing along behind the four dragons — to spend hugely on education at the secondary and tertiary level, and encourage more students to move into the science stream.

Goh's basic point was that the rate of savings and investment depended on successful export orientation. Increasing savings would find their way to neighbouring countries as investment.

How able investment-recipient countries downstream were in maximizing from this depended in turn on their investments in education and on how appropriately their population had been educated.

DOING BUSINESS IN CHINA (1994)

Goh was in Paris on 18 May 1994 to speak to the Institut De L'Enterprise. He informed his audience that he was chairman not only of the Institute of East Asia Political Economy, but also of a consultant firm called East Asian Consultancy, whose services included "collecting information, identifying possible joint venture partners and helping in getting negotiations started".

China's prospects were excellent, Goh said that day, and one could expect growth over the coming ten years to be as good as in the ten years just past. His optimism, he said, was based on the Chinese economy's similarities to Taiwan and South Korea. Repeating his argument that high rates of savings and investment were only a partial explanation for growth in these countries, he iterated that scientific, engineering and technical education in both these small dragons was the major factor spurring that exemplary growth. Thanks to the general population urbanizing and providing cheap labour, these countries were able to attain impressive results on the global market.

The same combination of factors could be found in China as well. However, the way growth had been attained in China differed in at least three ways from the smaller countries. First, China's products were aimed at the export market; second, its state-owned enterprises enjoyed virtual monopoly over output, and third; product improvement and cost reduction were not central concerns in the Chinese system, as was the case in Taiwan and South Korea. Understandably, the Chinese had been cautious about the reform process for fear that it would destabilize the country. The interface between economic reforms and political change would occupy the minds of reformists for years to come, Goh stated, as would the wage difference between the educational sector and the enterprise sector.

More immediate concerns included the banking system, which largely served as cashier for the government. Market-oriented production had caused a decentralization which then led to political pressure on banks now coming also from the provincial and local levels.

Just as Western industrial countries suffered business cycles, the Chinese economy also experienced periodic fluctuations. But while Western governments had access to macro-economic levers such as interest rates, national taxes and money supply for limiting fluctuations, the Chinese government did not.

What the Chinese reform economy was prone to was overheating, which occurred when supply bottlenecks and price increases appeared. In a crunch, steady defaults on payment among state-owned enterprises quickly created a debt-chain. In 1989–1991, when such a process began, Li Peng applied "emergency brakes" on the economy by tightly controlling the money supply, which led to certain economically detrimental effects. In 1993–1994, Vice-Premier Zhu Rongji was in a similar but worse position. But according to Goh, Zhu was succeeding through a "more moderate and discriminating approach" to money supply control. He was confident that under the new regime, inflationary pressures would be moderated and "a better balance between money supply and production" would be attained.

What Zhu did in mid-1993 was to issue a hurried macro-control policy consisting of "16 Measures". This identified the major areas where control needed to be exerted to cool the economy. Inflation dropped to 15% in 1995, down from 21.7%

two years earlier. By then, Zhu's macro-economic levers more obviously included the tightening of credit to reduce currency in circulation; the strengthening of bank reserves to limit money growth; the increasing of foreign exchange to stabilize exchange rates, and the optimizing of loan placements (Brahm 2002: 30–32).

Goh reminded his audience that Japan had also used central bank loans to finance industrial expansion, but took steps to control the balance of trade and domestic prices. This was possible if budget deficits were avoided. China did not have a good tax collection system and its state-owned enterprises often suffered great losses. It was therefore dependent on the country's ability to expand production. This ability, Goh said, rested on "the growing number of scientists and engineers combined with a large reserve of rural labour force".

This was in line with the "all but forgotten" Keynesian idea that "when there are unemployed resources available in any economy, a government [could] finance expansion by bank credit expansion without fearing runaway inflation". What was needed to keep things in check were countermeasures such as a large privatization programme and the centralizing of revenue collection. These were being undertaken by Zhu Rongji.

THE AWAKENING OF ASIA'S GIANT — CHINA (1994)

In a talk given on 12 September 1994, Goh, speaking at the 16th Asian Securities Analyst Council Conference in Singapore, elaborated further on his argument that the leap by an underdeveloped economy such as Taiwan into advanced economy status occurred through the provision of two key assets by a supportive advanced economy, in Taiwan's case, the

United States of America. These assets were technological production and human resource training.

Communist China was also a grateful recipient of these key assets from an advanced economy, Goh claimed. China's awakening, he said, actually started in 1949, and not in 1979. Throughout the 1950s, the Soviet Union was the Big Brother benefactor supplying China with the hardware and the experts needed to industrialize the new communist country. About 36,000 students were trained in Russia during that time, and China's gross industrial output went up by 34.8% in 1949–1952. The national income for the first five-year planning period (1953–1957) reached 8.9% annually, fell to 3.1% annually during the second five-year plan period (1958–1962), but then jumped to 14.5% each year in 1964–1965.

Despite China's chaotic development, figures actually show that between 1949 and 1980, her educational institutions tripled in number at all levels. The literacy rate also jumped dramatically. During those three decades, the number of students increased by six times at the primary level, by 45 times at the secondary level and ten times at the tertiary level. By all accounts, the increment rate continued to accelerate dramatically after 1980. And as was expected, a large percentage of these increases were in engineering and the natural sciences.

Despite her amazing success, China still suffered from several serious defects, Goh noted. First, the government continued to lack fiscal and monetary means to control the "boom-bust cycle"; second, the state-owned enterprises continued to suffer heavy losses but the option of closing them down did not exist; third, corruption among people in positions of authority continued, although the top-most leaders remained untainted; and finally, the central power had weakened in strength vis-à-vis the provincial governments.

> In effect what has happened over the years is that China has effectively become a Federal State as provinces increasingly acquire authority and wealth. As one Chinese scholar observes, post-Mao China has become a Federal State without a Federal Constitution. [...] Though China has a strong one-party regime, its capacity to formulate and implement economic policy is feeble.

Yet, despite all these serious problems, the economy grew by leaps and bounds. This, Goh argued, was due to the extraordinary growth of town and village enterprises (TVEs), whose collective output actually surpassed that of the state-owned enterprises in 1993.

He ventured several reasons for this phenomenon, unexpected even by Deng himself. First was the limitation placed on population movement to stop rural migration into the cities; second was the enormous concentration in the educational system on engineering and the natural sciences; third was the investment that had been put into "enlarging the scope of the machine building industries" which made it unnecessary for townships to import machinery with foreign exchange that they did not possess; fourth was the enormous shortage of consumer goods in the country; and fifth was the need felt by township leaders to create jobs for surplus labour that was growing restive.

Interestingly, the triumph of town and village enterprises, when seen on hindsight by later analysts, was but a stage in China's transition towards an economy driven by property rights. For instance, Kung and Lin argued in 2007 that these enterprises were "a crucial launching pad" for China's gradual marketization in the 1990s.

> But it is now clear that the success of TVEs thereafter was only part of a process of "self-destruction," where what initially appeared to be an aberration gradually moved toward the

common evolutionary path of property rights in market-driven economic development. (Kung and Lin 2007: 581)

Goh's explanation for China's ability to reform after 1979 was "the great effort made to accumulate knowledge in science and economy since 1949". This tied in neatly with his overall conviction that the modern world and its modes of production stemmed from technological innovations and from the scientific epistemology that had developed over time in Europe. In that sense, what other nations needed to do was to learn from the triumphs and the mistakes of the pioneering European nations. Indeed, that was the easy part of the equation. The tougher challenge was for less developed countries to change their population's mindset to one that was receptive of the primacy of economics and the efficacy of science and technology. His use of Japan as a benchmark for how an elite could direct modernization rested on an understanding of how bitter the pill was that a traditional society had to swallow in order to survive and thrive in a world transformed by science and technology and the capitalist mode of production.

This whole volume is an intellectual biography of Goh, and a concluding summary of it would not do his importance justice. His ideas are best savoured slowly and pensively. I shall instead end the story of this brilliant man by looping his later thoughts to his earliest ones.

Much of his thinking as an old man was concerned with changes in the political economy of Communist China. The reasons seem obvious. His retirement from government positions in Singapore took place just when both the Soviet Union and the Republic of China self-initiated economic and political change.

Being the macro-economist that he was, it was to be expected that he would be profoundly interested in such momentous events. For strategic reasons and in his search for a moral foundation for the Singaporean educational system, he had also been studying traditional Chinese thought and Chinese history. He had gone beyond his early interest in the Military School exemplified by Sun Zi and Wu Zi, to scrutinizing Imperial China's governance developed through the integration of the Legalist School and the Confucian School.

His intellectual interest in modern China had grown along with the economic growth of the four small dragons, and with Singapore's search for suitable moral principles that were not merely economic in nature. Goh's and Singapore's gradual shift in interest from ancient to modern China is most clearly manifested — as were most things that Goh showed an interest for — in specific institutions. The Institute of East Asian Philosophies founded in 1983 for the study of classical Confucianism evolved, as Deng's economic reforms progressed, into the Institute of East Asian Political Economy a decade later.

It is hard not to link the interest Goh expressed about China's progress in his young days to his later interest in modern China. He wrote in 1931 that he wished to be an engineer, because China badly needed "engineers, scientists, inventors and sailors". He also wanted China to become "one of the best nations in the world".

Since then, the political map of the region has changed in ways that no one could have predicted. When Singapore became an independent country in 1963, there was Goh, suddenly in a position to help build a new economy, a new defence and a new nation. This he did most admirably. However, one cannot deny that he retained a boyish affinity to China, old and new, that became evident in his later years.

One cannot deny either that he kept most luminously to the counsel he gave his schoolmates back in 1931:

> Our ambition must be to make ourselves useful to our country, our people and ourselves. To be ambitious we must have determination so that we may never slack or shirk in our work.

Goh suffered a stroke in 1998, and then another, two years later. He passed away in the early morning of 14 May 2010, and was given a state funeral on 23 May amidst moving accolades from all sides.

BIBLIOGRAPHY

Primary Sources and Magazines

ACS — *Anglo-Chinese Magazine* (Journal of the Anglo-Chinese School of the Methodist Mission, Singapore):

Vol. IV, No. 1, June 1931.

Vol. VIII, No. 1, July 1935.

Vol. IX, No. 1, July 1936.

Vol. XII, November 1939.

Vol. XVII, November 1948.

Vol. XXIV, November 1955.

Annual Report of Raffles College, Singapore, for the Academic Year 1938–39. Singapore: Malaya Publishing House, 1939.

Annual Report of Raffles College, Singapore, for the Academic Year 1947–48. Singapore: Malaya Publishing House, 1939.

Bulletin of the Malayan Students' Union Vol. 1, No. 1, February 1955. Bryanston Square, England: The Editorial Board.

CRO — Commonwealth Relations Office.

1965 Singapore (UK and the separation);

2 AED 72/701/2;

George McTurnan Kahin Papers, #14-27-3146. Division of Rare and Manuscript Collections, Cornell University Library.

GDC — *Gerald De Cruz* papers, folios 2, 42, 110 and 114, at ISEAS Library.

IAR — *The Tun Dr Ismail Abdul Rahman Papers*, at ISEAS Library, Singapore:

    CIA   — "Prospects for the Proposed Malaysian Federation". Central Intelligence Agency. Number 54-59/1962.

Drifting — *Drifting into Politics*. The unpublished memoirs of Tun Dr Ismail Abdul Rahman, chapters 1 to 16 (Folio 12a).

TS — *Top Secret*. Special Branch document (Folio 14; IAR/14).

ISEAS Papers — Documents concerning the Institute of Southeast Asian Studies (including the proposal on research institute for Indonesia affairs and other correspondence).

Parliamentary Debates, Official Reports:

First Session of First Parliament. Part III, 29 June 1967 to 24 January 1968.

First Session of Second Parliament, Part I, 6 May 1968 to 1 August 1968):

RCM — *Raffles College Magazine*:

Vol. VII, No. 1 and 2, Michaelmas Term, 1937.

Vol. VIII, No. 1 Trinity Term, 1938.

Vol. IX, No. 1 Trinity Term, 1939.

Suara Merdeka, magazine of the Malayan Forum (April–June 1954; December 1959; June 1959 Vol. 10, No. 1; June 1962, Special Issue Vol. 2).

CORD — *Oral Histories Collection* at Singapore's National Archives: Maurice Baker; Dennis Bloodworth; Gerald De Cruz; David Marshall; Eu Chooi Yip; Hon Sui Sen; Hwang Peng Yuan; James Puthucheary; Koh Sauk Keow; Lim Kim San; Rudy William Mosbergen; Tan Siew Sin; Toh Chin Chye; Albert Winsemius; Ya'akob bin Mohamed.

Interviews

Dr Moses Yu, August 2007; Dr Phua Swee Liang, October 2007; Mr Lim Ho Hup, November 2007; Mr Phua Bah Li, November 2007; Prof Lui Pao Chuen, 25 May 2007; Dr Soon Teck Wong, 29 May 2008; Mr Ngiam Tong Dow, 12 May 2008; Ms Patricia Lim Pui Huen, 26 May 2010.

Books, Speeches, Articles and Other Original Works by Goh Keng Swee

1996, July: "Beyond 'Miracles' and Total Factor Productivity", pp. 1–13.

In *ASEAN Economic Bulletin*, Vol. 13, No. 1 (With Linda Low). Singapore: ISEAS.

1995: *Wealth of East Asian Nations. Speeches and Writings by Goh Keng Swee*. Arranged and edited by Linda Low. Singapore, Kuala Lumpur and Hong Kong: Federal Publications.

1994, 12 September: "The Awakening of Asia's Giant — China", pp. 405–17. Speech delivered at the 16th Asian Securities Analyst Council Conference at Westin Stamford Hotel, Singapore. In *Wealth of East Asian Nations* (1995).

1994, 18 May: "Doing Business in China", pp. 395–404. Speech delivered to the Institut De L'Enterprise. In *Wealth of East Asian Nations* (1995).

1994, 7 March: "Into the 21st Century", pp. 380–94. Speech delivered at the History Teachers' Conference in Singapore. In *Wealth of East Asian Nations* (1995).

1993, 4 March: Speech delivered at the University of Hong Kong on the occasion of the award of Doctor of Letters, *honoris causa*.

1991, 21 December: "Li Peng on China's State Enterprises", pp. 369–79. In *Wealth of East Asian Nations* (1995).

1991a, November: "Why a Currency Board?". In Tan Pin Neo, Maggie, *Prudence at the Helm*.

1990, 8 January: "Economic Growth and the Intelligentsia — A Comparison of Experience in the Mainland and the Periphery, pp. 279–96. In *Wealth of East Asian Nations* (1995). Also published as a three-part series in *The Sunday Times*, Singapore, 11, 18 and 25 November.

1987, 22 October: "China's Economic Policies in a Historical Perspective". Speech delivered at the international conference, "China's Foreign Trade and Investment Policies: Expectations and Opportunities", p. 368. In *Wealth of East Asian Nations* (1995).

1985, 15 October: "The Human Element in Development Experience", pp. 47–54. In *Singapore Business* Vol. 9, No. 10.

1983, 28 July: "Public Administration and Economic Development in LDCs". Harry G. Johnson Memorial Lecture No. 4. Trade Policy Research Centre, London.

1981, 22 February: "Schools Council", pp. 212–19. In *Wealth of East Asian Nations* (1995).

1980, September: "The Dangers of Anomie", pp. 53–54. In *Singapore Paraplegics*. Society for Aid to the Paralysed.

1979, 26 July: Letter in response to the *Report on Moral Education 1979*, prepared by Ong Teng Cheong and Moral Education Committee, 1 June 1979.

1979, 20 May: Speech given at the 15th anniversary dinner of the Singapore Tourist Promotion Board at the Neptune Theatre Restaurant.

1979, January: *Business Morality in Less Developed Countries*. The Barbara Weinstock Lectures on the Morals of Trade, University of California, Berkeley. Berkeley: University of California.

1978, 23 June: "International Financial System". Speech delivered to the International Chamber of Commerce at Singapore's Shangri-la Hotel, pp. 153–61. In *Wealth of East Asian Nations* (1995).

1977 (1995): *The Practice of Economic Growth*. Singapore, Kuala Lumpur, Hong Kong: Federal Publications.

1976b, 3 November: "Adam Smith on Defence". Speech at Commissioning Ceremony at the Istana. In *The Practice of Economic Growth* (1977), pp. 238–40.

1976a: "A Socialist Economy that Works", pp. 77–85, in Nair, C.V. Devan (ed): *Socialism That Works...The Singapore Way*. Singapore, Kuala Lumpur and Hong Kong: Federal Publications.

1974, 26 August: "The Role of Civilians in National Defence". Speech delivered at the Commissioning Ceremony of SAF officers at the Istana. In *The Practice of Economic Growth* (1977), pp. 235–37.

1973, 30 November: "Qualities of a Strong Military Organisation". Speech delivered at SAF Promotion Ceremony at the Istana. In *The Practice of Economic Growth* (1977), pp. 229–34.

1973, 17 October: "Education in Singapore and the 'Teacher Image'". Speech delivered at the inauguration and convocation ceremony of the Institute of Education. In *The Practice of Economic Growth* (1977), pp. 213–19.

1973, 16 February: Speech as Minister of Defence at the opening of the Seiwaen (Japanese Garden).

1973: "Some Problems of Manpower Development in Singapore", pp. 7–19. In *Journal of Business* Vol. 2, No. 2. Business Administration Society and Department of Business Administration, National University of Singapore.

1972, 9 September: "Town and Gown". Speech delivered at the annual dinner of the Kesatuan Akademis Universiti Singapura, at the Mandarin Hotel. In *The Practice of Economic Growth* (1977), pp. 187–94.

1972, 16–17 June: Opening address at the seminar "Modernisation in Singapore; Impact on the Individual". Singapore: University Education Press. In *The Practice of Economic Growth* (1977), pp. 229–34.

1972 (1995): *The Economics of Modernization*. Singapore: Asia Pacific Press.

1971, 17 January: Speech at the opening of the "Seminar on Modernization in Southeast Asia". Singapore: Institute of Southeast Asian Studies.

1971, 4 January: Speech delivered at the opening of Jurong Bird Park.

1970, 25 October: Speech delivered at the 5th Anniversary Dinner and Dance of the Democratic Socialist Club (GDC Folio 110).

1969, 20 September: "Singapore's Monetary System, 1969". In *The Economics of Modernization* (1972), pp. 117–25.

1969, 1 August: "150 Years of Singapore". Speech delivered at the opening of the "150 Years of Development" Exhibition at Elizabeth Walk, Singapore. In *The Economics of Modernization* (1972), pp. 141–46.

1968, 2 December: Budget speech of the Minister of Finance at the sitting of Parliament.

1968, 30 March and 16 April: Radio and television broadcast on "The Crucial Years".

1968, 27 April: Opening of the Chartered Industries of Singapore Ltd.

1968, 18 January: Transcript of press interview on Minister of Finance's return from London.

1967, 5 December: *Two Years of Economic Progress*. Speech delivered as Minister of Finance at the Budget Session of Parliament. Ministry of Culture.

1967: Speech delivered at the PAP Bukit Merah Variety Show at Victoria Theatre.

1967, 13 March: Speech as Minister of Defence in moving the second reading of the National Service (Amendment) Bill in the Singapore Parliament.

1967, 11 March: "How the Intelligentsia Can Make their Contribution to Society". Speech at annual dinner and ball of The Australian Alumni, held at the Chinese Chamber of Commerce.

1967, 1 March: "Education Reform". Speech delivered at Anglo-Chinese School's 81st Founder's Day dinner.

1967a, 30 January: "Abolition of poverty". Radio talk show on Australian Broadcasting Commission network, pp. 36–39. In *The Economics of Modernization*.

1967, 28 January: *Communism in Non-Communist Asian Countries*. Singapore: Ministry of Culture Publication. Full title "The Nature and Appeals of Communism in Non-Communist Asian Countries", speech given at Australian Institute of Political Science, pp. 188–205. In *The Economics of Modernization*.

1966, 14 October: "A proposal to establish a research institute on Indonesian affairs". ISEAS Papers.

1966, 18 June: "Hard and Soft Armies". Speech delivered at the ceremonial opening of the Singapore Armed Forces Training Institute, pp. 215–18. In *The Economics of Modernization*.

1966, 7 May: "Creating an Officer Corp", Speech delivered at the first Instructors' Course graduation ceremony at the Singapore Armed Forces Training Institute, pp. 210–14. In *The Economics of Modernization*.

1965, 18 October: "Workers in developing countries", pp. 81–88. In *The Economics of Modernization*.

1965, April: "Social, Political and Institutional Aspects in Development Planning", pp. 1–15. In *The Malayan Economic Review* Vol. X, No. 1. The Journal of the Malayan Economic Society, University of Malaya Economic Society.

1964: "The Economic Problems of Democratic Socialism in Malaysia", pp. 137–40. In *Our First Ten Years*. Singapore: PAP Central Editorial Board.

1963: *Some Problems of Industrialisation*. Towards Socialism — Vol. 7. Singapore: Ministry of Culture Series.

1963, April: "Management in the Developing Society", pp. 7–13. Paper presented at the "Symposium on the Role of Management in Industrialization in Malaysia". In *The Malayan Economic Review* Vol. VIII, No. 1. Journal of the Malayan Economic Society, University of Malaya Economic Society.

1962, June: "Malaysia: The PAP View", pp. 2–6. In *Suara Merdeka* Special Issue Vol. 2. London: Malayan Forum.

1961, November: "Man and Economic Development". In *Commerce*, Journal of the Commerce Society of Nanyang University.

1960b, 29 September: *This is How Your Money is Spent*. Towards Socialism — Vol. 3. A Ministry of Culture Series.

1960a, 22 June: "My Election", pp. 4–5. In *Petir* Vol. III, No. 7. Singapore.

1959b, June: "The Social Revolution in Malaya". In *Suara Merdeka* Vol. 10, No. 1. London: Malayan Forum.

1959a, 22 March: "Our Economic Policy", pp. 19–27. In *The Tasks Ahead. PAP's Five-Year Plan 1959–1964*. Singapore: Petir.

1958: "Our Economic Future". In *Petir*, 4th Anniversary Celebration Souvenir. Singapore: People's Action Party.

1958, April: "Entrepreneurship in a Plural Economy", pp. 1–7. In *The Malayan Economic Review* Vol. II, No. 1. Journal of the Malayan Economic Society, University of Malaya.

1957, April: Book Review of Edward F. Scezepanik's *The Cost of Living in Hong Kong*; Hong Kong University Press, 1956; pp. 86–88. In *The Malayan Economic Review* Vol. II, No. 1. Journal of the Malayan Economic Society, University of Malaya Economic Society.

1956: *Techniques of National Income Estimation in Underdeveloped Territories, with special reference to Asia and Africa*. London School of Economics. Doctoral dissertation submitted to the University of London.

1956: *Urban Incomes & Housing. A Report on the Social Survey of Singapore, 1953–54*. Singapore: Department of Social Welfare.

1950, November: *Post-War Japan*. Book review of Honor Tracy's *Kakemono: A Sketch Book of Post-War Japan*. Harmondsworth: Methuen.

1940: *The Economic Front from a Malayan Point of View.* Singapore: Government Publishing Office. With an introduction by T.H. Silcock.

1938: "Capitalism versus Socialism", pp. 41–50. In *Raffles College Magazine* Vol. VIII, No. 1, Trinity Term.

1938: "College Personalities", pp. 61–62. In *Raffles College Magazine* Vol. VIII, No. 1, Trinity Term.

1937: "The Paradox", p. 4. In *Raffles College Magazine* Vol. VII, No. 2, Michaelmas Term.

1935, July: "Wanted — A Playing Field", p. 59. In *ACS Magazine* Vol. VIII, No. 1.

1931, June: "My Ambitions", p. 55. In *ACS Magazine* Vol. IV, No. 1.

Secondary Sources

Austin, Ian Patrick (2004) *Goh Keng Swee and Southeast Asian Governance.* Singapore: Marshall Cavendish.

Austin, Ian (2000) *Goh Keng Swee: His Contemporary Relevance to Corporate Governance in Southeast Asia.* S.l.; s.n.

Barber, Noel (1971) *Malaya 1948–1960. The War of the Running Dogs.* London: Fontana/Collins.

Barr, Michael (1998) "Lee Kuan Yew's 'Socialism' Reconsidered", pp. 33–54. In *Access: History*, Vol. 2, No. 1. University of Queensland. <http://www.uq.edu.au/access_history/two-one/lee.pdf>.

Bellows, Thomas J. (1970) *The People's Action Party of Singapore: Emergence of a Dominant Party System.* Monograph Series No. 14. Connecticut: Yale University Southeast Asia Studies.

Benton, George and Hong Liu, eds. (2004) *Diasporic Chinese Ventures. The Life and Work of Wang Gungwu.* London and New York: RoutledgeCurzon.

Brahm, Laurence J. (2002) *Zhu Rongji & the Transformation of Modern China.* John Wiley & Sons.

Central Provident Fund Board (2005) *Saving for Our Retirement. 50 Years of CPF.* Singapore: SNP Editions.

Chan Heng Chee and Obaid Ul Haq, eds. (2007) *S. Rajaratnam: The Prophetic and the Political.* Singapore: ISEAS and Graham Brash.

Cheah Boon Kheng (1979) *The Masked Comrades. A Study of the Communist United Front in Malaya, 1945–48.* Singapore: Times Books International.

Chee, Veronica (2002) "Port of Singapore Authority (PSA)". National Library Board of Singapore <http://infopedia.nl.sg/articles/SIP_577_2005-01-27.html>.

Cheong, Colin (1993) *New Frontiers. 25 Years of the Jurong Town Corporation.* Singapore: Times Editions.

Chew, Melanie, and Bernard Tan (2002) *Creating the Technological Edge.* Singapore: DSO National Laboratories.

Chew, Melanie (2005) *A Pyramid of Public Service. The Pyramid 1963–2005.* Singapore: SNP International.

——— (1996) *Leaders of Singapore.* Singapore: Resource Press.

Chin Kin Wah (1974) *The Five Power Defence Arrangements and AMDA.* Occasional Paper No. 23. July. Singapore: Institute of Southeast Asian Studies.

——— (1983) *The Defence of Malaysia and Singapore: The Transformation of a Security System 1957–1971.* Cambridge University Press.

Chin Peng (2003) *My Side of History.* Singapore: Media Masters.

Clutterbuck, Richard (1973) *Riot and Revolution in Singapore and Malaysia 1945–1963.* London: Faber & Faber.

De Cruz, Gerald (1993) *Rojak Rebel. Memoirs of a Singapore Maverick.* Singapore and Kuala Lumpur: Times Books International.

Dee, Maureen, ed. (2005) *Australia and the Formation of Malaysia 1961–1966.* Series: Documents on Australian Foreign Policy. Australian Department of Foreign Affairs and Trade.

Dirlik, Arif (1995) "Confucius in the Borderlands: Global Capitalism and the Reinvention of Confucianism", pp. 229–73. In *Boundary 2*, Vol. 22, No. 3. Duke University Press.

Domar, Evsey D. (1969) "Capital Expansion, Rate of Growth and Employment", pp. 33–44. In Joseph Stiglitz and Hirofumi Uzama, eds. *Readings in the Modern Theory of Economic Growth.* Cambridge, Massachusetts: MIT Press.

Emerson, Rupert 1937 (1970) *Malaysia. A Study of Direct and Indirect Rule.* Kuala Lumpur: University of Malaya Press.

Edgeworth, F.Y. (1925) *Papers Relating to Political Economy*. Oxford University Press.

Evans, Richard (1993/1995) *Deng Xiaoping and the Making of Modern China*. Penguin Books.

Fletcher, Nancy McHenry (1969) *The Separation of Singapore from Malaysia*. Data Paper No. 73. Southeast Asia Program. Department of Asian Studies, Cornell University, Ithaca, New York.

Flint, Peter B. (1989, June 16) "Honor Tracy, travel writer, is dead at 75". In *New York Times* <http://www.nytimes.com/1989/06/16/obituaries/honor-tracy-travel-writer-is-dead-at-75.html>.

Furnivall, J.S. 1948 (1956) *Colonial Policy and Practice: A Comparative Study of Burma and Netherlands India*. NewYork: New York University Press.

George, T.J.S. 1973 (1984) *Lee Kuan Yew's Singapore*. Singapore and Selangor: Eastern Universities Press.

Hardoyo (2007) "Two Councils", pp. 13–16. In McGlynn, John H. et al. *Indonesia in the Soeharto Years. Issues, Incidents and Images*. Jakarta: Lontar Foundation.

Harrod, R.F. (1969) "An Eassy in Dynamic Theory", pp. 14–33. In Joseph Stiglitz and Hirofumi Uzama, eds. *Readings in the Modern Theory of Economic Growth*. Cambridge, Massachusetts: MIT Press.

Heidenheimer, Arnold J. (1970) *Political Corruption*. New York: Holt, Rinehart and Winston.

Hon, Joan (1984) *Relatively Speaking*. Singapore: Times Books International.

Huxley, Tim (2000) *Defending the Lion City: The Armed Forces of Singapore*. St Leonard's, New South Wales: Allen & Unwin.

Ismail, Tawfik and Ooi Kee Beng (2008) *Malaya's First Year at the United Nations: As Reflected in Dr Ismail's Reports to the Tunku*. Singapore: ISEAS.

Josey, Alex (1968) *The Crucial Years*. Singapore: Times Books International.

Jurong Town Corporation (1969?) *Jurong Town Council*.

Katz, Rodney P. (1989) Library of Congress, Country Studies <http://lcweb2.loc.gov/cgi-bin/query/r?frd/cstdy:@field(DOCID+sg0152)>.

Keith, Patrick (2005) *Ousted*. Singapore: Media Masters.

Koh, Tommy, and Chang Li Lin (2005) *The Little Red Dot. Reflections by Singapore's Diplomats*. Singapore: World Scientific Publishing.

Kuah, Wee Jin, Adrian (2007) *Unchartered Territory. Dr Goh Keng Swee and the ST Engineering Story. A Tribute*. S. Rajaratnam School of International Studies and ST Engineering.

Kung Kai-Sing, James and Yi-Min Lin (2007) "The Decline of Township and Village Enterprises in China's Economic Transition", pp. 569–84. In *World Development* Vol. 35, No. 4. Elsevier Ltd.

Lam Peng Er and Kevin Y.L. Tan (1999) *Lee's Lieutenants: Singapore's Old Guard*. Sydney: Allen & Unwin.

Lai Ah Eng, ed. (2008) *Religious Diversity in Singapore*. Singapore: Lee Kuan Yew School of Public Policy, Institute of Policy Studies and Institute of Southeast Asian Studies.

Lau, Albert (1998) *A Moment of Anguish. Singapore in Malaysia and the Politics of Disengagement*. Singapore: Times Academic Press.

Lee Choon Eng (1936, July) "The Anglo-Chinese School, Singapore. A Short History". Singapore: ACS Magazine Vol. IX, No. 1.

Lee Kuan Yew (2000) *From Third World To First. The Singapore Story: 1965–2000*. Singapore: Singapore Press Holdings.

—— (1998) *The Singapore Story. Memoirs of Lee Kuan Yew*. Singapore: Singapore Press Holdings.

—— (1972, 16 February) Speech delivered at Fullerton Square, pp. 192–95. In C.V. Devan, ed., 1976: *Socialism That Works...The Singapore Way*. Singapore, Kuala Lumpur and Hong Kong: Federal Publications.

Lee Sheng-Yi (1983, January) *The Role of Singapore as a Financial Centre*. Department of Business Administration, National University of Singapore.

Leff, Nathaniel H. (1970) "Economic Development through Bureaucratic Corruption", pp. 510–20. In Heidenheimer, Arnold J. (1970) *Political Corruption*. New York: Holt, Rinehart and Winston. First published in November 1964 in *American Behavioural Scientist*.

Leifer, Michael (2000) *Singapore's Foreign Policy. Coping with Vulnerability*. Politics in Asia series. London: Routledge.

———— (1974) *The Foreign Relations of the New States*. Studies in Contemporary Southeast Asia. London: Longman.

Lewis, Arthur (1954, May) "Economic Development with Unlimited Supplies of Labour", pp. 139–91. In *Manchester School of Economic and Social Studies*, Vol. 22, No. 2.

Lily Zubaidah Rahim (1998) *The Singapore Dilemma: The Political and Educational Marginality of the Malay Community*. Shah Alam: Oxford University Press.

Lim, Pui Huen, P. (1998) *Institute of Southeast Asian Studies. A Commemorative History 1968–1998*. Singapore: Institute of Southeast Asian Studies.

Lim, Richard (1997) *Banking on a Virtue. POSBank 1971–1997. Celebrating 25 Years*. Singapore: POSBank.

Many Pathways, One Mission. Fifty Years of Singapore Education, 2007. Ministry of Education, Singapore.

MacIver, Robert M. (1950) *The Ramparts We Guard*. New York: MacMillan.

Marshall, Alfred 1890 (1956) *Principles of Economics: An Introductory Volume*. London: Macmillan.

Marsita Omar and Chan Fook Weng (2007, 31 December) "British Withdrawal from Singapore". In Singapore Infopedia, National Library <http://infopedia.nl.sg/articles/SIP_1001_2009-02-10.html>.

McGlynn, John H. et al. (2007/2005) *Indonesia in the Soeharto Years. Issues, Incidents and Images*. Jakarta: Lontar Foundation.

McVey, Ruth T. (1965) *The Rise of Indonesian Communism*. Cornell University Press.

Memorandum on Malaysia by the Malaysia Solidarity Consultative Committee, 23 February 1962. Appendix to Zainal Abidin bin Abdul Wahid 1984: "The Formation of Malaysia: The Role of the Malaysia Solidarity Consultative Committee", pp. 129–451. In Muhammad Abu Bakar, Amarjit Kaur and Abdullah Zakaria Ghazali, eds. *Historia. Essays in Commemoration of the 25th Anniversary of the Department of History, University of Malaya*. Kuala Lumpur: The Malaysian Historical Society.

Milne, R.S. and Diane K. Mauzy (1990) *Singapore. The Legacy of Lee Kuan Yew*. Boulder, San Francisco and Oxford: Westview Press.

Morais, J. Victor, ed. (1963) *The Who's Who in Malaysia 1963*. Kuala Lumpur: Solai Press.

Mukherjee, M. (1954 September) "The Technique of Social Accounting in a Pre-Industrial Economy", pp. 1–24. In *Sankhya: The Indian Journal of Statistics* Vol. 14, No. 1/2. New Delhi: Indian Institute of Statistics.

Myrdal, Gunnar (1968) *Asian Drama. An Inquiry into the Poverty of Nations*. Penguin.

Nair, C.V. Devan, ed. (1976) *Socialism that works...The Singapore Way*. Singapore, Kuala Lumpur and Hong Kong: Federal Publications.

Newman, John Henry (1845) *The Idea of a University*. Modern History Sourcebook <http://www.fordham.edu/halsall/mod/newman/newman-university.html>.

Ooi Kee Beng (2006) *The Reluctant Politician: Tun Dr Ismail and His Time*. Singapore: ISEAS.

Our First Ten Years, 1964, 21 November. PAP 10th Anniversary Souvenir. Singapore: PAP Central Editorial Board.

Pang Cheng Lian (1971) *Singapore's People's Action Party. Its History, Organisation and Leadership*. Singapore and Kuala Lumpur: Oxford University Press.

Patinkin, Don (1968) "A Nationalist Model". In Walter Adams, ed. *The Brain Drain*. London: Collier MacMillan.

Phillips, W.A. (1958, November) "The Relationship between Unemployment and the Rate of Change of Money Wage Rates in the United Kingdom, 1861–1957", pp. 283–99. In *Economica, New Series*, vol. 25. London.

Picard, Michel (1995) *Bali. Cultural Tourism and Touristic Culture*. (Original title: *Bali: Tourisme Culturel et culture touristique*. Editions L'Harmattan, Paris 1992). English translation by Diana Darling. Singapore: Archipelago Press.

Picard, Michel, and Robert E. Wood (1997) *Tourism, Ethnicity, and the State in Asian and Pacific Societies*. Honolulu: University of Hawaii Press.

Pigou, A.C. 1937 (1960) *Socialism and Capitalism*. London: MacMillan.
———— (1920) *The Economics of Welfare*. London: MacMillan.

———— (1912) *Wealth and Welfare*. London: MacMillan.

Phua Swee Liang (2008) *Goh Keng Swee. Public Figure Private Man*. Singapore: Goh Keng Swee Foundation.

Puthucheary, J.J. (1960) *Ownership and Control in the Malayan Economy*. Singapore: Eastern Universities Press. Reprinted in 2004 by INSAN, Petaling Jaya.

Report and Accounts of the Economic Development Board, 1 August to 31 December 1961. State of Singapore. 1962.

Report on the Ministry of Education 1978. Prepared by Dr Goh Keng Swee and the Education Study Team.

Report on Moral Education 1979. Prepared by Ong Teng Cheong and the Moral Education Committee, 1 June 1979.

Review of the Education Development Division, Ministry of Education. October 1979. Prepared by Chan Kai Yau, Director of Education.

Rigg, Jonathan (1988, March) "Singapore and the Recession of 1985", pp. 340–52. In *Asian Survey*, Vol. 28, No. 3.

Rosen, George (1975) *Peasant Society in a Changing Society. Comparative Development in Southeast Asia and India*. University of Illinois Press.

Schell, Orville (1999, 27 September) "With the official OK, Capitalism takes off". *Time Asia*, September 27, Vol. 154, No. 12 <http://www.time.com/time/asia/magazine/99/0927/shenzhen.html>.

Schumpeter, Joseph A. (1939) *Business Cycles; A Theoretical, Historical and Statistical Analysis of the Capitalist Process*. Two volumes. New York: McGraw-Hill.

Seah Chee-Meow (1980 February) "Singapore 1979. Dialectics of Survival", pp. 144–54. In *Asian Survey* Vol. 20, No. 2. *A Survey of Asia in 1979*. University of California Press.

Seow, Francis (1998) *The Media Enthralled*. London: Lynne Rienner Publishers.

Shamsul Bahrin & P.D.A. Perera 1977(?): FELDA — 21 Years of Land Development. Kuala Lumpur: Felda.

Shulman, Frank Joseph, and Anna Leon Shulman (2001) *Doctoral Dissertations on Hong Kong 1900–1997. An Annotated Bibliography*. University of Hong Kong Libraries Publications No. 12.

Silcock, Thomas (1985) *A History of Economics Teaching and Graduates in Singapore*. National University of Singapore: Department of Economics and Statistics.

Silcock, T.H. and E.K. Fisk, eds. (1963) *The Political Economy of Independent Malaya. A Case-Study in Development*. Canberra: The Australian National University.

Simandjuntak, B. (1969) *Malayan Federalism 1945–1963. A Study of Federal Problems in a Plural Society*. East Asian Historical Monographs. Kuala Lumpur: Oxford University Press.

Singapore Department of Social Welfare (1947 December) *A Social Survey of Singapore. A Preliminary Study of Some Aspects of Social Conditions in the Municipal Area in Singapore*.

Sree Kumar, Sharon Siddique and Yuwa Hedrick-Wong (2005) *Mind the Gaps. Singapore Business in China*. Singapore: Institute of Southeast Asian Studies.

Stone, Robert (1954) *Measurement of Consumers' Expenditure and Behaviour in the U.K. 1920–1939*. Cambridge.

Tan, Charlene (2008) "From Moral Values to Citizenship Education. The Teaching of Religion in Singapore Schools", pp. 321–41. In Lai Ah Eng, ed. *Religious Diversity in Singapore*. Singapore: Lee Kuan Yew School of Public Policy, Institute of Policy Studies and Institute of Southeast Asian Studies.

Tan Pin Neo, Maggie, ed. (1992) *Prudence at the Helm*. Board of Commissioners of Currency. Singapore 1967–1992. 25th Anniversary Publication.

Tan Siok Sun (2007) *Goh Keng Swee. A Portrait*. Singapore, Kuala Lumpur and Paris: Editions Didier Millet.

Tay, Simon, ed. (2006) *A Mandarin and the Making of Public Policy*. Reflections by Ngiam Tong Dow. Singapore: NUS Press.

The Asian Dollar Market, 1973. First National City Bank.

Tien Mui Mun (2002) "Dr Goh Keng Swee". Singapore Infopedia, National Library <http://infopedia.nl.sg/articles/SIP_662_2005-01-11.html>.

TowardSTomorrow. The Singapore Technologies Story, 1995. Singapore Technologies.

286

Times-Chambers *Combined Dictionary Thesaurus* 1995 (2001). Singapore: Times Media.

Vasil, Raj (2000) *Governing Singapore: A History of National Development and Democracy*. Sydney: Allen & Unwin.

Wagner, Adolf (1891) "Marshall's Principles of Economics", pp. 319–38. In *Quarterly Journal of Economics*, Vol. 5. Harvard University: MIT Press <http://socserv.mcmaster.ca/econ/ugcm/3ll3/marshall/Wagner.htm>.

Wang Gungwu (2005) *Nation-Building. Five Southeast Asian Histories*. Singapore: Institute of Southeast Asian Studies.

Wee, Jane (1997) "Singapore Institute of Standards and Industrial Research". Singapore: National Library Board <http://infopedia.nl.sg/articles/SIP_26_2005-01-09.html>.

Wee Kim Wee (2004) *Wee Kim Wee. Glimpses and Reflections*. Singapore: Landmark Books.

Wells, A.F. (1956, June) "Urban Incomes and Housing", pp. 60–61. In *The Malayan Economic Review* Vol. 1, No. 1. University of Malaya Economics Society.

Yap, Sonny, Richard Lim and Leong Weng Kam (2009) *Men in White: The Untold Story of Singapore's Ruling Political Party*. Singapore: Singapore Press Holdings and Marshall Cavendish.

Yeo Kim Wah (1973) *Political Development in Singapore 1945–1955*. Singapore University Press.

Yong, C.F. and R.B. McKenna (1990) *The Kuomintang Movement in British Malaya 1912–1949*. Singapore University Press, National University of Singapore.

Yusuf Hasyim (2007) "Killing Communists", pp. 16–27. In McGlynn, John H. et al. *Indonesia in the Soeharto Years. Issues, Incidents and Images*. Jakarta: Lontar Foundation.

Internet Sites and Mass Media Sources

Aseansec — The ASEAN Declaration <http://www.aseansec.org/1212.htm>.

ATS — Australian Treaty Series 1971 No. 21 <http://www.austlii.edu.au/au/other/dfat/treaties/1971/21.html>.

CEE — The Concise Encyclopaedia of Economics <http://www.econlib.org/library/Enc/bios/Pigou.html>.

CS — Country Studies. "Singapore: Patterns of Change" <http://www.country-studies.com/singapore/economy — patterns-of-development.html>.

EDB — EDB Singapore <http://www.edb.gov.sg/edb/sg/en_uk/index/about_edb/our_history/the_1970s.html>.

Encyclopaedia Brittanica <http://www.britannica.com/EBchecked/topic/460259/Arthur-Cecil-Pigou>.

HKU HDG — Hong Kong University, Honorary Degrees Graduation <http://www3.hku.hk/hongrads/index.php/archive/graduate_detail/164>.

IMDB — Internet Movie Database <http://www.imdb.com/name/nm0001791/bio>.

Infopedia — National Library of Singapore <http://infopedia.nl.sg>.

MAS

"Introduction to MAS" <http://www.mas.gov.sg/about_us/Introduction_to_MAS.html>;

"Heritage Collection" <http://www.mas.gov.sg/currency/currency_info/Heritage_Collection.html>.

NOL — NOL website <http://www.nolweb.com/about/history.html>.

NPIA — Nobel Prize Internet Archive <http://www.nobelprizes.com/nobel/nobel.html>.

NWC — New World Encyclopaedia <http://www.newworldencyclopedia.org/entry/Arthur_Cecil_Pigou>.

PGE 72 — Parliamentary General Elections 1972 <http://www.singapore-elections.com/parl-1972-ge/>.

Prime Minister's Office, Press Release, 14 May 2010 — "President Nathan's tribute to Dr Goh Keng Swee" http://news.asiaone.com/News/AsiaOne%2BNews/Singapore/Story/A1Story20100514-216317.html>.

PSA — Port of Singapore Authority <http://www.singaporepsa.com/>.

PW — Property Wire, "Singapore aims to attract 1.7 million tourists" <http://www.propertywire.com/news/asia/singapore-aims-to-attract-17m-tourists-20080305621.html>.

SE — *Singapore Elections* <http://www.singapore-elections.com/parl-1979-be/>.

SEIN Quarterly <http://sienquarterly.icwip.hu/htmls/download/magazine/sienq_30.pdf>.

ST — *The Straits Times*, Singapore.

Today — *Weekend Today*, Singapore.

WFDY News — World Federation of Democractic Youth, June 2008 <http://wfdydemo.kne.gr/wp-content/uploads/2009/01/wfdy-news-june-2008-digital.pdf>.

INDEX

information and communication
    technologies, 125
Institute of East Asian
    Philosophies (IEAP), 235
    conference, 250
    study of classical
        Confucianism, 269
Institute of Education, 222
Institute of Southeast Asian
    Studies (ISEAS)
    establishment of, 112
Institute of Southeast Asian
    Studies Act, 215
intellectual sterility, 184
intelligentsia
    contribution to society, 203–
        209
    economic growth, 250-256
inter-ethnic relations, 77
inter-racial harmony, 82
Internal Security Act, 101, 140
    arrest of Gopalan Krishnan
        Raman, 145
Internal Security Department
    (ISD), 140
Interchangeability Agreement,
    160
international brigandage, 33
International Chamber of
    Commerce, speech at, 165
international financial system,
    165–68
international tenders, 129
investments, British, 121

Iron Curtain, ban on travel, 66
iron rice bowl, 253
    structure, 257
Ismail Abdul Rahman (Dr), 90

Japan
    achievements of, 175
    advantages, 239
    central bank loans, 265
    invasion of Manchuria, 7
    praise for, 100
    surrender, 44
    tourism out of, 150
Japanese Garden, 156, 186
Japanese invasion
    third stage of social
        revolution, 92
Japanese multinationals
    information flow globally, 257
Japanese Occupation
    Tax Office, 43, 208
job creation
    as proposed by Keynes, 76
Jomo, K.S., 63
Jurong Bird Park, 112
Jurong Country Club, 156
Jurong Hill Park, 156
Jurong Industrial Estate, 154
Jurong Port, 154
Jurong Town Corporation (JTC),
    151, 155

Kahin, George McTurnan, 210
    letter to, 213

ABOUT THE AUTHOR

OOI KEE BENG was born and bred in Penang, and received his basic schooling at La Salle School, St Xavier's Institution and Methodist High School. His first career was in journalism, and he was attached to *The Star* and *The Straits Echo* in the mid-1970s.

His entire tertiary education was done at Stockholm University, with Public Administration (in the Swedish system) being his first degree. After several years studying Practical Philosophy, he concluded his academic studies with Chinese Philosophy and a doctorate in Sinology. He is now a Swedish citizen.

He is currently a Senior Fellow at Singapore's Institute of Southeast Asian Studies (ISEAS), and a regular columnist for Singapore's *Today* newspaper.

His books include *Between Umno and a Hard Place: The Najib Razak Era Begins*; *Arrested Reform: The Undoing of Abdullah Badawi*; *March 8: Eclipsing May 13* (co-authored with Saravanamuttu and Lee); *Malaya's First Year at the United Nations* (co-compiled with Tawfik Ismail); *Lost in Transition: Malaysia under Abdullah*; *The Era of Transition: Malaysia after Mahathir*; *Chinese Strategists: Beyond Sun Zi's Art of War*; *The Reluctant Politician — Tun Dr Ismail and His Time*; and *Continent, Coast and Ocean: Dynamics of Regionalism in Eastern Asia* (co-edited with Ding Choo Ming).

The Reluctant Politician won the "Award of Excellence for Best Writing Published in Book Form on Any Aspect of Asia (Non-Fiction)" at the Asian Publishing Convention Awards 2008. *Continent, Coast, Ocean: Dynamics of Regionalism in Eastern Asia* was named "Top Co-published Academic Work" in 2008 by the ASEAN Book Publishers Association (ABPA).

He has also translated Chinese war manuals into Swedish, such as *Sun Zis krigskonst* and *Weiliaozis krigskonst*.

He is Adjunct Associate Professor at the Southeast Asian Studies Programme, National University of Singapore, and Visiting Associate Professor at the Department of Public and Social Administration, City University of Hong Kong. He is also the Editor of the *Penang Economic Monthly*, published by the Socio-Economic and Environmental Research Institute in Penang.